Editor's Note

Jonathan Wilson, Editor

It's a strange world in which Juventus can be cast as an underdog, and yet modern football has achieved it. When the other three teams comprising the last four of the Champions League are all in their third consecutive semi-finals, though, it was the 31-time Italian champions who flew the flag for the little man, or at least for the giant who's not quite as big as some of the giants. When *The Blizzard* began in 2011, it was apparent that the age of the super-clubs was upon us; as we begin out fifth year, and so welcome our fifth different cover, the only surprise is that the coagulation of money at the elite and the consequent stratification of the club game has happened so quickly.

On the one hand that means that the quality of football in the latter stages of the Champions League is probably the best football that has ever been played: all four legs of the semi-finals this year were of an exceptionally high standard. On the other, it means predictable domestic league campaigns – the inevitable march of Juve, Bayern Munich and Paris St-Germain to victory, the eternal tussle of Barcelona and Real Madrid, the Chelsea-Manchester United-Manchester City carve-up. It's possible that domestic championships in Europe will soon become as meaningless and wearisome as the state championships in Brazil: leagues that once were the priority that become almost irrelevant alongside the continental/national championship.

There are those to point to the examples of Borussia Dortmund and Atlético Madrid,

and it is true that they show how a team from slightly below the elite (but only slightly: they're still along the 20 wealthiest clubs in the world) can challenge, and the successes of both are remarkable, but both have then found their best players snaffled by the true elite. The process of regeneration can be sustained for only so long before they inevitably fall back into the second tier again; where the elite can spend and spend, replacing players who don't fit in with new purchases, the second tier cannot afford mistakes in the market.

What that means is that, rather than national elites who then meet in European competition, there has emerged an international elite of six to eight sides. If the process carries on for another five years, it's hard to see how, for those clubs (and for fans and thus TV networks) domestic tournaments could retain their appeal.

Whatever happens, hopefully *The Blizzard* will be there to see it and offer the sort of in-depth analysis we've been providing since we launched. It seems vaguely incredible that we're still here and for that I – again – thank all our writers and editors and the various other people in the office whose jobs I don't really understand, as well as you, the readers. And again I ask that you tell as many people as you can about us. We may be in our fifth year, but we're still not wealthy enough for a marketing budget: word of mouth is all we have.

May 2015

Contents

The Blizzard, Issue Seventeen

Introduction

3. Editor's Note

Beyond the Game

11. **Igor Rabiner, The Player of the People**

    The death of Igor Cherenkov last year prompted an astonishing outpouring of grief from Spartak fans

24. **Philippe Auclair, The Man who Sacked Himself**

    Gabriel Hanot was a player, a coach, a journalist and a pioneer who remains oddly neglected in France

29. **Brian Oliver, Looking Forward**

    How the former Chelsea defender John Dempsey left football behind to work in a care home

34. **Shaul Adar, The Complicated Symbol**

    Bnei Sakhnin's journey to establish themselves as an Arab team in Israel's top flight

43. **James Corbett, Namesakes**

    Everton have had two Alex Youngs: one's the subject of a Ken Loach film, the other killed his brother

Interview

56. **Miguel Delaney, Paul Breitner**

    How a Bayern Munich defeat paved the way for West Germany's 1974 World Cup triumph

Belfast

61. **Levkos Kyriacou, A Patchwork City**

    Mapping the fan-bases of the major club's in Northern Ireland's capital

76. **Keith Baillie, Requiem for a Stand**

    A history in seven key moments of the short life of the Kop at Windsor Park

86. **Conor Heffernan, Before the Shopping Centre**

    How crowd violence brought an end to the existence of Belfast Celtic

Theory

95. **Alex Holiga, The Man who Built White Ships**

    Stanko Poklepović, the oldest coach in Europe, and the importance of spiral impostations

101. Simon Curtis, The Whisky Option

Malcolm Allison's time at Sporting was brief but fans remember him fondly

107. Richard Fitzpatrick, Messi and the Machine

Could playing video games be shaping the present generation of footballers?

113. George Caulkin, Not at All Costs

Paul Tisdale has not only revolutionised how Exeter City play, but how they think

121. Charlie Eccleshare, Wrestling with the All-Blacks

How Declan Edge is trying to make New Zealand take football seriously

● Polemic

129. Alexander Shea, Against Sanitised Football

Can fans fight back against clubs who seek to ignore their history for bland branding?

136. Paul Brown, The Trials of Baghdad Bob

Can Roberto Martínez restore his reputation after a season of wilful blinkeredness?

⇔ Fiction

141. David Ashton, The Tackle

John Brodie, the former winger turned detective, returns to hunt down some stolen medals

● Greatest Games

169. Paul Brown, Scotland 3 England 1

Home International, Hampden Park, Glasgow, 17 April 1937

● Eight Bells

179. Michael Yokhin, Unexpected relegations

A selection of giants who have unexpectedly lost their place in the top tier

Information

190. Contributors

192. *Blizzard* Subscriptions

193. About *The Blizzard*

FSC
www.fsc.org
MIX
Paper from
responsible sources
FSC® C008152

GOALS ARE OVERRATED...
THE BEAUTY IS IN THE STRUGGLE.

Exclusively available online from **www.theblizzard.co.uk** and **www.goalsoul.net**

THE BLIZZARD BY GOALSOUL
A PARTNERSHIP BORN OF FOOTBALL

In celebration of our most popular design, The Blizzard and goalsoul have decided to release 'Goals are overrated...' across three stunning new colour combinations.

The Blizzard by goalsoul partnership is a commitment to style and substance in equal measure. Our stunning and original graphic tees look and feel great. Lovingly hand screen-printed on 100% combed-cotton and shrink-resistant fabric — you can be sure of the highest possible quality, durability and wearability.

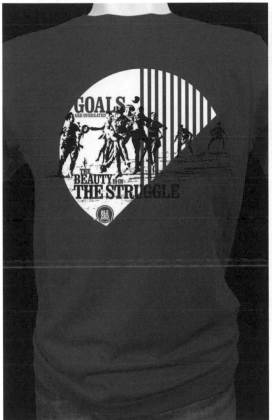

Calling All Writers

Your chance to tell the story of a football great

For almost fifty years, John Toshack has been one of the biggest figures in Welsh football. As a bustling centre-forward he formed a lethal partnership with Kevin Keegan at Liverpool, where he won three league titles and two Uefa Cups. As a manager he led Swansea City from the fourth division to the first in four seasons, won a Copa del Rey with Real Sociedad and La Liga with Real Madrid. His career has since taken him to Turkey, France, Macedonia FYR, Azerbaijan and Morocco. He remains a profound and provocative thinker about the game. Now he's looking for a reader of *The Blizzard* to help write his autobiography.

Ghost-writing a book is hard. It's a long-term project that will probably take at least a year; discipline and dedication are essential. It's not simply a matter of conducting a few interviews and transcribing the tape. A successful ghost must be able form a coherent narrative while drawing memories from the subject, finding key moments of colour and detail that bring the work to life. He or she will require excellent writing ability and the capacity to speak with the voice of another. Although John Toshack will give his time readily, ghosting demands hours and hours of research, speaking to players, managers and others who may be able to jog the memory or confirm facts, watching videos, poring through books, checking details in old newspapers and magazines.

But if you can do all that, while working with *The Blizzard's* editorial team, this represents a tremendous opportunity, whether for an experienced journalist or a first-timer. *The Blizzard* has always been determined to promote high-class football writing wherever possible and we're delighted that somebody of John Toshack's stature has joined us in pursuing that goal.

The Prize

The winning author will work with John Toshack on writing his autobiography, which will be edited and published by *The Blizzard*. The writer will be paid a percentage of profit under the standard *Blizzard* protocol.

To enter

Email **toshack@theblizzard.co.uk** before August 31 with:

- Your C.V.
- A covering letter of no more than 1000 words explaining why *you* are the best person to write this book.
- An outline of no more than 2000 words demonstrating how you envisage the book being structured, the tone it would take and key themes to be explored.

The Panel

Entries will be considered by John Toshack, Guillem Balague and Jonathan Wilson and a winner announced in *The Blizzard* Issue Nineteen, due to be published in early December.

10

Beyond the Game

"A good man is always unlucky."

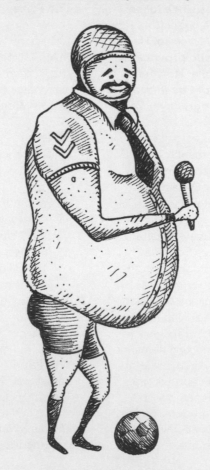

The Player of the People

The death of Igor Cherenkov last year prompted an astonishing outpouring of grief from Spartak fans

By Igor Rabiner

Sometimes in football, a funeral says far more than matches and goals, wins and losses.

In October 2014, around 20,000 people gathered at Spartak's indoor stadium in Sokolniki, in the north-east of Moscow, for the funeral of the People's Footballer, Fyodor Cherenkov, who had died at the age of 55. The ceremony lasted an hour and a half longer than planned.

The tail of the queue stretched far into the distance. There were people there not only in the red-and-white scarves of Spartak, for whom Cherenkov played a club record 498 games, but also fans in the colours of CSKA, Zenit, Dinamo and Lokomotiv. Spartak even received a message of condolence from Dynamo Kyiv – an astonishing act given the political relationship between Russia and Ukraine.

Former players, journalists and fans all agreed on one thing: only one other footballer had ever been accompanied on his final journey by so many people. It was not, as might have been expected, Lev Yashin, but Eduard Streltsov, Edik, the tragic genius who was sentenced to twelve years in jail on what many believe to have been trumped-up charges of rape. He missed the 1958 World Cup as a result, served five years

of his sentence and returned to become Soviet Player of the Year. As the master of ceremonies, Grigory Tvaltvadze, noted, "Only two players have been called in our country by only their first names, by the diminutive, without use of their surnames. There's no need to explain to anybody who are we talking about: Edik and Fedya..."

Neither were well-known abroad. Neither ever played at a World Cup. Both survived great personal trauma, which, as often happens in Russia, made them even more loved.

Initially two hours had been allocated for the farewell. But people kept coming for three. Three and a half. Even more would have come if police outside, near Sokolniki metro station, hadn't cut off access. Some of those turned away had flown from other cities, even though they had never met Fedya in person.

I've never seen so many adults not just crying but sobbing.

There was a man of about 40, in glasses, tie and a red-and-white scarf, with a totally pale face. "My adolescence has died," he whispered.

There was an old man with a huge grey beard, dressed in khaki and a Spartak scarf. He covered his face with his hands, not wanting to see the outside world.

There was a very old family, holding each other's hands. They came with their son, who was himself more than 50.

There were women of all ages; who, seeing this, could say football is not a women's sport in Russia?

There were no police inside the hall, and they weren't needed. Laying flowers by the coffin, anybody could have stepped over the red-and-white ribbon that separated football people from everybody else. They could have talked, for example, to Alexei Paramonov, almost 90 now, who won a gold medal at the Melbourne Olympics in 1956. "I didn't have football talent or abilities," he said. "I wasn't Fedya Cherenkov." And this was a man who once marked Ferenc Puskás out of a game.

The president of the Russian Football Union, Nikolay Tolstykh, compared Cherenkov's technique with Garrincha and announced that he had arranged with Uefa that Russia would wear black armbands during the international against Sweden.

Sergei Rodionov, a prominent striker, a long-time teammate and close friend of Cherenkov and now the president of Spartak's academy, which is named after Cherenkov, said, "We will always miss your kindness, honesty and decency."

Everybody was there. From Paramonov, the 87-year-old Nikita Simonyan and the 82-year-old Anatoly Isaev (all members of the great Spartak team of the fifties and Olympic champions)

to the kids from Spartak academy. Who didn't understand, of course, the scale of the person whose coffin they approached, but who saw for the first time in their lives how a football player could be loved by the whole country.

Even Fabio Capello changed the time of training to allow national team players to attend. And you could see in the guard of honour the current Spartak and Russia players – Roman Shirokov and Artyom Rebrov, Dmitri Kombarov and Denis Glushakov, Artyom Dzyuba and Sergei Parshivlyuk. – as well as the non-Spartak players Sergei Semak, Sergei Ignashevich and Aleksandr Kerzhakov.

After putting down his flowers, the current Spartak manager, Murat Yakin, modestly stepped aside. I hope that, looking at the endless flow of people, the Swiss coach understood much more about this club.

The owner of Spartak, who had already promised to build a statue of Fyodor at the club's stadium and to name one stand in his honour, was not present, but he was there a few hours later at the burial...

I was standing a few dozen meters from the coffin and talking to a musician, the long-time Spartak fan Yuri Davydov, who tried to explain why there were so many more people there for Cherenkov than for the club's founder, Nikolai Starostin, who died in 1996, or for the great manager, Konstantin Beskov, who died in 2006. "Starostin or Beskov, when they passed, were very old men," he said. "People who came to Cherenkov's farewell represented four generations. He still was a boy for older supporters.

For his generation he is a contemporary. For the next one, mine, an idol. For the youngest one, a legend."

At 1.23 pm, three and a half hours after the beginning of ceremony, the storm of the ovation began. Fyodor Cherenkov's coffin was brought through a corridor of hundreds of applauding fans. The same happened a few hours later at the Troekurovskoe cemetery.

Not long after I heard the terrible news I received a call from a colleague. We exchanged condolences and then he told a story. "I saw this with my own eyes," he said. "I immediately called the paper, but they didn't believe me. But I swear, it happened."

This was the story he told me. Before Spartak's 4-1 win over Arsenal in the Champions League in 2000, a security guard at the Luzhniki, indifferent to football and its legends, refused to let Fyodor in, demanding to see his ticket. He didn't have one and, modestly, turned to leave. But fans saw what had happened and dozens of them lifted Cherenkov up and surged by the security guard, carried him into the stand. Did it really happen? Who knows? But if I want to believe it, it happened: Cherenkov's personality always attracted half-legends; fact and myth were always difficult to disentangle, the desire to express an inner truth often over-riding documentary reliability.

Imagine this. Spartak were playing Dynamo Kyiv, their biggest rival. On the same day, Cherenkov, a student at the Moscow State Mining University, had an exam. "Konstantin Ivanovich [Beskov] let me go," Cherenkov once told me. "At that time there was no way to avoid it. I passed the exam, then went to my class-mates' hostel. I even caught a taxi as a celebration: usually I used a trolleybus. Then I asked the driver to switch on the radio, and heard that Spartak had won – 2-1. So, I celebrated two events at the same time!"

That was real, but the next story is obviously a legend – even if it is a beautiful one. Once Fyodor went to an exam, as usual, without any favour or preference. His teacher had no idea about football and Cherenkov never told anyone who he was. He successfully passed the exam and later somebody explained to the professor who the student was. He didn't believe it, so the other students took him to the Luzhniki. The professor took a closer look and exclaimed, "Yeah, this is the student Cherenkov." A fan sitting nearby said, "Sir, you yourself are a student. And Cherenkov is a professor!"

Of course, this didn't happen, but it might have done. Because it's one of the fairy tales that are more real than anything real. And when I shared my grief on social networks, a Spartak fan called Oleg Skvortsov replied, "We studied at university with Cherenkov. Teachers always used him as an example – he passed exams and never used his status or fame."

Meanwhile, about the trolleybuses... 13 years after Fyodor finished his playing career, he mentioned in an interview that he used public transportation.

He didn't complain: "I go by tram and watch how people are dressed. I listen to what they are talking about, feel their emotions. This way you feel the life better. I need it."

A couple of months later some unknown supporter, who has never revealed his identity, presented Cherenkov with a Lada Model 10 (his number on the pitch). What sort of footballer, what sort of man, do you have to be that a fan will present you with a car so long after you finish playing?

In March 1990, Cherenkov, at the time the Spartak captain, led the team in an away match against Chornomorets Odessa. It was the second game for the red-and-whites for a 21 year old, signed from the provincial side Fakel Voronezh, Valery Karpin. The only goal in the game came from a mistake by Karpin. "To be honest, I even cried in the dressing-room," he told me years later. "At that moment Fyodor Cherenkov, the kind soul, approached me and said, 'Don't cry, Valera. I know that you will help us a lot.' Could you imagine what those words meant to me?"

A few decades later, when Cherenkov was left without anywhere to live, Karpin, then the Spartak manager and CEO, agreed with the owner, Leonid Fedun, that the club should buy him an apartment. Everybody who knew Cherenkov, at least a little bit, could confirm how light – not just good! – a person he was. Not from this world, as we say. When we asked him in an interview for *Sport-Express* about his attitude to money, he replied, "I remember a parable from my childhood. A rich man sits on a bag of money. He thinks: 'Where should I put these rubles?'

Then he hears how a smith knocks with a hammer and sings songs. He is surprised: 'I'm so rich, and I'm silent. And this beggar smith sings and sings. Let's give him money.' And he gave it to him. And the smith got angry. He started to think how he could spend the money. And he stopped singing.'

We in Russia call this kind of person 'God's man'.

What kind of a player was Cherenkov? Just one recent analogy. You probably remember the magical goal by James Rodríguez against Japan at the 2014 World Cup, when the Colombian, as Russian footballers say, "made clowns" out of a defender and the goalkeeper with a few feints and softly tossed the ball into the net? Cherenkov scored dozens of goals like that in his career.

The secret of his football art was in its outdoor nature. The trouble with today's players is that most of them are from incubators: very early they are sent to football schools, where their imagination is killed, where they are educated professionally but impersonally. And everybody ends up looking like each other.

Once Cherenkov, by then already an adult, heard this story from his mother. When he was very small and ran about near his home in the Kuntsevo district with something shaped like a ball, he was spotted by a passer-by who was so impressed that he found out where the Cherenkovs lived and presented Fedya with his first proper football. "I liked just to feel he ball," Fyodor told me. "When the guys went home, I remained alone. It wasn't boring for me because I had a ball. I carried it as much as possible up on my foot. I juggled the ball, trying to keep it up 500 times in a row. Sometimes it had got dark but I hadn't reached the target and so I wouldn't go home."

When I watched the robotic Russia side at the 2014 World Cup, I recalled that story from Fyodor, how the ball became an animated subject for him and he learned to speak to it in his own personal language. Today's children, at least in Russia, are collectively urged towards some uniform, grey mode of expression.

"In terms of individual skills I put Cherenkov in first place in all Spartak history," the great goalkeeper and television announcer Vladimir Maslachenko, who died years before Cherenkov, told me. "He is a genius, who wasn't fully understood. In terms of pure football qualities Cherenkov is even not Streltsov; Cherenkov is Pelé."

You could say that Maslachenko went too far. But in this case I don't care about the opinion of objectivists. Because I probably would never have loved football so much if I hadn't seen Cherenkov. And I would have never gone into sports journalism, if I hadn't wanted to find words worthy of describing the art of Fedya.

I have no right to forget that until the end of my life. And if I forget, this "objectivism" should be regarded as a betrayal of my childhood and my first football love. That's why I would sign up with pleasure to the words of Oleg Romantsev, Fyodor's teammate and then manager: "Fedya for me is the greatest player in the world, ever!"

Cherenkov is one of the few Soviet players who scored at the old Maracanã. In June 1980, Brazil, with Socrates, Zico, Junior and Eder, hosted the USSR in a match to celebrate 30 years of the stadium and 10 years since the Selecão's last victory at a World Cup. Brazil opened the scoring, Zico missed a penalty kick and it looked as though the Soviet team would be destroyed.

But all of a sudden there came a beautiful attack, led by Spartak players, that swept across the whole pitch. Vagiz Khidiyatullin started it, Cherenkov continued it, Yuri Gavrilov made an amazing backheel pass... and Fyodor ran in to the box and with a one-touch strike equalised. A few minutes later Sergey Andreyev scored a second goal, the winner.

Cherenkov scored at the Maracanã, he scored against the France of Michel Platini and Alain Giresse, he scored in four games in a row during the Moscow Olympics in 1980, as well as many decisive goals in Europe.

And I've never forgotten how once in the autumn of 1983 late on a midweek evening my dad forced me, a 10 year old, to go to bed. It was bedtime with school the next day. But how was it possible to go to bed with Spartak playing the second leg of a Uefa Cup tie away against Aston Villa? For half an hour I resisted, tiptoeing to the door and listening for any fluctuation in the sound from the radio.

But finally I got to sleep and only the next morning did I find out that two goals by Cherenkov, the second of them scored in the last minute, had taken Spartak to the next round. The disappointment that I didn't experience that crazy happiness live is still with me. Since that day I've hated to watch games that have already been played.

It's sad that few people outside Soviet Union remember him. It's a monstrous injustice. As is the fact that he never played at a World Cup. We wanted so much to share our happiness in watching Cherenkov, but Fate said, "No". When 35-year-old Fyodor announced in 1994 that he was quitting the game, I asked the 92-year-old Spartak founder Nikolay Starostin his thoughts. He breathed deeply and said, "A good man is always unlucky".

"At the student internship in the Elbrus Mountains I talked for a long time with mountain engineers and other people," Cherenkov told me once. "The toughness of spirit that I gathered from them has helped me in the hardest moments."

He had enough of them.

After the physical disruption he first suffered in spring 1984, when he was 24, his whole life was an ordeal. Cherenkov took it stoically. "If the illness is given to me, it's given for something," he said. "There is nothing accidental. I have to overcome it, and never ignore God's precepts. I have to always remember that good elevates and evil destroys."

When Cherenkov played, nobody publicly discussed his disease and it was impossible to do so in Soviet times. Of course, there were rumours: how could the Soviet Footballer of the Year

of 1983, who played that time with a memorable hairstyle like a Russian Fellaini, suddenly disappear for several months the following spring? Officially he had suffered an injury, but nobody believed that story. But nobody at that time knew the truth. And the poignancy of this ignorance, what happened to the idol, made the people's love for him even stronger.

The USSR defender Alexander Bubnov, a TV announcer with a controversial reputation, who played for Spartak with Cherenkov, revealed some sensational details that no one had spoken about before. Nobody has confirmed it since, but who knows?

Bubnov outlined what he said had happened when Spartak played Anderlecht in the quarter-final of Uefa Cup in March 1984. In the away game, Konstantin Beskov fielded Cherenkov on the right wing, which, in Bubnov's opinion, was a mistake because Fyodor usually played in the middle and, from a physical point of view, Frank Vercauteren, the Anderlecht left winger was much stronger. After a 4-2 defeat loss, Beskov said, "Fedya, you are the best player in the country. And Vercauteren is the best player in his country. Now you've played against each other, and it showed who is really the best." After that, Bubnov said, Beskov even gave Cherenkov a match programme and suggested he get Vercauteren's autograph on it.

Cherenkov, in Bubnov's version of events, began to behave strangely. In Tbilisi, where the second leg was played, he told a waiter that he would not eat the food because it was poisoned. And when Bubnov went with Sergey Rozhkov, an assistant coach, to Cherenkov's room, they found Fedya sitting on the bed, smoking three cigarettes at the same time. After that Sergey Rodionov, Fyodor's friend and room-mate, was moved to another room, and members of coaching staff stayed with Cherenkov instead. Doctors advised Cherenkov shouldn't be sent straight back to Moscow, reasoning he would feel better with the team.

Cherenkov was at his best in pre-game training but Beskov didn't risk putting him on the pitch. Spartak won 1-0 but it wasn't enough. Amid all the noise and discussion in the dressing-room afterwards, Cherenkov went missing. He was finally found on the team bus. Only later did it emerge that Cherenkov had actually gone to Anderlecht's dressing-room and got Vercauteren's autograph.

After they got back to the hotel, the team went for dinner. Beskov's table was near Bubnov's. Suddenly Cherenkov approached the manager's table and put the programme from the game in Brussels, with Vercauteren's autograph, on Beskov's plate, turned around and went away. Beskov was shocked and couldn't say anything. According to Bubnov, Beskov's taunt about the autograph had been the final straw that led to Cherenkov's nervous breakdown. When he got back to Moscow, Fyodor was admitted to the Institute of Psychiatry and returned to the pitch only a few months later.

It's hard to know whether the story is true. Nobody has confirmed it. I even spoke to Vercauteren, who is now working in Russia as manager of Krylya Sovetov, but he couldn't recall signing the autograph. That doesn't mean it didn't happen – he was a famous player, who probably signed dozens of autographs for opponents – but it still means there's no confirmation. I never heard Cherenkov criticise Beskov, but then that was never his style.

Whatever the cause, Fedya fell ill. For my book *Spartak Confessions*, he said, "I used to think that my illness wasn't caused by overdoing it in 1983, when I played not only for Spartak in every tournament but also for the Soviet national side and for the Olympic team. I guessed at other reasons. But in the end I came to the conclusion that the reason was definitely that I'd overloaded myself. I remember how hard it was to recover that first time. My body dried up with the medicines I took. I had the sense that weights were hanging from my legs."

He often had to have treatment – In 1984, 1986, 1990... but he kept on coming back. In 1987 he scored the winner against Dynamo in Kyiv with a rare header. A few weeks later, he scored the vital goal against Guriya Lanchkhuti as Spartak ended seven years without a trophy by winning the championship.

In 1989, by which time Oleg Romantsev had become manager, Cherenkov became captain after the goalkeeper Rinat Dasayev had moved from Spartak to Sevilla. Spartak beat Valeriy Lobanovskyi's Dynamo 4-1 in Kyiv. When the sides met again in Moscow, Spartak knew a win would seal the title. Valery Shmarov scored the winner with a last-minute free-kick; Cherenkov described that – rather than any of his own heroics – the best moment of his career. That year, aged 30, Fyodor became Soviet Footballer of the Year for the second time.

The success never changed him. In the summer of 1987 he scored the 100th goal of his career from a very controversial penalty. "For many years my conscience tortured me over that 100th goal," he said.

Many Spartak fans hated Lobanovskyi not just because he was manager of Dynamo Kyiv, their biggest rivals, but because he didn't take Cherenkov to the World Cup in 1986 or 1990. But they didn't know the truth.

Georgy Yartsev, a teammate of Cherenkov at Spartak and later Russian national team manager, explained: "Part of the phenomenon of the people's love for Cherenkov is the unwillingness of a manager to select the best player of the country in the national team. People didn't know some of his problems and thought it was a sign of disrespect to a person who made millions happy."

Lobanovskyi couldn't disclose the truth, and so he had to accept the hatred. Many Spartak fans couldn't forgive him for that. We saw that Cherenkov tended to play better in odd-numbered years, but we didn't know that was because he kept falling ill in even-numbered years. When Cherenkov became player of the year in 1989, and still Lobanovskyi didn't pick him in the squad for the 1990 World Cup, everybody understood: that was it – there was no chance of Fyodor playing at a World Cup. All the *spartakovtsy* cried and cursed Lobanovskyi. But two decades later Cherenkov told me, "In 1990, people told that Lobanovskyi should have taken me to the World Cup.

I didn't even give it a thought. Why? Because after the successful season of 1989, when we became champions, I suddenly felt awful inside with exhaustion. In 1990, my thoughts were not about the national team but how to get the strength to start willing myself to play football again. That's why I wasn't hurt by Lobanovskyi."

Rinat Dasayev had another theory. "I think Lobanovskyi just was afraid to overload Fyodor, knowing his health problems. He always asked, 'How is Fyodor?' but he never did it formally." I don't see any reasons not to believe the goalkeeper.

In the summer of 1990 Cherenkov accompanied Sergei Rodionov to play for Red Star Paris in the French second division. But Fedya's journey lasted just six months. He didn't feel comfortable at all outside his native country and came back to Spartak. He produced some more brilliant flashes in 1991 and 1993, the final year of his career. Both were odd years, and in 1992, an even one, he didn't play at all.

As soon as I asked people on social networks to tell me their personal memories Cherenkov, the stories rained in.

Sergei Borisov, the Uefa press officer, wrote about how, while Guus Hiddink's Russia team were training in the Austrian town of Leogang during Euro 2008, he and a colleague heard a soft, confused voice. They turned around and saw Cherenkov. Extremely quietly, as though expecting to be turned down, he asked if he could approach the pitch, just to stand near the bench, near the training footballers.

Borisov and his colleague stopped breathing: Cherenkov himself was asking them to be allowed closer to the players – when the current players of the national team should have been asking to stay closer to Cherenkov.

My colleague Mikhail Evseev told me how five or six years ago Cherenkov visited a tournament for blind kids. He approached him for a comment and suggested it was good of him to find time to attend such events. "You have to conduct interviews with these guys who are real heroes," Cherenkov replied. "Who am I? Just a former footballer..."

Maxim Bolshov, a supporter, spoke of how four or five years ago he was waiting for the buffet in the same queue as Cherenkov at half-time of an Under-21 game. Everybody recognised him and urged him to go the front, but he refused and stayed in line.

Erkin Baidariov, another supporter, from Uzbekistan, recalled how in the early eighties, when Spartak arrived in Tashkent, the local boys ran to the hotel for autographs. One of hotel staff learned that Fedya was in his room and brought a group of boys upstairs. They knocked on his door and heard a voice: "You can enter: the door is open." They went in and saw Fyodor, who had just had a shower, dressed in just a towel. He smiled, signed everything, chatted with the boys and didn't show any signs of irritation that they'd disturbed him.

Several decades later, Fyodor, who lived extremely modestly, would say,

"Everything in my life is settled, I have everything I need. I try to improve myself, to get rid of sins – for example, despondency and gluttony."

At the memorial ceremony, Spartak veterans and ordinary fans approached me and told stories. For instance, in 2009 there was a pre-New Year meeting of four generations of Spartak champions who won the Soviet and Russian leagues in 1969, 79, 89 and 99. Almost everybody arrived in cars and the younger the players were the more expensive the model. Then suddenly Fyodor appeared from the bushes. He was very modestly dressed and obviously frozen. Those who saw him were astonished: "Fedya, couldn't anybody drive you here?" He, as usual, waved his hand: "What for? I could come by myself." He was doomed to carry his disease until the end. This illness, as well as the medications which accompanied it, undermined his energy and health every year.

In summer he played with pleasure for Spartak's veterans teams. In spring and autumn, very rarely.

In the nineties, Oleg Romantsev, as president and manager of Spartak, tried to include him on the coaching staff of the reserve team. Fyodor could have shown players at the training pitch more than anyone, but the job couldn't have lasted for a long time.

His wife Irina would sometimes look into his eyes and decide: "Fedya, it's time to go to the hospital." And he went there. Every single spring, every single autumn. And it was getting worse and worse.

The club cared for him as much as possible. The Spartak youth academy was named after him during his lifetime, which says a lot. The decision was taken after dozens of Spartak veterans signed a letter urging the club to honour him. Spartak also paid for Cherenkov's medical care.

For the last nine months of his life Cherenkov lived alone after his second marriage broke up. There can be no doubt that life was hard for his wife. For us, Fyodor was an idol and the greatest footballer of all time. For her, he was a partner every day.

In those final nine months, he lived — let us give the address — at Samora Machel street, 4/3, apt. 18. Nobody there knew him well. He didn't have a neighbour like *tyotya*[1] Valya, who regularly visited him in his apartment at Kuntsevo about five years ago, boiled a pot of *shchi* (cabbage soup) and didn't allow him to starve. In those last months, Fedya probably only ate till he was full when he travelled with Spartak veterans.

It hurts a lot that Cherenkov never saw the long-awaited Spartak stadium in the Tushino district, the result of almost an unbelievable twist of circumstances. The Otkrytie Arena, which will be used for the 2018 World Cup, was opened on 30 August 2014 by Spartak veterans. It had been planned that Fyodor would play in an exhibition game, but for some reason he didn't appear. Nor did he turn up for the opening match, a friendly against Crvena Zvezda, or for the first league games, against Torpedo and Terek.

It was a strange story. Alexander Belenkov, Cherenkov's friend, who played with him until he was 16 at Spartak's football school — a group managed by the 1956 Olympic champion Anatoly Maslyonkin — arrived at the stadium at 2.30 pm. Fyodor had promised to bring his friend a ticket before going to play — and he always fulfilled his promises.

At 3pm Belenkov, who was still waiting, dialled Fyodor's mobile and was told, "The traffic police stopped me. But don't worry, I'll deal with it. I'll come about 4."

4pm was kick-off time of the game in which Fedya was the player most people wanted to see. But he didn't arrive and didn't answer further calls.

He never arrived at the stadium. A few days after his death somebody posted a video on Facebook showing him arriving with the veterans team in Samara, where he again didn't play. He was invited to the local TV station along with another former Spartak player, Alexander Mirzoyan.

Fyodor looked awful. His eyes didn't move. He barely spoke and when he did it was extremely quietly. And he said that somebody told him that the Otkrytie Stadium was built on an old graveyard (actually it was built on a former airfield). It seemed like an explanation for why he had avoided the stadium; in his final years he had become extremely religious.

Belenkov told me that on August 19 he visited Fyodor at his apartment and they

---

[1] *"tyotya" literally means "aunt" but the term is used in Russia of any older woman who offers support.*

spoke for five hours. He showed me a photo of both of them aged 11 and there were tears in his eyes.

On August 31 Fyodor played for Spartak veterans in Kotelniki. On September 22 he was found unconscious just inside the front door of his apartment building. He lived for a further 11 days, but there was nothing to be done. Some people say that conditions in the hospital were poor and blame the club.

He died on 4 October 2014, at 1am.

The end of July 2014, perfect weather, a cloudless mood. As in childhood, I'm not just walking, I'm almost jogging from Sportivnaya Metro station to the Luzhniki. To a football game.

But now this is not an official game, attended by thousands, many chanting abuse. This is the football of kind faces and gentle smiles, and everybody who is going to Kid's Town at Luzhniki, not the Bolshaya Arena, feels happy. Because it's a football match dedicated to the 55th birthday of Fyodor Cherenkov.

Fedya himself, though, doesn't get onto the pitch. What a pity! He would have given at least one pass of genius. Or he would have kicked the ball between somebody's legs. Or would have shown some other trick he practiced at Kuntsevo, dozens of which he light-heartedly transferred to 'proper' football many years ago. That's why so many serious men fell in love with him. Because for 90 minutes he made them kids.

But now, on his birthday, he doesn't even play and avoids offering explanations. He

makes people get lost in guesses, and his health, unfortunately, is one of the main topics of speculation. Cherenkov, for whom a ball is a god, doesn't want to play football? Nonsense. It can't be anything good.

But anxious thoughts are rapidly cleared away: the hero of the day looks cheerful. He stoically signs autographs for more than an hour. He addresses everybody with his usual shy smile – although now it's hidden behind a thick beard, which makes Fyodor somehow different.

Then there is a banquet in a restaurant on a ship on the river. There's a moment at which I'm hugging him. Then giving him a copy of my article, "The Magic Country of Cherenkovia," written for his birthday. And for maybe the 100th time in my life, I'm repeating to him, "Fedya, you always were my idol. Thank you for being born and for being with us."

And then I heard him reply with a line from the Bible: "Do not worship anything or anybody blindly."

He was a rare person – a man of God a, saint, an ethereal person from anywhere but the cynical 21st century. That evening when I got home, my wife said it was a long time since she'd seen me looking so enlightened.

And now there is no more Fedya. As I think about this, I'm walking on the street. I'm wrapped up against the cold, but I begin shaking. It's the shake of an irretrievable loneliness. So far I haven't been able to imagine how to live, knowing that there is no Fedya on this earth. Probably somehow it's possible. But how much warmth and light each of us lost with his exit. It's impossible to bring them back.

But it's possible to bring back some memories. Fate bookended my acquaintance with Cherenkov in a surprising manner. My first meeting with him was also at the Kid's Town at Luzhniki.

In June 1990 I, a novice 17-year-old reporter, went there to some charity game of athletes and actors in which he was playing. And I asked him in a trembling voice if it was possible to do an interview.

Fyodor gave me his home phone number. You remember only very important details from your distant past, and I'll never forget how I tried to reach him from a public phone on the railway station at Pavlovsky Posad, a town two hours by train from Moscow, where my students group practised on the local paper.

You had to throw a two *kopeiki* coin down the throat of that phone, and after you'd spoken for few minutes, you had to throw in another one. I reached him, and just as he was thinking when he could talk to me, the last *dvushka* (two kopecks) disappeared inside the phone. There were just a few seconds until the

connection would be cut off and my dream would disappear. I was totally alone at the station, there was nobody to give me another coin.

But Fyodor's pauses were always perfectly timed. He managed to tell me the day, the time and the magic word "Tarasovka" – Spartak's training ground – and immediately afterwards the connection was cut.

Now I'm looking at this black and white picture. That old wooden players' hotel building behind Cherenkov's back isn't there any more. The monument to Lenin isn't there any more. And now Fedya, my beloved Fedya, isn't there any more.

I still remember the last words that I heard him say: "Do not worship anything or anybody blindly."

I'm sorry, Fedya. I did it. And thank God, I wasn't shy of my feelings and told you them two months before your exit.

I'm proud that I had such an idol in my life as you. Thank you that you were.

No one like you will ever be born again. But somebody else maybe will. It couldn't be any other way. Because this is life. And it goes on. Ⓑ

HOME TAPING IS KILLING MUSIC

AND IT'S ILLEGAL

The Man who Sacked Himself

Gabriel Hanot was a player, a coach, a journalist and a pioneer who remains oddly neglected in France

By Philippe Auclair

The France national team which lined up against Spain at the Stade de Colombes on 19 June 1949 had very little to show for its season to that point. A weakened Switzerland had been beaten 4-2 a fortnight earlier, but the four previous games had brought three defeats and a draw[1], while Yugoslavia lay in wait for a double-header that would send its winner to the 1950 World Cup. The last opportunity to build some momentum before then was given by the visit of Spain, who offered a much sterner test than the Swiss. That chance was blown, emphatically so. The French capitulated 5-1 in front of their public, giving the sports daily *L'Équipe* every reason to publish one of the most violent editorials in its history two days later. The headline summed up the belligerent mood of its anonymous author.

"AN UPHEAVAL IS FRANCE'S ONLY CHANCE OF SALVATION!"

What followed was a two-page reform plan which addressed every single symptom of the disease at the heart of French football, from overpaid professionals ("120 000 francs and more per month", almost ten times the minimum wage which would be introduced in France soon afterwards) to the reduction of the League calendar ("a maximum of 14 or 16 teams in the top division", no games to be played less than three days apart), the prohibition of friendlies in the close season and the free access of children to stadiums ("under the constant supervision of a coach, even if there are cases of truancy" – no half-measures, then). But, lucid and visionary as this diagnosis of French football's ills was at the time, it was not as striking as the identity of the man who suggested that nothing less a revolution was required to remedy them[2]: he was none other than Gabriel Hanot, the paper's editor – who'd doubled as the

---

[1] *3-3 v. Belgium, 1-4 v. Netherlands, 0-2 v. Scotland, 1-3 v. England.*

[2] *The necessity of reform would always be one of the points Hanot advocated most passionately throughout his long career as a journalist. What irked him most of all was the lack of attention given to youth development and the "physical deficit" of French players, a theme he didn't need much encouragement to write variations about. In 1957, six months before what would be a splendid World Cup for Albert Batteux's team, he asked of its players: "are they athletes or bourgeois?" calling for a "long-term policy" of improvement in their fitness. It was not implemented until Ştefan Kovács and Robert Boulogne took charge of the team in the 1970s and built the foundations of the system that produced a World Cup-winning team – putting into practice a number of the*

national team's de facto manager since December 1945. And this is what he had to write about himself. In capital letters. On the front page.

"THE SOLE MANAGER HAS NOT SUCCEEDED THIS SEASON. IF THIS IS ENOUGH TO CONDEMN A MAN, LET US REPLACE HIM. IN THESE CONDITIONS, A NEW TECHNICAL ADVISOR MUST BE FOUND, SAYS ONE OF US, AS THE PREVIOUS ONE HAS NOT MANAGED TO GET THE NECESSARY PERFORMANCES FROM THE CHOSEN PLAYERS."

In other words, Hanot ("one of us") was calling for his own sacking.

His wish was fulfilled. His resignation from the position of *conseiller technique du sélectionneur*[3] was accepted within twenty four hours. It's not that the Colombes disaster had forced the hand of the French Federation's panjandrums; it is more that they had no desire to stand in Hanot's way, just as none of the journalists who'd written scathing reports of France's obliteration in the columns of the paper he ruled over had had the guts to offend their *patron*. For fear was the foremost feeling Hanot inspired in those who came close to him. Respect and admiration were present too, but fear always came first –

perhaps because he himself ignored the meaning of that word.

This was a man, after all, who, after escaping from a German prison camp in the First World War, volunteered to join the flying corps of the French army, the equivalent of playing Russian roulette with two bullets instead of one. Of the 17,300 French soldiers who climbed in their open-cockpit aeroplanes between 1914 and 1918, 5,533 were killed in action. That is a casualty rate of 31%. Once you'd lived through that, there are a number of social niceties you do without. Handshakes, for example (as Hanot put it: "not only are they unhygienic, but they serve no purpose whatsoever"). He was a man of few words, who did not mince them when he felt someone needed to be taken down a peg or two. Jean Prouff, one of the key players in France's post-war team, has spoken of how, in April 1949, Hanot phoned him in his Rotterdam hotel room at 4am after a 4-1 defeat against the Netherlands. Prouff had been France's captain for the first time on that occasion. "I hope you're not sleeping after the game you've just played," his manager said. "As for me, I can't. Tomorrow, at breakfast, you'll explain to your teammates why you're not worthy to stay with us for the next game[4]. And you'll take the first train

---

recommendations Hanot had made in his famous editorial.

[3] *The official sélectionneur was Gaston Barreau, a teammate of Hanot's in France's pre-First World War national side. The word 'sélectionneur' shouldn't fool anybody: Barreau's duties never extended beyond those of an assistant coach during Hanot's managerial tenure. He survived Hanot's resignation and played a role in the affairs of* Les Bleus *until his death in 1958, having spent the last thirty-six years of his life with the French team.*

[4] *Hanot used his knowledge of English to publish the first French translation of the International Board's* Laws of Football *in 1921.*

home." (Hanot used the formal *vous*, a sure sign a bollocking was to follow). A few hours later, Prouff happened to meet Hanot in the hotel lift. The conversation was brief.

"You're still here?" the manager asked.

Yet Prouff's admiration for and loyalty to Hanot were not blunted by that episode. "That was his way to convey his displeasure," he recalled. "But as he was right, what could I possibly answer? Nothing. And perhaps he'd wanted to show all the players that even I, one of his favourites, was not granted special privileges. I find this remarkable. And it didn't prevent him from phoning me several times after that." Hanot, "tough" and "cold" as he was (two adjectives which pop up more often than not in the recollections of those who knew him) was neither a brute nor a bully. What he could be was impatient with those who had not been graced with as diverse an array of gifts as himself. He was opinionated, too, imperious, a man of convictions. Looking at his achievements, it is easy to understand why: he was a living embodiment of the maxim *mens sana in corpore sano*. He had achieved excellence in whatever he'd tried his hand at. Physical accomplishment, intellectual rigour and moral rectitude were what he expected from those who worked with him, be they journalists, football players or sports administrators – and especially from himself. If he could do it, why couldn't others do the same? Which constitutes perhaps, come to think of it, the only form of egalitarianism such an exceptional man could espouse.

Hanot received as good an education as any lower-middle-class Frenchman could hope for at the turn of the century (he was born on 6 November 1889 in the northern town of Arras), showing an unusual aptitude for mastering foreign languages. He spoke English with some fluency[5], but had an even better command of German, which made him a rarity in French society at a time of escalating tension with the victor of the 1870-71 Franco-Prussian war. His love of German culture made him move to Münster when he was only twenty years old, at no small cost to his football ambitions. It cannot be a coincidence that, having established himself as one of France's best wingers (and an automatic pick for the national team) when he

[5] *Against Scotland, at Hampden Park, four days after the defeat at De Kuip. Prouff re-joined the France team after Hanot's resignation, playing both legs of its World Cup qualifier against Yugoslavia in the autumn of 1949 (both drawn 1-1, the Yugoslavs edging the subsequent play-off 3-2 after extra time). These were his last two caps with Les Bleus. Prouff was quite an extraordinary man himself: in the summer of 1944, he was asked by the FFF to take part in an unofficial game against a British Army Select XI in just-liberated Paris. Prouff, then stationed in Rennes, thought nothing of covering 350km in two days on his bicycle, from which he jumped to start warming up on the touchline, to the astonishment of teammates who thought they'd never see him, much less that he'd show such freshness and enthusiasm after that gruelling journey. Prouff went on to become one of France's finest coaches, taking Standard Liège to the semi-finals of the European Cup in 1962 and to the Belgian league title a year later. This very proud Breton also led Stade Rennais to two French Cup trophies (1965 and 1971). He died in 2008.*

was only eighteen[6], he wasn't called once to the national squad during the two years he spent studying beyond the Rhine, despite winning the league title with US Tourcoing weeks before travelling to Westphalia[7] and playing elite football for FC Preußen throughout his voluntary exile. It's been said that he was a victim of the quarrel between the two governing bodies which were then vying for the right to be the sole administrators of the game in France, the CFI and USFSA, but it is difficult to see why this remarkably talented footballer would have been singled out when most of his other teammates were not. It is far more likely that the French football authorities didn't want to reward a young man who'd chosen to live in the land of the *Boches*. Whether this exclusion bothered him unduly is another matter altogether. In any case, it proved only temporary. Hanot resumed his international career shortly after his return to France and, in all likelihood, given his age and his qualities, would have accrued considerably more than his twelve caps if war had not broken out – and if his playing career had not been curtailed by a flying accident shortly after he collected the last of them (as captain, for the first and only time) in a 2-2 draw with Belgium on 4 March 1919, when he was not yet 30.

To Hanot, typically, this sudden end to his playing days did not represent the end of the world, but the chance to enter several others. His status as one of his generation's most accomplished players was beyond doubt; so was, soon, his reputation as a formidable journalist for *L'Auto*[8] and *Le Miroir des Sports*, who did not restrict himself to football, but also covered golf and, naturally, aviation[9]. He went on to invent the *Ballon d'Or*, the European Cup, the *Concours du jeune footballeur* (a series tests for young

---

[6] *Hanot was a member of the French 'A' squad which took part in the 1908 Olympic tournament in London (a 'B' team was also sent to England to make up the numbers) and endured a torrid time there, being on the receiving end of a record 17-1 defeat by silver medallists Denmark, Sophus Nielsen helping himself to ten goals on that occasion – an Olympic record which should stand for a while. Hanot had been rested for that match; it is not obvious that his presence on the field would have changed anything, however. The French were obliging opponents at the time. Several months earlier, in March 1908, Hanot had taken part in a friendly played at Royal Park against England, in which they conceded twelve goals without reply.*

[7] *The French national side played eight games during that period (1910-1912).*

[8] *L'Auto morphed into* L'Équipe *in 1946, after a brief hiatus caused by the paper's closeness with collaborationists during the Occupation. Hanot himself was never suspected of any unpatriotic act, as is proved by his official accession to the position of* conseiller technique du sélectionneur *after the 1945 armistice.*

[9] *One of Hanot's closest friends was Antoine de Saint-Exupéry, famous the world over for writing and illustrating* The Little Prince, *but also remembered in France as one of his age's most daring (and dashing) pilots, whose disappearance somewhere over the Mediterranean on 31 July 1944 is still shrouded in mystery. 'Saint-Ex' was flying an unarmed P-48 from a Free French base in Corsica towards the Rhône valley and was probably shot down by a German fighter plane as he was approaching Marseille. His body was never recovered.*

players staged before the kick-off of the French Cup final, held from 1930 to 1979, which revealed talents such as Raymond Kopa, Jean-Michel Larqué and Christian Sarramagna); lobbied for the introduction of professionalism in French football (and was successful in doing so, as could be expected, in 1932); organised the first coaching seminars ever held in Europe; carried on bossing everyone as if it were his birth right, which he never believed it was, as he remained an elitist egalitarian, a son of the Republic, and this rarest of animals: a powerful man who had no time for those who defined themselves by the power they wielded. To wit, the blank years of the German occupation. The Vichy regime considered professional football to be a game played by degenerate cosmopolitan types, far too many of them Jews, hoboing from Budapest to Bordeaux, and preferred the wholesomeness of mass gymnastics. Hanot kept his counsel, lay low and waited for the Normandy landings.

You would think that such an extraordinary man, a towering figure who shaped the French and European game more than any other individual in the 20th century, and did so so wisely, so forcefully, so imaginatively, would be celebrated in his own country. After all, the French are not slow to wrap the tricolour flag around one of their own when he or she has achieved a measure of international recognition. But this is not the case with Gabriel Hanot, who achieved so much more. No street, no school, no stadium bears his name. 46 years after his death at the age of 77, no statue has yet been erected in the city where he was born. No portrait or photograph of the visionary greets the visitor at the headquarters of *L'Équipe* and *France Football* in Boulogne-Billancourt. And if you think that is a pretty poor show, wait for this: the official website of the French FA gives his date of birth as 13 December 1901. Hanot was therefore six years old when he earned the first of his 12 caps for France. Ⓑ

Looking Forward

How the former Chelsea defender John Dempsey left football behind to work in a care home

By Brian Oliver

He played against Pelé, Cruyff and Beckenbauer. George Best was suspended for his testimonial match but Eusébio came instead and played alongside Bobby Moore and Geoff Hurst. He scored against Real Madrid in a European final, and was one of the outstanding performers in a classic FA Cup Final. But there is much, much more. He has, through sport, enriched the lives of many people with Down's Syndrome and learning difficulties. He has occasionally had to change the nappies of vulnerable adults who are incapable of caring for themselves. He knows all about wheelchair maintenance, lifting disabled people with a hoist, autism, epilepsy and challenging behaviour. He was a day centre care worker for 25 years. He is John Dempsey – a remarkable man who has led a life quite unlike anything expected of a top professional footballer. And he has enjoyed every moment.

Dempsey was a Chelsea legend of the 1970s, though he has an affinity, too, for Fulham, where he started his career. He was a stalwart centre-half in a team that featured Ron 'Chopper' Harris, Peter Bonetti, Charlie Cooke, Peter Osgood and Alan Hudson. It was the 'Blue is the Colour' era, when the song of that name added to the allure of the 'glamour' team of English football. Dempsey had no idea, throughout a busy playing career, what he would do after football.

"None of us ever thought about what we would do next," said Dempsey. His father was a big influence on him when he started, and "even he never mentioned it. None of us did. When you're playing, all you think about is football. But we all had to find something afterwards because we didn't earn so much back then."

That is something of an understatement. Dempsey's wages as an apprentice at Fulham were £6 a week. His first professional contract took him to £15 a week and by the time he finished at Chelsea in the late 1970s he was on £125 a week. With bonuses he earned little more than the average national salary. He did not have an agent, nor did he have any sponsors.

After Chelsea, Dempsey spent three years playing for Philadelphia Fury in the United States. He had helped to stop Pelé scoring in a friendly in Kingston, Jamaica in 1971, in which Santos beat Chelsea 1-0. In the North American Soccer League he shut out Gerd Müller of Fort Lauderdale – "a surprisingly small bloke" – and in four games against Cruyff (Los Angeles Aztecs, Washington Diplomats), the Dutchman scored only once. Other opponents included

Rodney Marsh (Tampa Bay Rowdies), and a trio of loan players at Detroit Express – Trevor Francis, Alan Brazil and a young Mark Hateley.

In 1979 Dempsey was voted the NASL's defender of the year. The runner-up was Franz Beckenbauer.

In 1980 he was awarded a testimonial, in which Chelsea beat an International XI featuring Moore, Hurst, Alan Ball and Eusébio. Best had promised to play but was banned by his club, Hibernian, shortly before the game.

Dempsey then tried management, without much success. He had played for the Republic of Ireland 19 times, qualifying through his parents, and led Dundalk in the League of Ireland for two and a half seasons. He returned to London and managed the non-league sides Maidenhead and Egham before he "drifted into work" for Barnet Council. He did not drift out again until he retired, aged 65, three years ago.

"I became a care worker and stayed for 25 years," he said. "I have had a very rewarding job, a rewarding life, after football. I must admit I got as much enjoyment doing that as I did playing football."

Few, if any, of his 1970s Chelsea teammates would say the same thing – that they had as fulfilling a life after football as they did while playing. Sadly, one of them, Peter Houseman, did not have a life after football at all: he was killed, with his wife, in a car crash in 1977. "I look at some of the others and while some of them did work they enjoyed, others have been angry and still are in some cases," said Dempsey. "They

think the club, or the game, should have helped them but it isn't like that. You finish playing and another lot come in. Once your time's finished you're soon forgotten. That's how it is. It's very, very sad when people get like that."

Sitting at his home in Hemel Hempstead, Dempsey ran through what he knew of his fellow players who featured in the famous FA Cup replay win against Leeds in 1970. The first game was a 2-2 draw at Wembley. "They'd had the Horse of the Year Show at Wembley the week before and the pitch was terrible, the ball bobbled all over the place. We could have lost that first game. Leeds had so much possession, and they were a good team.

"The pitch wasn't great [at Old Trafford] for the replay either, but we played better then, we deserved to win. I think I played well in both games."

The winning goal was scored by David Webb, who had a successful business career after football. "He spends a lot of time abroad and has done quite well. He used to dabble in buying and selling cars when he was playing, and always had a head for business."

Ron Harris, who trained greyhounds for years, has also done well in business, said Dempsey. One of Harris's top dogs was called Dempsey Duke. Peter Bonetti was a postman on the Isle of Mull for a while "and is now a Chelsea ambassador for home games, like Ron."

"Marvin Hinton, last I heard, had been a baggage handler at Gatwick for a while. Tommy Baldwin was a minicab driver. John Hollins did the best of those who stayed in football." Hollins managed Chelsea, Swansea, Rochdale and Crawley. "Peter Osgood and Ian Hutchinson ran a pub in Windsor but it went bankrupt. They're both dead now; so is Keith Weller."

Weller, who owned a coffee shop and worked as a van driver after settling in the United States, died 10 years ago. He did not play in the 1970 team but, a year later, was in the side that beat Real Madrid to win the Cup-Winners' Cup in Athens. That went to a replay, too – and Dempsey volleyed a spectacular goal in the second game. He learned his goalscoring skills early in his career, when he played a few games for Fulham as a centre-forward.

"Charlie Cooke runs football skills courses in America, and Eddie McReadie lives there too." McReadie, who managed Chelsea from 1975-77, coached and managed in the United States. He lives happily on a farm in Tennessee with his wife, a renowned quilt maker, and two dogs, one of which is called Chelsea. He became a Christian eight years ago and sounds as though he could run Dempsey close for contentment in later life.

The player who most feels hard done by is Alan Hudson, whose fall into a desperate lifestyle has been well documented. Hudson, who spent four years in the United States at the same time as Dempsey, had problems with gambling and alcohol. He was in a coma for two months after being hit by a car in London in 1997, was recently diagnosed with cancer and is living on benefits and a small pension. He is bitter that Chelsea never gave him a testimonial match. "I have always got on with Alan, and I went

to see him a couple of times when he was in hospital," said Dempsey. "The doctors thought he wouldn't survive. It's very sad, what's happened to him."

While Hudson was heading for a troubled future in the 1980s, Dempsey found his way into a new career. He did a bit of coaching at schools in north London. "Tony Jarrett did athletics, so did Donovan Reid [both were Olympians] and Lloyd Cowan, who is Christine Ohuruogu's coach. I did football," said Dempsey. "One afternoon a week I started going to Broadfields in Edgware, a centre for people with learning difficulties. They had autism, Down's Syndrome, challenging behaviour. After six or seven months one of the staff said a vacancy was coming up to teach PE at the centre. I quite enjoyed the schools work but I was interested. I didn't have a lot of qualifications but they said what I was doing, the one afternoon a week would count in my favour. I went for an interview and got the job. And I stayed for 25 years.

"The main part of it was running groups and there was a lot of personal care. I would have eight regular clients. I'd have people in wheelchairs who might have to wear nappies and I'd have to change them, lift them on to a bench. If it was really bad I had to take them into the showers too.

"It was an unusual job – a lot of people have told me they wouldn't fancy it, but I would say to them, 'Go and have a look and you'll see why I enjoy it.' None of my old teammates ever did come and see for themselves, though.

"Back at that time people didn't really talk about it a lot, about caring for these sorts of people. Some of my old teammates would say, 'I don't know how you can do that job.' A lot of them didn't realise what I was doing. I don't know of any other players who ever did anything like it. They won't be doing it now either, with all the money they're earning!"

One man who did go to Broadfields was Matthew Harding, the wealthy Chelsea director who died in a helicopter crash in 1996. "I went to see him in his office in Fenchurch Street to ask him for a donation. We needed a minibus, and to buy it and adapt it would cost about £23,000. I said anything would help, but asked him for £500. He said, 'You get the bus and I'll pay what it costs.' All he wanted was reassurance that I wouldn't be leaving the centre in the near future.

"He wanted to come along and present the bus. He had lunch at 12.30 and stayed till half past four. As he was leaving he said, 'Now I can see why you don't want to leave. This visit has really made my day.' His secretary rang a couple of days later to say Matthew wanted to come back in a couple of months. He did, and again about a year later. Then, sadly, he had his helicopter crash.

"He was different. People would look at you funny back when I started. They didn't like to see adults with Down's Syndrome out in public. At the swimming pool, at the bus stop, they'd just look at you. They didn't realise what warm loving human beings these people are. Coming to the centre once a week was something they really looked forward to, the highlight of their week.

"We had about 135 coming every week. You built up quite a relationship with some of them. Eight of the clients were under my wing, in my key worker group. It wasn't just working directly with them, though. Once a year we'd see their parents, would have to write a review for every one of them. We'd sit and talk about their progress, with the centre manager and a social worker there.

"I like to think I improved their lives. About seven months ago, long after I'd retired, one of my old group had her 50th birthday. Her parents invited me along on a Saturday night, and they told her I was coming. They told her a few words to say to her guests and after a short while she just kept talking about John Dempsey. I was so embarrassed, but it brought back happy memories. It was good to know that, even though I'd left, she hadn't forgotten what I'd done for her. It was all about trying to give to them something they hadn't had in life."

His care group became aware over time that Dempsey had been a famous footballer and would sometimes start singing 'Blue is the Colour'. He remembers one football match particularly fondly.

"We had a team from Broadfields that played in a league of 12 teams, all from similar care centres," he said. "I'd referee the home games and give them a bit of help. You had to make sure they kicked right way because sometimes they'd just kick whichever way they wanted. We had one player, Danny Kirkham, a centre-half, who was quite good. He had behaviour and learning problems. In one game against St Albans their centre-forward was about 6ft 8in and every time he got the ball everyone started running out of his way. The big fella came storming through again and I said, 'Danny, Danny, come on, tackle him.' He turned round to me and said, 'You fucking tackle him!'"

He sometimes had to deal with challenging behaviour. "They particularly liked routine, and if anything ever changed they might not react very well. They might fly off the handle, try to scratch you. You got used to it. It was a demanding job, long hours, but very rewarding."

Except financially.

When Dempsey finished his 25 years service in 2011, his salary was £25,000 a year. Three years before that, he was given a 'personal recognition award' by Chelsea at Stamford Bridge. It was presented by another man who played in central defence for Chelsea in a European final – John Terry. At the time, Terry would earn Dempsey's annual salary in two days.

The club invite him to two games a year, and for others he can buy tickets to take his son or daughter. The last game he saw was against Leicester this season. He follows Chelsea closely on television, too.

"Of course I think the money they earn nowadays is far too high," he said. "I watched the Youth Cup Final at the end of last season, when Chelsea played Fulham. One of the defenders, Andreas Christensen, is supposed to be earning £20,000 a week and he's 18, he's never played in the first team. Then there's Ruben Loftus-Cheek, the midfielder – they say he's on a lot of money too. In five years they can earn so much that they never have to think about working again, in or out of football."

That is bad for their development as people, Dempsey believes. "What will they do with their lives? I can genuinely say that in all my years as a care worker I never once went to work without looking forward to it.

"They're lucky to have been born in this era. But I'm lucky to have led the life I've had." Ⓑ

The Complicated Symbol

Bnei Sakhnin's journey to establish themselves as an Arab team in Israel's top flight

By Shaul Adar

Sammy Ofer Stadium, September 2014, Maccabi Haifa v Bnei Sakhnin

Haifa, northern Israel, summer 2014. The 30,000-seater Sammy Ofer stadium, light years ahead of any other venue in Israel, was full for its opening game. The majority of those there were emotional Maccabi Haifa fans, draped in green flags and banners, but one corner was populated with the travelling fans of Bnei Sakhnin, a team from a nearby Arab town.

Sakhnin fans had one huge banner: a drawing of a barefoot 10-year-old child in ragged clothes with his hand clasped behind his back — Handala, the creation of the Palestinian caricaturist Naji Al-Ali, which symbolises the resistance of Palestinian refugees who lost their homes to the state of Israel in 1948. The writing on the banner said "Sakhnin el Arab" — Arab Sakhnin. It was an apt reminder to the Israeli football fans that the stadium may be 'European' (the overused adjective when it comes to describe quality) but Israeli football is still rooted deep in the Middle East.

"[El Ali] was assassinated by the Israelis because of a drawing. A drawing!"' says Mahmud Galia, a journalist from Sakhnin. According to credible Israeli sources, the artist was actually murdered in London

in 1987 by a Palestinian hit squad after he insulted Yasser Arafat, the leader of the PLO at the time. Mossad was well aware of the plot but did nothing to stop it.

This is Israel, where life revolves around the Arab-Israeli conflict and everyone has a narrative to follow. Football is not exempt and Bnei Sakhnin tells that story better than any other team.

Ihud Bnei Sakhnin in Hebrew or Ittihad Abna Sakhnin in Arabic (Sons of Sakhnin United) began as a local team of a small town but are now a team that represents the minority in Israel. With a squad composed mainly of Arab-Israeli players, Sakhnin has become *kul al Arab* — an all-Arab team in the top league. The club used to nurture up-and-coming players on loan from Maccabi Haifa and had a mix of Jewish and Arab players, but now Jewish players hesitate to sign for them. The team draws fans from all over Israel's Arab communities. While most Arab-Israeli institutions are careful not to overstate their Palestinian identity, Sakhnin sometimes can't resist it.

Before a league match in October 2014, club officials handed framed honorary diplomas to people who had helped the team and raised money for it. Among the recipients was Azmi Bishara, but he wasn't there. He was a prominent Arab member of the Knesset, the Israeli parliament, but fled Israel when he was suspected of helping Hezbollah, the Shi'a Islamist militant group, in its conflict with Israel in the summer of 2006, a claim he has always denied. Today Bishara is an advisor to the crown prince of Qatar and for many Israelis a symbol of the Arab enemy within the state. When Sakhnin chose to honour him for his fundraising work in Qatar, it shook Israeli football and public mayhem ensued.

Fans, media and politicians turned against the club that used to be the darling of Israeli sport. "I don't understand what the fuss is about," said the Sakhnin chairman Muhammad Abu Yunas. "Dr Bishara helped raise money for Bnei Sakhnin while the establishment didn't give us anything, so why shouldn't we look for money from abroad? What's wrong with that?"

"A fine or games behind closed doors is not a sufficient punishment for the vile act of Bnei Sakhnin," said Limor Livnat, the sports minister. "Only an expulsion from the league will make clear to the innocence-pleading heads of the team the severity of their act in organising a ceremony in honour of someone suspected of treason and espionage for one of Israel's worst enemies."

In Gaza, the Hamas spokesperson wrote, "I wish to congratulate Ittihad Abna Sakhnin which has stood up and honoured Dr Azmi Bishara despite all threats."

After the conflict against Hamas in the summer of 2014, a continuation of 15 years of bloodshed following the collapse of the peace process in 2000, Israel is a place short of hope. Many Israelis believe there is no solution to the Arab-Israeli conflict and that sporadic wars will happen every few years. The rise of Isis and atrocities on Israel's doorstep in Syria has done little to improve the already fragile sense of security.

In Israel itself, relationships between the Jewish majority and the 20% Arab minority (not including Palestinians in the West Bank and Gaza Strip under Israeli occupation) are fast eroding. Systematic discrimination, mainly around housing and land issues, is a constant source of resentment among the Arab-Israelis. In the 2015 general election, the prime minister Benjamin Netanyahu based his campaign on fear of and hatred towards the Palestinians and the Arab world. "Arab voters are coming out in droves to the polls. Left-wing organisations are bussing them out," was his shocking rallying call on polling day. It was effective as the fear of a Labour government backed by an Arab party drove many Israelis to vote for Netanyahu.

It leaves the Arab population between a rock and a hard place. They are citizens of Israel but part of the Palestinian people and the greater Arab world. Some of them (but fewer and fewer) see themselves as Israelis, others as Arab-Israelis and many others as Palestinians. [In this article I will use the term Arab-Israelis as a neutral description of citizenship and ethnicity.] For the Jewish majority they are a potential enemy while for Palestinians outside Israel they are Israelified Arabs. With hatred and racism now out in the open, the country sometimes resembles Yugoslavia just before it fell apart.

The Israeli sociologist Dr Tamir Sorek of Florida University looked into the subject in his book *Arab Soccer in a Jewish State – the Integrative Enclave*. His research took place around the turn of the millennium and his findings are illuminating. "There's a power struggle around the club, and while the board wants to keep the definition of an Israeli team there is a significant group of fans who want to bring in elements which were not seen until 2008," he wrote. "There is an inclination to emphasise Palestinians' foundations and identity. In the unwritten code in Israel, it is seen as defiance when they call themselves Palestinians. For them the success of the team allows them to imagine integration in the Israeli society from a position of power. Emphasising the Arabness is not disconnected from the desire to be valued as citizens."

The town of Sakhnin sits in Galilee, a region of natural beauty and historical importance. In this small hilly piece of land, Jesus is said to have performed miracles, Saladin beat the crusaders in the Battle of the Horns of Hattin and the Israeli Army fought and won major battles. However, there is a feeling that one site to the south of Sakhnin casts a shadow over the land: Har Megiddo (Mount Megiddo) – Armageddon. It is a time of despair and you don't have to look for long to find people who think that World War III will start from here. Some messianic Jews, Islamists and evangelical Christians even want the war to erupt so their God will smite their enemies once and for all.

In the meantime, Bnei Sakhnin are becoming an important symbol of how complicated life in Israel can be. The formation of the club in 1992 now looks almost prophetic. In the 2015 general election, a united Arab party ran for the Knesset for the first time. Communists, Islamists, secular Arabs and a token Jew shared one political front. Bnei Sakhnin led the way on the football front. In 1992, Maccabi and Hapoel Sakhnin rose above years of rivalry and formed one united team. Instead of engaging in petty local politics and conflicts along the lines of the town's clans, Bnei Sakhnin took a different route. It was no coincidence it happened in Sakhnin. "There is something proud about Sakhnin," says Galia. "Land Day started here, it's the first town to embrace the Arabs of the West Bank and the Gaza Strip."

Sakhnin have been a bastion of struggle over the years. "We have given up many martyrs," Nidal, a political activist, is quoted as saying in Sorek's book, "whether it was in October 2000, in 1976 or 1948. Our entire history is a history of people who love their land, who always identify with the Palestinian people." Nidal referred to Israel's War of Independence in 1948 that brought the destruction of Palestinian life and two major events that followed. In 1976 a protest rose after the government announced its intention to confiscate lands from Sakhnin and neighbouring villages. A general strike and demonstrations were called and in violent clashes with the border police, six people were killed, three of them from Sakhnin. That day, March 30, was declared Land Day, an annual day of memorial and protest by the Arab minority in Israel. "By blood, by spirit, we will redeem you, oh Galilee," has been the rallying call ever since.

Sakhnin's place in the centre of the narrative of struggle was cemented in October 2000 when 13 Arab demonstrators in Israel were killed by the police during the first few days of the second Intifada. Two of the victims were from Sakhnin. Even in the bloody history of the conflict the events of October 2000 had a longstanding impact. Arab-Israelis took them as a proof of how fragile their human rights were, while mainstream Israelis saw it as treason. Both views added to Sakhnin's status as the Village of Martyrs.

The new team climbed the leagues steadily and after only 11 years made it to the top flight, only the second Arab-Israeli team to do so. Hapoel Tayibe had been the first, gaining promotion to the top tier in 1996. Tayibe suffered immediate relegation, financial collapse and vanished into the nether regions of Israeli football. The plan was to become a leading Arab-Israeli team with a squad based on Arab players and fans from across the Arab community in Israel. Tayibe never achieved the success on the pitch necessary to make that possible.

That year I came up with a number of scenarios of how Hapoel Tayibe's first season in the top league would go. One was immediate relegation and another the team becoming *kul al Arab*. In a way, both came true. Tayibe failed and never got beyond the status of a local team as it was too early for such plans. There weren't enough top-quality Arab players, the team didn't have the financial muscle to compete while Arab players were, at the time, deemed inferior to Jewish players at Arab clubs.

These processes later came to fruition with Sakhnin. The team, vitally, avoided

relegation, which turned out to be a tipping-point. It wasn't pretty, though. Under the manager Eyal Lahman, Sakhnin played tough, aggressive and sometimes brutal football. Even by English standards it was harsh, and when the team played against Newcastle United in the Uefa Cup in 2005 the tackles were followed by winces, gasps of astonishment and then rage by the Newcastle fans at St James' Park. Still, Sakhnin became part of the league. Since then the team has been relegated once but bounced back immediately.

A greater achievement was reaching the Cup final in 2004, the first Arab team to do so. In a packed National Stadium near Tel Aviv they beat Hapoel Haifa 4-1. "It was an unforgettable night," says Galia. "My father is still celebrating in his grave." Fans from all over the country made the pilgrimage to Sakhnin that night and the Israeli media celebrated with them. "*Sakhteyn* [an Arabic word used by Hebrew speakers meaning 'well done') Sakhnin," was the headline in one tabloid. "An achievement which will open doors" and "This is how one creates coexistence," said others.

Yedioth Ahronoth, the biggest paper at the time, went with "Mabruk ['congratulations' in Arabic, a word also used in Hebrew]: a historic achievement for the Arabs of Israel."

Zohar Bahalul, a well-known Arab journalist and now newly elected member of the Knesset, famous for his over-the-top Hebrew, wrote, "No more the same simplistic, supercilious and arrogant view of him [the Arab]. Perhaps from today onwards the attitude will be more respectful, more human and decent. There is hope. A new chapter in the cultural conflict between Arab and Jewish citizens of the state was written yesterday. A chapter of reconciliation. A sport has succeeded where others, for so many years have failed. The educational system in Israel never learned to inculcate the values of coexistence... Behold! Sport overcame the historic obstacle, disposed of the stereotypes, sowed pride and new hope in the Arab population."

Limor Livnat, the Minister of Education, Culture and Sport described the achievement as a "championship for a team from the Arab sector – a certificate of honour for Israeli society." The team of Arabs, Jews and Christians was hailed as a groundbreaker.

The website of Beitar Jerusalem's Ultras was shut down for 24 hours as a gesture of mourning.

The reactions were genuine. Israeli football, for all its faults, was far more open than most public spheres for Arab-Israelis. The best Arab players found their way to the top teams (apart from Beitar Jerusalem, where the racist fans won't allow it) and to the national team. During a 2006 World Cup qualifying match against Ireland, Abbas Sawan, Sakhnin's cup-winning captain and probably their finest ever player, scored a wonderful last-minute equaliser. Among the celebrating fans was Galia. "I was always against Israel's national team but with that game I was happy," he said. "Not for the team but for Sawan. We are an inseparable part of this country and we do have influence. Some fans put on an Israeli scarf on me and I went home with it. I

woke up the next morning, saw it, and thought, 'Oh dear, what have I done?'"

Sorek explains in his book: "Soccer provides many Arab men with a secure sphere of competitive masculinity and identification with flags and emblems and at the same time it avoids both Palestinian and Israeli national narratives ... The soccer sphere is constructed to serve as an enclave of integration, in which the Palestinian citizens of Israel attempt to suspend their national identification as Palestinians and in doing so maintain inwardly and outwardly circumscribed display – in time and place – of civic partnership with the Jewish majority."

For many years that was the model. Arab national symbols were kept away from the football stadiums; the chairmen of the teams spoke frequently about coexistence and the fans chanted, cursed and sang in Hebrew, even in games between two Arab teams. In the Arab press the tone was often far more nationalistic, but the football enclave was flourishing. The state and the FA were happy to show the world that Israel is a fair society and the Arab-Israelis enjoyed success and recognition. Walid Badir, a long-serving Arab player in the national team (who played at Wimbledon for one season) was the captain of Hapoel Tel Aviv, who won the 2010 Championship in the last minute of the season against Beitar in Jerusalem. The irony wasn't lost.

So, how has Israeli football changed from an example of integration to another arena for the conflict to be played out upon? Sorek explains,

"The significance of people who are afraid to challenge the Jewish public's sensitivities is fading. The events of October 2000 demonstrated the fragility of the Arab's civil rights. The events contributed to the trend that shows of protest that were once deemed a danger to the relationship with the Jews are now more common because the Arab citizens feel they have less to lose. Because of football's historical importance as a place of integration, it took more time for those trends to filter through. The war between Israel and Hezbollah in 2006 that was portrayed in the Arab media as a major defeat for Israel caused satisfaction among the Arab citizens of Israel and led to more defying ways of protest.

"Since the assassination of the prime minister Yitzhak Rabin in 1995 and, especially, since the beginning of the Second Intifada in 2000, the gradual extension of Palestinian citizenship rights in Israel has ended and even been reversed, a policy expressed in a wave of discriminatory legislation against Palestinian citizens. This wave, along with frustration over the failed emancipatory process of the 1990s, has pushed many Palestinians in Israel to reconsider their integrative aspirations. In addition, the widespread feeling among Palestinians that the two-state solution to the Israeli-Palestinian conflict has reached an impasse has also contributed to an imagining of alternative political solutions in which Israeli citizenship would be replaced with the citizenship of a future bi-national, non-national, or Islamic state."

And there's Beitar Jerusalem. Once the team of the people and now a club under the spell of a proudly racist nationalistic Ultras organisation called La Familia.[1] The club that had the potential to become Israel's most popular turned into a nasty organisation in which no Arabs or Muslims can play.'Beitar Jerusalem, forever pure' read a banner after two Chechen players were signed. The transfers resulted in games in front of empty stands and the club offices being burned down. The fascists won that round. Things got so bad that many fans found it unbearable and formed 'a new club, Beitarin Jerusalem, based on' their love of the old Beitar and humanistic values.

Over the years, Beitar v Sakhnin has become the Israeli *clásico*, the Terra Santa's derby of hate. Both teams have fallen from their previous state of grace but the game has become one of the focal points of the season. It usually comes a few days before or after a terror atrocity, a military offensive or election (just by probability) to add more heat to the encounter.

The match in November 2014 was probably the most policed match ever in Israel. Around 900 policemen and stewards tried to control fewer than 5000 fans (800 of them supporting Beitar) and 22 players, to no avail. The match in Sakhnin took place a few months after a military conflict in Gaza and only a few days after a terror attack in a Jerusalem synagogue in which five Israelis were murdered. Tension in Jerusalem had been brewing for months.

[1] *See* The Blizzard *Issue Two*.

The city of peace — at least that's its folk etymology — turned into the city of fear where no one, Jew or Arab, knew if they'd make it home in the evening. Every local skirmish had the potential to turn into a regional war.

At the Doha Stadium, a gallery of Arab politicians took their places while right-wing extremists stood among the Beitar fans. Never before had a top-flight match had so many Palestinian flags on display (an act illegal until 1992) while Beitar fans brought Israeli flags and one of the Golani Brigade — the fearsome infantry brigade of the Israeli Defence Army.

"By spirit, by blood, we'll redeem Al Aqsa," called out the local fans, referring to the heart of the conflict — Temple Mount in Jerusalem. There were songs about Palestine and the chant of "*Allahu Akbar*" [God is great]. Beitar fans answered in the usual way with nationalistic and anti-Muslim chants.

The annual matches are the much needed adrenalin rush for two mediocre football teams. "This is why we are in this league," said a local fan. "During the game we can express our identity." They are 180 minutes a year that crystallise the essence of Ittihad Abna Sakhnin.

The game last November ended in a 1-0 win to Sakhnin and five added minutes of fouls, flying umbrellas and other objects, and players pleading for some restraint from the fans. Three Beitar players should have been sent off but the referee decided to ignore their fouls. Later the Israeli media complimented him for using his common sense and preventing a riot. Beitar fans took their rage out on the public toilets and the buses instead.

One Beitar player later told the press that "We said to each other, 'We can't believe we lost that game.' It was like a war for this country, more than sport and we should have won it.'" Another player said, "It drove me mad to see the media after the game. Did you forget you are the Israeli media? What we went through should be the headlines and not some broken sinks. 5000 people singing, 'By blood we'll redeem Al Aqsa,' and you let them get away with it? If they could they would have made their way to the pitch and killed us all."

Israeli football is still waiting for a moment equivalent to Zvonimir Boban kicking a Yugoslav policeman at the Maksimir but it's most likely to happen at a Sakhnin v Beitar match. In the last round of the 2013 season, Sakhnin hosted Beitar for a match that might have resulted in Beitar's relegation. The game ended in an uneventful 0-0 draw and with Beitar safe in the league. It was the most boring game between the two teams in many years.

Doha Stadium, December 2014, Bnei Sakhnin v Hapoel Be'er Sheva

It was match day in Sakhnin and fans flocked to the stadium, passing memorial sites for the town's *shahids* [Islamic martyrs]. Doha stadium has three stands and one wall covered with ads and oriental arches like a shabby Stade Louis II of AS Monaco. Qatar financed the building of the humble yet practical stadium — much to the chagrin of many Israelis.

Their opponents were Hapoel Be'er Sheva from the south of the country who at the time were second in the league. Be'er Sheva, a much better team with some excellent attacking players and about 1500 travelling fans, were expected to win easily. The visitors and Sakhnin's vocal fans sat behind the two goals and ignored each other. Be'er Sheva fans sung their version of "Bad Moon Rising" while the locals chanted some generic support for their team, almost all of it in Hebrew. Among the Sakhnin fans was a group of Bedouins from the south, once part of Be'er Sheva's heartlands but much less so since the rise of Sakhnin.

Uri Aviram, a famous Jewish fan of Sakhnin for over 20 years told me, "I took my kids and we were warmly welcomed, as at no other club, with coffee and a barbecue. I liked it and I said to myself, 'I want to be here.' The talk was still about coexistence then. I found wonderful people here, warm and caring. They are not 'pet Arabs' like the ones the Israeli left is looking for."

And what does he think about the current trend? "The whole league missed the chance to have a team like that as a calling card for Israeli football. Sakhnin could have represented the country in a great way with players of all religions. We've missed it. Now it is a political team. Too political. I wish it was the team of old."

Galia is outspoken. "Can I smoke?" he asked me during the game when we were sitting in the small press box. "You can do whatever you want, it's your home," I said.

"No, you are my guest so now it is your home," he joked. "Just like you did to us with the country."

Galia thinks that the waving of Palestinian flags started at the games against Beitar and took off from there. "People saw that they could express their opinion in football grounds," he said. "It's a stage where you can protest against everyday life, the killing of *shahids*, the situation in Jerusalem and to do it in front of TV and press. It's the only time that the national media are here."

Sakhnin started the game without a single Jewish player but midway through the first half, the goalkeeper Muhammad Kandil was injured and replaced by Ran Kadosh, formerly of Barnet and one of only two Jewish players in the squad. On his Facebook page you can see a picture of Kadosh celebrating a Sakhnin goal with a Jewish prayer, while his teammates bow for Muslim prayer and another player makes the sign of the cross. "Three religions, one team and one game we all love!" says the caption. "Each man shall live by his own belief! Bnei Sakhnin 2015 is the writing on the wall."

Sakhnin are no longer the brutal team of the early years. They're a team of short and fast players. Hapoel's game is primitive and looks like pre-modern football with the defenders having to defend on their own while forwards stay upfield most of the time. Soon enough Be'er Sheva's right-back was exposed and left facing two Sakhnin players. A foul in the box led to a penalty that Firas Mugrabi converted. Mugrabi bowed while the announcer and fans celebrated the goal in Hebrew.

At the start of the second half, Be'er Sheva switched to three at the back and the game was over. For a team that couldn't defend with four, trying to hold the fast Sakhnin counter-attacks with only three was impossible and Muhammad Gadir, on loan from Maccabi Haifa and the best player on the pitch that day, made it 2-0 minutes after the restart. By then Be'er Sheva were playing in a 3-1-6 formation (with two Arab subs) that led to endless counter-attacks from the home side. Minutes from the end, the visitors won a free-kick near the Sakhnin goal and pushed seven players into the 18-yard box, but still the fans weren't happy. "He's a coward," they said bitterly about Be'er Sheva's manager Elisha Levy.

Sakhnin won the game 2-0 against a much stronger opponent and in the streets around the Doha, Be'er Sheva fans shook hands with Sakhnin fans and said, "*Mabruk.*" Last season when Be'er Sheva won 3-0 there, the scenes after the game were similar. A few local fans tried to provoke the away fans, chanting, "This is Palestine," but they were ignored. Sometimes, even in Israel, football can be, however fragile it is, just football.

"We tried to get into the league but we were rejected," says Galia. "For us it was more than a football league, it was an acceptance league but we were rejected. It's like in politics, like those offensive words by Netanyahu. We are citizens of this country, not refugees! But thanks to him the unity of the Arab society will continue after the election."

Namesakes

Everton have had two Alex Youngs: one's the subject of a Ken Loach film, the other killed his brother

By James Corbett

May 1967 and the denouement of a disappointing season. Player by player Everton's manager Harry Catterick was dismantling his so-called 'Mersey Millionnaires', who had brought the 1963 League Championship and 1966 FA Cup to Goodison. The likes of Roy Vernon, Alex Scott and Billy Bingham were being replaced by a new generation of homegrown players, such as Colin Harvey and Joe Royle, supplemented by young big-name signings like Alan Ball and Howard Kendall.

Going into the final game of the season, a Tuesday night home match against Sunderland, sixth place was already secured. There had been disappointing exits in the European Cup Winners' Cup and the FA Cup quarter-final, but terrace disgruntlement was muted by a general acknowledgement that this Everton team was a work in progress. And for the last match, there was joy that the Gwladys Street's idol, Alex Young, was back.

It had been six weeks since he had last been seen playing for Everton, and four months since he had played in his favoured number nine shirt, but it was like he had never been away. Young – Everton's Golden Vision – demolished Sunderland with a display of virtuosity, grace and skill. "Young spread destruction through their ranks with his

wonderful ball distribution, artistry and sheer cheek," wrote Michael Charters in the *Liverpool Echo*. Young didn't score but had a hand in each of Everton's four goals and only over-elaboration and a fine display by Jim Montgomery kept the score down to 4-1.

According to his captain Brian Labone, it was the best individual performance he had ever seen from Young and Alan Ball wanted him – and not Johnny Morrissey, who had scored a hat-trick – to keep the match ball at the end. "Young beat Sunderland almost on his own that night," claimed Labone "He played on the wing and I never felt so sorry for a man as I did for the Sunderland left-back [John Parke]. For him, it was a nightmare. For Young, it was a great personal triumph."

Cast your eye through any club history and legends tend to fall into distinct categories: goalscorers, playmakers, artists, mavericks, leaders, genius managers. In the pantheon of Everton greats, however, Alex Young is a special case because he transcends such ready categorisation. A sublimely gifted centre-forward, he assumed many of these characteristics. Lacking the physicality of the blood and thunder player who typified his position, Young was a slim, delicate, fragile player possessing more the physique of a winger or inside-forward. He was a great goalscorer, one of Goodison's finest, but also a creator of goals. For Evertonians, he typified a footballing era where the club's status as 'The School of Science' was beyond question.

If Dave Hickson is Everton's most loved player and Dixie Dean their most iconic, it's no exaggeration to say that Young is their most adored. He is to Everton what Kenny Dalglish is to Liverpool or Éric Cantona to Manchester United. Like Cantona, he inspired an eponymous Ken Loach film, but not even Cantona's adulation prompted an attack by fans on his manager after being dropped, as happened when Harry Catterick left out Young in January 1966. One of the most enduring images of the era is an Evertonian being led off the Goodison pitch by a bobby, still defiantly holding up a placard with the legend, "Sack Catterick, Keep Young."

This adulation bred suspicion in his manager, who dropped him, played him out of position and tried on several occasions to sell him. "It turned out that the more the fans loved me, the more the manager disliked me," Young recorded in his memoirs. "I was engaged in a constant battle with Harry and learned not to trust him." Where Bob Paisley and Alex Ferguson talked up Dalglish and Cantona, Catterick downplayed the role of his talisman. Perhaps this is why Alex Young lacks the effect on the wider football consciousness today.

Because footage of this era is limited by its graininess, the single-camera angle, the cliché-ridden Pathé newsreel, it remains difficult to get a full idea of Young's repertoire. The nuance is lost and YouTube, frozen frame by frame, leaves us with mere glimpses. Here's Alex, gliding over a mudbath. There's a swivel of the hips, but the floating leap, the dart of the eyes sending a defender the wrong way, the feint and dummy are left mostly in an ageing generation's memories.

Young was born in Loanhead, a coal mining village in Midlothian, in 1937. It was a time when an astonishing array of talent was bred in Scotland's central belt: in Young's junior school team alone were Ian King, later of Leicester City, and Malcolm Howieson, who would play for Grimsby Town; John White, who played with Young at Hearts and for Tottenham, went to a neighbouring school.

As with many from his background, Young seemed destined for life down the coal mine and was taken on as a colliery apprentice aged 15. His escape from such drudgery came via football. Spotted by Hearts playing junior football, he initially combined playing with work at the coalface. Aged 18, at the start of the 1955-56 season he made his Hearts debut in a League Cup tie; by the season's end he was an established Tynecastle favourite and had played a part in Hearts' first Scottish FA Cup win in half a century.

This would emerge as the greatest team in Hearts' history. As well as Young and White it boasted players such as Dave Mackay, Ian Crawford and Willie Bauld. Twice they lifted the Scottish League title, in 1958 – when they scored an astonishing 132 league goals and finished 13 points clear of Rangers – and 1960, and would also claim the League Cup in 1959 and 1960. Young cultivated a reputation as a forward of grace and élan. In 1960 he won his first Scotland cap, against Austria; just seven more would follow – the majority of them while still playing for Hearts.

The move to Everton came later in 1960 as Hearts' greatest team began to break up and the wealth of pools magnate John Moores started to make an impression at Goodison. As an 11 year old, Joe Royle – who would later replace him as Everton number 9 – watched Young's debut against Tottenham in December 1960 and recalled, "We all had our mouths open that night. We were all goldfish watching a wonderful talent."

Injuries meant he had a slow start to his Everton career, but his pedigree was never in question. "Young is a thoroughbred, a great mover with the ball, fast, active, razor sharp in his reactions," reported the *Liverpool Echo* of an early performance. "For his size, he is a good header of the ball. He is clever, artistic and can score goals." Everton finished the 1960-61 campaign fifth – their best since the war – but it was not enough to save their manager, Johnny Carey, who was sacked.

Although his relationship with Carey's successor, Catterick, was never easy, his form was astonishing. He and the Wales captain Roy Vernon would score 116 league goals between them over the following three years. Vernon, clinical and whippet-like – the ultimate penalty area predator – was the perfect foil for the Scot and they built up a subliminal understanding. Everton lifted the league title in 1963 – Young's brilliant header

in a late-season clash with their nearest rivals Tottenham effectively sealing that crown. His club were unlucky not to retain it a year later, after ailing late in the campaign when they were undermined by a match-fixing scandal involving their captain, Tony Kay.

Catterick by then had signed Fred Pickering for a British domestic transfer record and consigned Young to the reserves. Fan anger was initially quietened by Pickering's prolific form. Young asked for a transfer but later withdrew the request. Roy Vernon was sold to Stoke City and Young reverted to an inside forward or wing role, while 'Boomer' Pickering banged in the goals. Looking back in Young's 2008 biography there was a wearied tone in describing Catterick's management. "I thought of him as a canny businessman who bought and sold livestock, usually at a profit, and enjoyed the thrill of deal-making more than football," he recalled. "I don't think it was a case of him disliking me – more a case of him hating me."

Still he hung in there. The 1966 FA Cup win saw a revival in fortunes. Pickering, through injuries and loss of form, became a marginalised figure and Young was restored to the number 9 shirt. Yet football was evolving. Don Revie's Leeds had introduced a new style of play to the First Division characterised by cynicism and other clubs, to a greater or lesser extent, began to adopt what would euphemistically be termed 'professionalism'. As Brian Labone wrote in his 1968 autobiography, "An examination of Young today, is at the same time, both a joy and a sadness. A joy because he is just about the most perfect ball playing footballer around...

But sad because for all that skill and sheer natural talent, Alex is becoming a misfit in modern soccer. He belongs to a breed that is almost extinct... that can no longer survive and flourish in the hard-driving, hustling and ruthless business we are in now."

The facts demonstrated that Labone's lament wasn't simply ghostwritten sentimentality. In 1960-61, Young's first season, Everton scored 87, conceded 69, finishing with 50 points; in 1967-68, Young's last campaign at the club, they gained 52 points, having scored 67 and conceded just 40 goals. Young's last game in an Everton shirt came on 11 May 1968, a month after the screening of *The Golden Vision*, Loach's film about Young.

His career wound down very quickly. A potentially lucrative move to the short-lived New York Generals franchise fell through after Catterick obstructed it. Instead he was briefly player-manager at Glentoran. The move was ill-fated, however, and Young was uneasy at Northern Ireland's rising sectarian violence. He returned to England with Stockport County, but the Third Division was no fitting stage. After making just a single appearance in the 1969-70 season he called time on his illustrious career.

Young returned to Scotland, where he lived a quiet post-football existence, first running a pub, then working for his family's soft furnishings business, making occasional pilgrimages south to Goodison. His son, Jason, was a forward for Scotland's youth teams alongside Duncan Ferguson, but after breaking his leg was consigned to a career in the Scottish lower leagues with Livingston and Stranraer.

The Golden Vision is – and was – at once accepting, ambivalent and surprised about his fame. His friend and biographer, the historian and philanthropist David France, describes walking with him through Liverpool city centre one night in 2007 when it was "late, dark and raining": Young had the effect of the Pied Piper on fans who kept appearing by the dozen "from every nook and cranny" to have autographs signed. "In spite of these experiences he remains genuinely surprised that the younger fans know who he is, never mind that they know so much about him," France said.

Young was always aware of his greatness, no matter how disarmingly modest he remained. In his 1968 autobiography *Goals at Goodison* he claimed – or at least his ghostwriter did – to keep in his wallet a photograph sent to him by a fan, of a wall bearing the legend "Alex Young The Great". Nearly 40 years later I casually mentioned this to him as we were about to go in to a dinner and he blushed with a look of incredulity.

"Och, no," he replied. "That's a load of mumbo-jumbo. Where on earth did you hear that?"

The Golden Vision was not the only significant Alex Young in Everton's history. Separated by 57 years, a player of the same name, same position, same mining heritage, from the same part of Scotland preceded him: Alex 'Sandy' Young, a fellow Scot whose achievements arguably outstripped even the Golden Vision's.

Yet off the field the parallel lives of Alex Young diverge. While the 1960s player was the subject of Loach's social realism, so dramatic were the life and times of Sandy – free scoring centre-forward, FA Cup Final hero, murderer, felon – that, if they were made into a film, they would be better suited to a Ron Howard-directed Hollywood epic.

His was an extraordinary life which traversed the peaks and troughs of human existence. Although no relation to the 1960s idol, he was born just 30 miles away, in 1880 in the Stirlingshire coal mining village of Slamannan. Like the Golden Vision he started working life down a pit, the 1901 census recording his occupation as a miner.

That was the year that he signed for Everton. Having made a name for himself with Slamannan Juniors, Young had spent the 1899-1900 season in Scottish League Division One with St Mirren, where he scored six times in 19 appearances. St Mirren had struggled in the league, however, winning just three of their 18 league matches, and avoided demotion only after beating St Bernard's in a play-off. Young left at the season's end to join Falkirk, then still competing in amateur leagues. Combining football at Brockville Park, just 6 miles from Slamannan, with work down the mines was presumably easier for Sandy, who scored 16 goals in 36 games. In May 1901 Everton paid Falkirk £100 to sign Young and St Mirren £20 for his league registration.

At Goodison he was paid £2.10s per week – comfortably more than the 30s he would have earned at the coalface, but hardly a life-changing salary. He was never prolific in his first few campaigns for Everton, but it is clear that his selfless play allowed others – notably Jimmy Settle and Jack Sharp – to thrive. Everton were perennial nearly-men in this time and they ended Young's debut season – in which he played in 30 of the club's 34 league matches – runners up to Sunderland. Twice more, in 1904-05, and 1908-09, they would finish second as well as third in 1903-04 and 1906-07, the year they also finished FA Cup runners-up.

Young led the Everton forward line through these years. He was a regular goalscorer, but only in 1906-07 – when he topped the First Division scoring charts with 28 goals – could he be described as outstandingly prolific. A *Liverpool Echo* pen portrait of the period was revealing of how he divided some opinions: "Sandy Young, the centre-forward, is a variable sort of man who plays one good game in three on average. He takes the bumps a centre-forward must inevitably expect smilingly and determination makes up for lack of skill at times." Others were more enthusiastic: "I have been a regular attender at the Everton matches since the days of [Alec] Dick and [George] Dobson [in the 1880s], and I unhesitatingly affirm that Sandy Young is the greatest forward that has ever played under the club's colours. Young has been and still is the club's greatest asset," wrote one fan to the same newspaper.

"He was idolised by the public of Liverpool, and his career is something of a romance," recalled Ernest 'Bee' Edwards, who was the *Liverpool Echo's* sports editor through much of the first half of the last century. Young, he wrote, "at once made his name by brilliant foot-work and curious little artistries of dribbling that make a footballer a hero in the eyes of the public." Sandy's "twisting and turning and feinting were a delight to the football enthusiast's eye."

And yet for all the adulation, he remained an aloof individual, a man whose personality was at odds with his growing fame. An unnamed former teammate of Young's declared that he "was very highly strung, had peculiar habits and was a very sombre man." Young, according to this account, "would live alone, as far as possible and many a time when out training he slinked off to some long walk and no one could get a word out of him. If one was not satisfied with his game one never offered any remarks on the point as Sandy would straightway have curled up, and played any sort of tosh."

The defining moment of Sandy's career came in 1906 when Everton met Newcastle United in the FA Cup Final at Crystal Palace. It was the club's third final and following two finals defeats in the 1890s as well as losing out on the league title by a point to their opponents the previous year, Everton were desperate to overcome their also-ran status.

With the exception of a second round strike against Chesterfield, goals had proved elusive to Young throughout Everton's Cup run, but on this April day he was on fine form. On 53 minutes he found the net, but the goal was ruled out for offside. ("He was standing almost under the bar," reported the *Mirror*.) 25 minutes later Jack Sharp was sent free down the wing, evading the pursuit of the Newcastle left-back Carr. Sharp beat Carr and another defender, and sent in a beautifully weighted cross which Young slotted home for the game's only goal.

"I doubt," the Football League's founding father, William McGregor, said "if we have ever had a final in which there has been more loose play... [It was] one of the poorest finals." The *Daily Mirror's* reporter accused Young of marring his "dashing display" with "a good many petty tricks, which Mr Kirkham [the referee] generally noticed and always promptly penalised." But as the invariably partisan *Liverpool Daily Post* put it, "Thrice has the battle been waged, and twice the victory denied, but the third time pays for all: Bravo the Blues!"

Although Young's scoring spree a year later almost elevated Everton to a league and cup double and he still managed a goal every other game through the 1907-08 season, by then Everton had dropped to eleventh and there was a need for change. In an effort to revive fortunes, Bertie Freeman was signed late in the campaign from Woolwich Arsenal and took Young's berth. Thereafter the Scot would find himself overshadowed by Freeman's prolific exploits and left to play as an inside-forward. He managed just two league goals during the 1909-10 season and although he showed signs that he may wrest back the centre-forward berth the following season, Everton's selectors deemed Young – by then aged 30 – to be past his best.

In the summer of 1911 Young was sold to Tottenham Hotspur for £500. At the time he was Everton's highest ever goalscorer with a total of 125, a tally surpassed just three times in the following century. His spell in London was brief, the highlight being his return to Goodison where he was still idolised. When he scored the equaliser in a 2-2 draw, Edwards reported, "of all the receptions I have ever heard that day's volume led the lot."

He returned north within a year, signing for Manchester City. There followed spells with South Liverpool and Burslem Port Vale, but the earlier heights were never hit. By the outbreak of the First World War Young had dropped out of professional football and emigrated to Australia.

Football, until the 1990s, remained a sport short on literature, save for match reports and the ubiquitous match day programme. Books, beyond usually anodyne autobiographies and club-produced annuals, remained few and far between. Everton, in the club's first century, possessed just two club histories, published on the occasions of its half centenary and, in 1978, centenary. By contrast, the last decade alone has seen nearly twenty such publications.

Instead, oral tradition kept the legends of the game alive and because it was a relatively young sport, those stories retained a first- or second-hand aspect for many fans. A child of the 1980s, I first went to the match with men who had witnessed every player since Dixie Dean, and for anything before that era those supporters could offer their fathers' or grandfathers' memories. However, with a history kept alive by alehouse yarns it was unsurprising that some myths perpetuated, and so it was with Sandy Young.

What happened after Young retired from playing and moved to Australia was until a couple of years ago occluded

by a combination of mystery and urban legend. One newspaper report claimed that Young was hanged for sheep rustling, a story which always seemed scarcely credible. Nevertheless, it was mentioned in several publications and thus gained some credence, becoming one of those self-perpetuating fables; a yarn that was complicated and further misconstrued by the fact that a rival and equally dramatic account emerged that Young was jailed for the murder of his brother John. Further uncorroborated details suggested that Young spent years in a lunatic asylum after this apparent crime. The story sometimes became confused or exaggerated – the footballer who ended up in the loony bin after stealing sheep – and Everton's early hero was tarred by unsubstantiated infamy.

Indeed when I wrote a history of Everton in 2003 still no evidence had surfaced to contradict or confirm these versions of Sandy's latter years. It was only later, thanks to the detective work of an Everton fanatic, that the truth emerged.

If you step into the darkened corner of Liverpool Central Library where the microfiche machines are located, on any given day there is a good chance you will encounter Billy Smith, a 48-year-old security guard and amateur historian who has made it his life's work to record every detail of Everton's 136-year long history. The self-styled 'Blue Correspondent', Smith is a modern equivalent of what Hugh McIllvanney once described as "the sort of magnificent obsessionists who suspect that when Jesus performed the miracle of walking on the waters he was bouncing a ball on his instep at the time." According to the Blue

Correspondent's account, Jesus would probably have been wearing a royal blue shirt at the time.

Smith's research started in 2000 and was initially focussed on Everton's 1980s halcyon era. He became the first person to document accurately all the club's penalty takers and buoyed by the success of this early project then "decided to go the Full Monty on Everton." The 'Full Monty' according to Billy is every single report on the Blues, most painstakingly transcribed from old microfiche and then published on the internet. By Smith's own admission he is not a writer, his aim, instead, "is to get information out to historians and researchers so that they can get accurate information." His research now encompasses millions of words and currently documents everything from the club's formation in 1878 to February 1954. He reckons he has another "six or seven years left" before he has every game recorded, adding "and then I'll start on the statistics."

"I devote far too much time, if the truth is told," he admits. When asked how much, he replies: "Around six hours a day on average; however, sometimes, before I know it 12 hours can go flying past." He jokes about needing to "get a life," but his work has been invaluable to anyone with a serious interest in Everton history. And it was Smith, in 2012, whose research separated the truth from the myths about what happened to Sandy and John Young in Australia.

"My true passion is Everton from 1879 to 1888," says Smith. "However, the truth about Alex gives me a lot of satisfaction."

In Australia, Sandy Young joined his brother, John, who was a dairy farmer in Victoria. While still playing, Sandy had advanced him more than £300 to emigrate there in 1912 and establish a farm. He set up near Tongala, 150 miles north of Melbourne, and Sandy joined him when he left Port Vale. However their partnership was swiftly undermined by squabbles over money. Court accounts later revealed how Sandy did not get on with his brother, who threatened him on several occasions. John had hit him on the head with a bucket on two occasions and on the body with a stick. On another occasion he chased him with a fork and threatened to shoot him.

On 1 December 1915, their relationship spiralled tragically out of control. The previous night the brothers had fought again. John had hit him without provocation and warned, "You or me will have to enter heaven tonight." That warning proved prophetic.

The following morning, with tensions high, Sandy heard a noise in the house, and thought it was his brother. He got up and loaded a double-barrelled shotgun gun. He found John milking a cow in their barn, Sandy approached him and warned that he was going to shoot.

According to a police statement, John replied, "'Put the gun away. You are only trying to frighten me.' Alexander, however, took no notice, and fired at me." Sandy then returned to their house, turned the gun on himself and shot himself in the head. That was his last memory.

A week later he regained consciousness, physically scarred but very much alive, in Echuca Hospital, some 20 miles deeper into the outback. John was dead, having bled to death after suffering an internal haemorrhage. He left behind a widow, Agnes, and five children. Sandy was placed under arrest, facing a murder charge.

According to a police statement he made before he passed out (and which he couldn't subsequently recall making), Sandy confessed, "I was driven to this; I am sorry. I shot him on the spur of the moment. Can the doctors not do anything for him?" Told that John had just hours to live Sandy buried his face in his hands and cried out, "Poor Agnes and the bairns. What will become of them?"

When news of the killing reached Britain some two months later, it was met with shock even at a time when newspapers were filled with the catastrophic losses being suffered daily on the Western Front. As much as the tragedy itself, focus was on Young's character and personality. Edwards wrote of Young's "curious temperament" adding that "there were periods when he stroked the single lock of hair that adorned his forehead which suggested that he suffered severe pains in the head."

In Stirlingshire, the Youngs' elderly mother read of John's death in the press. Two of his sisters were sent to Liverpool to meet the Everton secretary, Will Cuff, to see if the club could assist in Sandy's defence. To a local reporter they spoke of Young's "melancholy temperament", a theme developed over subsequent months.

Cuff, who combined his duties at Goodison with a prominent local law

practice, immediately telegraphed Tongola's mayor and may also have instructed a solicitor on Young's behalf. In England he contacted counterparts at Young's former clubs and secured affidavits from Manchester City's secretary-manager Ernest Mangnall and representatives from South Liverpool on the subject of Young's mental condition. He got testimony from an unnamed Everton captain of the era stating that Young was "a morose fellow, quiet, sombre, and touchy". He added that "it was never possible to chide him in the dressing-room after he had played a '45', or he would curl up and sulk palpably if one did happen to suggest that be should put more life into his game." All this was apparently evidence of Young's mental unsoundness and was submitted to the Australian judge ahead of the trial.

When the case went to court in June 1916, the question was not Young's guilt, but his sanity. At one stage the judge asked, "Why did you try to blow your brains out when you considered you had only shot your brother in self defence?"

"I cannot say," replied Young.

The jury, after an hour's deliberation, returned a verdict of manslaughter. It seems likely that Cuff's intervention saved Young's life. Instead of the hangman's noose, he was sentenced to three years in prison, divided between Pentridge Penitentiary – a notorious island jail – and Ararat Lunatic Asylum.

In Liverpool, Cuff invited donations to help pay Young's £200 legal bills. On his release Young was sent £20 by the Everton board, but beyond that the trail went cold. In October 1945, the Everton board received a letter regarding his "circumstances", but after considering it, decided to refer the matter to the public assistance officer in Stirlingshire, where Young was seemingly based.

The next years remained a blank, until news of Young's death in September 1959 in an Edinburgh nursing home. His passing went entirely unnoticed at the time and for the best part of the next 50 years. It seemed as though no one mourned him and no one ever asked: whatever happened to Sandy Young?

When Smith uncovered details of Young's fate in Australia, the *Liverpool Echo* picked up on his research. Things then started to move apace. Paul Wharton, chairman of the EFC Heritage Society – another of McIllvanney's school of "magnificent obsessionists" – tracked down Young's burial site in Edinburgh. What he found shocked him. Young was buried in an unmarked grave with two Italian immigrants. "Where these people fit in with Alex I don't know yet," Wharton wrote to me at the time. He also visited Young's last known address in Portobello. The owner invited him to see what was now a family home and Wharton learned it had previously been a mental health care home. "This sadly ties in with Alex's state of mind," he added.

Wharton resolved that something should be done as it was "not befitting that someone who had made such a contribution to Everton history be buried in a poor house grave." He petitioned Everton to help fund the cost of a headstone and when the club agreed to go halves with the EFC Heritage Society, the remainder was raised prior to an Everton match in December 2013.

At this stage, members of Young's extended family began making contact with Wharton and, for the first time in many cases, with each other.

"I think because of the mental health issues he had and what happened in Australia he became the black sheep of the family, if you like. We knew very little about what happened when he came back to Scotland," says Bryan Cleeton, the footballer's great-great-nephew.

"The tragic events in Australia put a dampener on Sandy and buried his football career," he adds. "It was only when a picture of Sandy appeared in a Panini sticker album in 1987 that we really realised that he was held in such high regard at Everton and his actual accomplishments, such as scoring the winning goal when they won the FA Cup."

The new focus on Sandy Young, assisted by social media, suddenly united parts of his family that had never known each other. It also ultimately unravelled the remaining mysteries of his later, lonely wilderness years.

September 2014 and the last of the summer sun shines gently through the oak trees at Edinburgh's Seafield Cemetery. It is a lovely spot, with birdsong chattering over the distant hum of traffic. In the tranquillity of the graveyard the wave of political debate washing over the country ahead of its independence referendum the following week seems very distant.

With Paul Wharton and Billy Smith, the two unsung heroes who had lifted the shroud of mystery from Sandy's demise, I walked along a tree-shaded path and there, watched over by a solitary piper, it is: a permanent memorial to the footballer; a black headstone, as dark and shiny as onyx, bearing Young's details, a small portrait at its top and the impression of his 1906 FA Cup winner's medal underneath it.

Around 100 of us – descendants of Young, a handful of football officials, enthusiasts and members of the press – await the start of the dedication ceremony and admire the work of the stonemason. It is almost 55 years to the day since Young died and at last his final resting place is properly marked.

As we wait, I fall into conversation with an old man. I ask him what had brought him to Seafield Cemetrery.

"I remember him only too well," he told me. "Sandy was my uncle."

The old man was Cyril Cleeton, whose mother was Sandy's sister. Then in his mid-80s, he recalled his uncle's hermit-like existence on his return from Scotland in 1920. "Sandy had reached the depths. If he had reached the pinnacle of his profession, he had reached the depths of his own depravation," said Cyril. "He lived alone in abject poverty. No one to care for him. He was a recluse, there's no question about that.

"He used to do odd jobs about the place. We had a bungalow with quite a big garden that took a bit of tending, so Sandy would do that. But his career as a footballer was not brought up."

Cleeton said that he had an "inkling" of his uncle's fame, but admits that he "didn't know he was the esteemed footballer we talk about now."

"It was only later when my niece came down to Everton and researched his past that I had any idea. It came as a surprise."

I asked him about the shooting in Australia. Cyril said that as a boy he would help shave his uncle with a single edge razor and was aware of the gouge on the right side of his face where Sandy had shot himself. If he asked about it, "The reply I got, more often than not, was, 'Oh, we don't talk about that.'"

The sound of 'Flower of Scotland' from the bagpipes indicated the dedication ceremony was underway. Tributes were made to Sandy and wreathes laid, including one by John's great-granddaughter, Catherine Yarham, who had travelled from Australia to attend the ceremony.

Everton's chaplain, Henry Corbett, dealt sensitively with the complexities of Sandy's "tough story" – the brother who died at his hand, the years of suffering from mental illness – but spoke of the need for forgiveness and moving on.

"The Christian faith says that forgiveness is possible and that we believe in a God who understands and in a God who offers hope," he said. "Alex 'Sandy' Young's family and friends and the football family of Everton Football Club rededicate his grave."

On the edge of the gathering was a familiar figure. The tight blond curls –

grey when I'd last set eyes upon him a few years earlier – had now turned to white, but there he was, unmistakable, elegant, iconic – the Golden Vision.

He was 77 by then and rumours about his declining health had periodically filtered down to Merseyside, where he was seldom seen. But on this day at least, Alex Young – a little deafer, a little older – was on fine form. We passed a couple of minutes chatting about Everton, his family, a mutual friend in America; inanities really, but then Alex the Great was never one to hold court grandiloquently. The Golden Vision's status as a footballing deity, while accepted in his modest way, was one that never sat easily with him. If I'd learned anything from him over the years it was

that his greatness as a footballer did not define him, rather his humility as a man.

It seemed so extraordinary, that the lives of these two footballers had shared so many parallels and yet their fates had so little in common. Both had become mythical creatures for very different reasons and here they were, united at last.

The piper gave a second burst of 'Flower of Scotland' and the Golden Vision made to leave. He shook everybody by the hand and bade farewell to his congregation of adorers. Then he was gone, shuffling through the graveyard, his wife Nancy at his side, into the sun-bathed afternoon and on his way. Ⓑ

55

Interview

"We played just for winning."

Paul Breitner

How a Bayern Munich defeat paved the way for West Germany's 1974 World Cup triumph

By Miguel Delaney

The 1974 World Cup final is a signpost match in football history, yet, for all the famous images and impressions from that game, they are not what Paul Breitner immediately recalls. His memory doesn't focus on the Netherlands' astounding first minute, nor on Franz Beckenbauer remonstrating with the referee Jack Taylor, nor on Gerd Müller's scuffed winner.

What Breitner remembers first is an emotion, but it is not the emotion you would expect. It certainly isn't the exhilarating feeling of victory, as West Germany defied expectation to defeat the Dutch.

Rather, it is the emotion that fired that win: anger.

Breitner recalls the rage he felt just after the Netherlands' opening goal. In what had seemed the most sensational expression of Rinus Michels's Total Football, the Dutch went ahead without any West German player touching the ball. Johan Cruyff had been taken down in the box, leaving Johan Neeskens to score. Except, the Dutch players apparently didn't think that was the most sensational expression of Total Football. They wanted total humiliation and began to try to embarrass the Germans through open play, rather

than actually beating them with goals. It provoked a response.

"This is the moment you want to go home, that you want to leave the stadium," Breitner says. "You start the game convinced you will win the final and with very concentrated emotions... and then you are losing after two minutes. Then they start playing, laughing at us. 'Here's the ball, there's the ball.'

"They were playing so arrogantly that we started to respire, we started living again. We saw they don't want to kill us, they just want to laugh at us, so we thought, 'you will not play the way you like to do.'"

What happened next has ensured that World Cup final has become one of the most analysed events in sport, but almost completely from a Dutch point of view. It has been placed in the context of everything from the exact application of a philosophy to the nature of how you best beat an opponent, and even the effect of the Second World War and the countries' mutual history on a mere 90 minutes of sport.

Within all of this, West Germany have almost been caricatured as mechanistic winners who neither valued the victory in the way they should have nor proved fully worthy winners when set against the quality of the Dutch. The parallels with 1954, when the Germans defeated an equally admired Hungary team, made that feeling all the more pronounced.

It was almost as if they weren't seen as a team undergoing their own development but mere cyphers just waiting to take advantage of any slip by anyone else and spoil the party.

That World Cup victory was a peak in terms of German victories, with the country itself represented by one of the most successful cores of players the game has seen. Bayern Munich supplied six of West Germany's starters in that final and at the final whistle those players held the World Cup, the 1972 European Championship, the 1974 European Cup and the Bundesliga, having claimed the domestic title for the third successive season.

Breitner was one of the key members of the squad and, as he sits in Bayern's Säbener Strasse base talking to *The Blizzard*, he expands on the other side of the psychology of that 1974 final – the psychology of winning and what forges winners. The anger illustrated the very human side of West Germany's own development, which is so often underplayed. They had their own long nights of the soul.

There are few so well equipped to talk about the process as Breitner. He has not just won more than most players in history, but tends to think about these things more than most players.

Occasionally, he sounds like Roy Keane, not least when he's asked about the differences between Bayern

and an even greater side from that era: Cruyff's Ajax.

"They didn't just want to win every match," Breitner says of their Amsterdam contemporaries. "They wanted to create a spectacle. They wanted to give the crowd a spectacular match. We, Bayern Munich, we played just for winning. We were not interested in giving fans a spectacle. Spectacular is winning!"

This is relevant to so much of that 1974 World Cup final. The Dutch did not want just to offer a spectacular win. They also wanted to make a spectacle of West Germany, for so many reasons.

Had Michels's team done that, and properly built on that brilliant start to hammer Breitner and his teammates, it would have been the second such experience for those Bayern players. They had been battered by many of the Dutch squad just 16 months earlier in the European Cup quarter-final. Just as Bayern provided the core of the West German team, the Netherlands were based around Ajax. The two clubs met in the 1972-73 quarter-final, with Ajax winning the first leg 4-0. Breitner feels that was almost as important to winning the 1974 final as the Netherlands' offensively good opening spell. Setbacks set up both Bayern and West Germany.

"After five or six minutes [in 1974], we saw that they were not interested in killing us," Breitner explains. "In the match against Ajax [in 1973], they did kill us. They won 4-0. This [World Cup] final, they could also have won 4-0, 5-0, 6-0, maybe, if they had scored the second or third goal in the next few minutes.

"It [the European Cup match] was one of the most important defeats you can have. Sometimes, a defeat is very important for your future. I think this was the moment when we [this core of players] started to understand what we had to improve to win the European Cup the following year. We had to learn.

"I think it was the key moment for winning the European Cup the next year, and the World Cup. We played a quite open football. We changed sometimes from playing just man contra man, so we made some important tactical changes. We also needed them for the World Cup to play in the national team.

"It was maybe a moment, a defeat you can compare with the final against Chelsea here in the Allianz Arena [in 2012]. I would compare it. The team that lost against Chelsea went through the defeat, learnt from the defeat and did better the next season, and the same happened with our team that lost 4-0 against Ajax."

The comparison with the modern Bayern is all the more relevant because they are a rare instance of that special dynamic and duality having been replicated. For Ajax/Netherlands and Bayern/West Germany in the 1970s, read Barcelona/Spain and Bayern/Germany over the last five years.

As with many of those teams, Breitner traces the start of their rise to one critical match. Important defeats may finish a team's development, but a crucial victory was what first took them to that level. The latter makes them regular winners, the former transforms them into relentless winners.

"The important moment was winning against England in April [1972, at Wembley in the European Championship quarter-final]. That was the birth of the great German team and also for Bayern Munich. This was the moment in which the young players - especially Uli [Hoeneß] and I — started to become stars, started to become dominating players, decisive players, for the national team and also for Bayern Munich. This international match was one of the biggest highlights in the history of Bayern Munich."

In that 3-1 win over England Gerd Müller scored the clinching third goal, setting a trend that was to become even more frequent than Bayern and West Germany winning. In fact, many of those wins came directly because of Müller goals. The striker followed on from that goal against England to hit the opening goals in both the semi-final and final of that European Championship, two goals in the 1974 European Cup final against Atlético Madrid, the winner in the World Cup final and then the second in the 1975 European Cup final.

That was a clutch player. Müller came almost to personify this German era of victory for the purity of the way he just kept doing the single thing that would guarantee victory. His performances were all the more remarkable because he was maintaining goal ratios from the fifties — hitting more than one a game — at a time when catenaccio and the increased systemisation of football made scoring so much more difficult.

Even a man as forthright as Breitner remains in awe of Müller. "I tell you what I tell everybody. Gerd Müller was the most important German football player after 54, after the German team who won in 54 the World Cup in Switzerland. Gerd Müller was the most important, not Franz Beckenbauer, not Uwe Seeler, Gerd Müller because he gave Bayern Munich and the national team all the titles, all the cups, all the victories. He was the winner. He is the man who is responsible for all this we have here as Bayern Munich. Those are the basics. Without Gerd Müller, Bayern Munich would now be a quite normal club but not this super, super club we are right now.

"We had Gerd Müller. In 19 of 20 matches he was able to score a decisive goal.

"We knew it, we knew it, and even if he had a very bad day and it was, 'Oh my God, what a bad day he's having today!' we gave him the ball, we gave him the ball, we gave him the ball, and maybe he lost the ball 10 times, 15 times, 20 times, but the 21st time he scored. It was crazy."

It led to an era with a crazy return of trophies, when the overriding emotion was not rage. It was glory.

"A supporter doesn't want to see his team play a spectacular match," Breitner says. "He wants to see a victory."

It feels all the more special when it comes with righteous vindication.

60

Belfast

"BBC Northern Ireland cleared the schedules to show a full re-run of the match just four hours after the full-time whistle."

A Patchwork City

Mapping the fan-bases of the major club's in Northern Ireland's capital

By Levkos Kyriacou

'On alien soil like yourself I am here;
I'll take root and flourish of that never fear,
And though I'll be crossed sore and oft by
the foes
You'll find me as hardy as Thistle and Rose,'

So goes the verse recited by the Irish Patriot Michael Davitt at the symbolic planting of Irish turf and shamrocks in the new pitch at Glasgow's Celtic Park in 1892. Composed from the point of view of the turf, this is an early example of the longstanding and potent relationship between football clubs in Scotland and Ireland and the capacity of sport and conflict to intertwine. On a broader level it reveals how the spread of football, not unlike the spread of religion, has the capacity to absorb new and distant places into local lore, in this case into the tradition of clubs and their grounds. The drawing together of football fandom and Catholic and Protestant identity through the Old Firm in Glasgow has been reciprocated in Belfast through some of the city's senior football clubs. For the Catholic, nationalist community in Northern Ireland, the genesis of Celtic and its development into one of Europe's most storied clubs has been the inspiration for the formation of Belfast clubs taking on the Celtic name, colours and customs. This essay looks at the impact of the Celtic identity on Belfast football and the wider city.

A note on the maps that accompany the sites discussed in this essay:
The importance of football in Belfast is not easily defined. The sport is immensely popular yet its senior clubs are small and face significant challenges. The teams themselves are not selected through exclusionary policies but there is no club that can be identified as truly mixed in terms of its support. The city has suffered from years of conflict and remains divided yet footballing competition between the two main communities has endured. Today, two of the strongest club sides in Northern Ireland, Cliftonville and Crusaders, are situated in predominantly Catholic and Protestant neighbourhoods of North Belfast separated by a so-called 'Peaceline' (the walls that divide Belfast), Belfast's football clubs are, to varying degrees, associated with one or other of the city's conflicting communities and affected by their location within a divided city. It is important here to note that branding Belfast's football clubs with overarching ethno-national identities requires caution. The city's clubs do not operate exclusionary policies with respect to the players that represent them rather the association with Protestant and Catholic communities reflects the predominant demography of the club's fan-base. The location in the city is intrinsically linked to this given the highly segregated working class neighborhoods in which most of Belfast's football clubs are based.

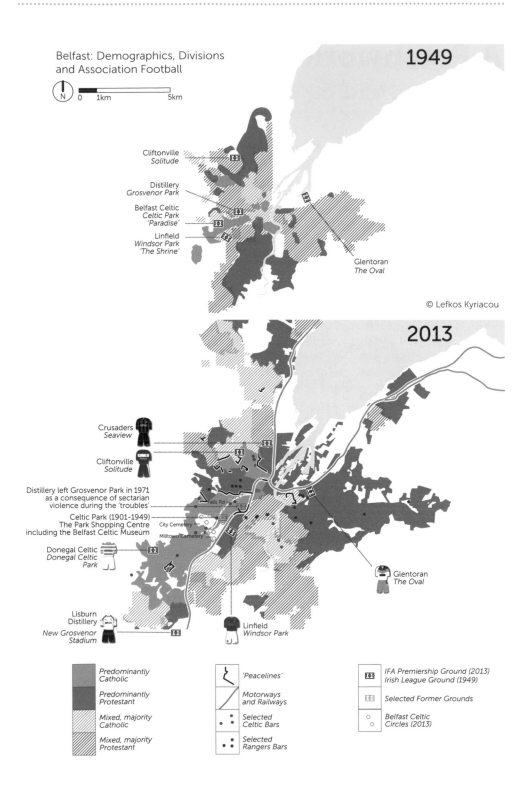

Belfast: Demographics, Divisions and Association Football

1949

0 1km 5km

Cliftonville
Solitude

Distillery
Grosvenor Park

Belfast Celtic
Celtic Park
'Paradise'

Linfield
Windsor Park
'The Shrine'

Glentoran
The Oval

© Lefkos Kyriacou

2013

Crusaders
Seaview

Cliftonville
Solitude

Distillery left Grosvenor Park in 1971
as a consequence of sectarian
violence during the 'troubles'

Celtic Park (1901-1949)
The Park Shopping Centre
including the Belfast Celtic Museum

City Cemetery

Milltown Cemetery

Falls Rd

Donegal Celtic
Donegal Celtic
Park

Lisburn
Distillery
New Grosvenor
Stadium

Linfield
Windsor Park

Glentoran
The Oval

Predominantly
Catholic

Predominantly
Protestant

Mixed, majority
Catholic

Mixed, majority
Protestant

'Peacelines'

Motorways
and Railways

Selected
Celtic Bars

Selected
Rangers Bars

IFA Premiership Ground (2013)
Irish League Ground (1949)

Selected Former Grounds

Belfast Celtic
Circles (2013)

The disappearance of Belfast Celtic, one half of the city's 'Big Two' along with Linfield until its disbandment in 1949, is a notorious example of the impact of urban conflict on sport. Yet despite its death as a sporting entity over 60 years ago, the club has followed an unusual trajectory and maintained a presence in today's Belfast. In British cities football clubs have proven to be enduring institutions and their grounds resilient urban spaces. It is accepted wisdom that attempting to move a club's ground beyond the area of its local fanbase will be met with major resistance. It is difficult to even countenance the notion that a club and team can completely disband. So for a major football club and its ground to be completely erased as with Belfast Celtic is unusual and traumatising for both the sport and the city.

Established in 1891, three years after Celtic of Glasgow, the club were based in Catholic West Belfast and for the most part at Celtic Park off the Falls Road. Belfast's own 'Paradise' was said to hold up to 50,000 and have one of the finest playing surfaces of the time. Belfast Celtic enjoyed a significant level of sporting success including 14 league titles and 8 Irish Cups in their fifty-eight year history. Such was the standing of the club in the 1940s that striker Jimmy Jones turned down an offer from Matt Busby to join Manchester United. Inextricably linked to the Belfast Celtic story was the sporting rivalry with clubs supported by predominantly Protestant communities, most notably Linfield, who played a short walk away across Donegall Road.

Windsor Park, the home of Linfield, is situated in the Belfast neighbourhood of The Village. During Linfield's rivalry with Belfast Celtic, this was a predominantly working class Protestant neighbourhood. Furthermore Linfield operated a longstanding, unofficial sectarian recruitment policy, the only club to do so over an extended period, and despite the prominent signing of a local Catholic player in 1992, Windsor Park has long been identified as an iconic site for unionists and in turn an inhospitable place for most nationalists.

In 1920, Belfast Celtic along with football clubs from Dublin withdrew from competitive football during the Irish War of Independence as a consequence of violent flashpoints at matches. This cartoon depicts such an incident at an Irish cup semi-final between Glentoran and Belfast Celtic at Solitude in 1920. The club returned to the Irish League in 1924, now severed from the south, and a trophy-laden period followed until their board took the decision to leave the League again after the annual Boxing Day/St Stephen's Day fixture against Linfield in 1948. The match at Windsor Park pitted Belfast Celtic, the reigning champions against their closest rivals. Linfield scored a late equaliser despite astonishingly being reduced to eight men through a series of injuries. The tragedy was that this full-blooded, high stakes sporting encounter erupted into a violent pitch invasion by the home supporters. Several Celtic players were attacked, most notably Celtic's Protestant centre-forward Jimmy Jones who was pulled from the pitch into the terraces and suffered a broken leg.

EX-BELFAST CELTIC SELECT TEAM v. CELTIC
At Celtic Park, Belfast, 17th May, 1952
Back Row (left to right)—A'HERNE (Luton Town), CURRIE (Bradford City),
McALINDON (Belfast Celtic), DOHERTY (Huddersfield Town).
Front Row (left to right)—BONNAR (Barnsley), DENVER (Glenavon),
McMORRAN (Barnsley), VERNON (West Bromwich), O'NEIL (Walsall),
LAWLOR (Fulham), CAMPBELL (Fulham).

Following the events at Windsor Park, Belfast Celtic's position
was deemed untenable by their board who set about selling
the team's leading players to English and Scottish clubs before
announcing a withdrawal from the league. The club's board
and Irish Football Association may not have envisaged the
decision to be permanent, but once the team had disbanded
in 1949 Belfast Celtic never reformed competitively. A
combination of factors meant there was never a 'right time'
for the club to reform: sectarian tensions would have needed
to de-escalate and logistically there were administrative
procedures to undertake for the club to re-enter senior
football (Crusaders from North Belfast had taken their place).
A select team of former players, mostly now plying their trade
for English clubs, returned to Belfast in 1952 for an exhibition
match against Celtic but this proved to be a final goodbye
rather than the sign of a homecoming.

After the club's demise, Celtic Park functioned as a greyhound track until 1983, when the ground was redeveloped as a shopping mall called the Park Centre; a long, slow death for a major urban institution. Commemorative plaques at the entrance to the centre now mark the site of the former ground. Despite not kicking a ball for over sixty years, Belfast Celtic lives on through a society established in 2003 that maintain an active website and social media presence. The society, largely comprised of people that never saw the team play claims that is is 'living proof that the Grand Old Team is not forgotten' **(www.belfastceltic.org).**

The cultural activity of the Belfast Celtic Society centres on commemoration of the club in West Belfast, the focal point of which is the Belfast Celtic Museum. Incongruously located within a commercial unit in the Park Centre between a clothing and gift card store, the museum exhibits tell the story of the club from the society's collection of club memorabilia and archival material.

In 2012 the society launched the Belfast Celtic Trail in West
Belfast comprised of fifteen commemorative green plaques
called 'Belfast Celtic Circles' that were erected along the
length of the Falls Road. The plaques take in the broad
hinterland of the club including the Park Centre, the graves
of its most famous players (both Catholic and Protestant)
along with clubhouses, bars and shops historically associated
with the club. Belfast Celtic are not a living football club but
they remain rooted in the urban memory of the city and are
actively commemorated in the streets, bars, cemeteries and
commercial spaces of West Belfast.

Donegal Celtic are a nascent footballing institution, establlished in 1970, situated in and founded during the urban expansion of West Belfast during the Troubles. The club have not come close to the success of Belfast Celtic but have enjoyed several seasons of top-flight football and were playing in the Irish Premiership as recently as 2013. The club's identity and name emerged from the Catholic, Nationalist community settling into the surrounding housing estates named after places in County Donegal. A renewal of the city's longstanding association with the Celtic football tradition was embodied in the team's colours, crest and pre-match huddle and captured in a mural at the entrance to their ground. Although the similarities between Donegal and Belfast Celtic are evident, Donegal Celtic was never conceived as a revival of the Belfast club. The club's importance grew during the Troubles as Catholic communities avoided travelling outside their neighbourhoods making the clubhouse and its facilities an important social hub for the local area. Unsurprisingly the team's identity led to flashpoints at fixtures during the Troubles. The clubhouse was also also subjected to arson attacks and shootings and the two-foot deep masonary wall that shielded the entrance from gunfire during the Troubles is a stark reminder of darker times.

Belfast's football fanbase was eroded and fragmented in a number of ways by the impact of the conflict on their sport. This no doubt contributed to many fans, from both communities, looking overseas to British clubs and a great number to Glasgow. Among Belfast's numerous bars and pubs with declared Old Firm affiliations, certain establishments celebrate their heroes, sportsman and combatants alike, loudly and in tandem. In these instances, such as this Rangers Pub in North Belfast, the shop fronts and drinking rooms are transformed into shrines for fallen combatants while the 'proxy warriors' of sport are depicted alongside them. Possibly the most significant impact of Belfast Celtic's disbandment is that the city lost a great inter-communal sporting rivalry but the sport did not lose its sectarian rifts. Now the major sporting rivalry between Belfast's conflicting communities is played out through a footballing frontier in Glasgow and separately within the social clubs of Belfast.

This essay is part of an independent piece of research investigating the role of sport in cities affected by conflict. Nonetheless, the work is closely related to and partly funded by the ESRC Large Grant project, 'Conflict in Cities and the Contested State' (RES-060-25-0015). Ⓑ

Requiem for a Stand

A history in seven key moments of the short life of the Kop at Windsor Park

By Keith Baillie

20 August 1997 – Northern Ireland 1 Germany 3

When Michael Hughes lifted the ball above the sprawling Andreas Köpke and into the back of the Germany net, he couldn't have possibly known what he had started. At the time, the goal had obvious significance. The West Ham United midfielder had given Northern Ireland a 1-0 lead over the reigning European champions with half an hour left. It was also Northern Ireland's 500th goal and, better still, it was the first international goal scored in front of Windsor Park's new West Stand.

It was August 1997 and Belfast was a city on the precipice of major change. Almost 30 years of the Troubles had left Northern Ireland's capital city beleaguered, divided and downtrodden, but the peace process had at least given the country's residents some hope of a brighter future. With the IRA's ceasefire reinstated a month before the World Cup qualifier, the Good Friday Agreement was less than a year away.

Football was changing too. Northern Ireland played their last game in front of Windsor Park's old Spion Kop in May of the previous year. The huge swath of open terrace that had witnessed the glorious adventures of Peter Doherty, Danny Blanchflower, George Best, Pat Jennings and Norman Whiteside watched on for one last time. St Johnstone's George O'Boyle and Bayern Munich's Mehmet Scholl exchanged goals in a 1-1 draw that served as a warm-up game for Germany's successful Euro 96 campaign.

A year later and Germany were in Belfast again. The venerable terraced end had been replaced by a modern but modest seated stand. The 'new Kop' held just 4,000 spectators but, unlike many behind-the-goal renovations of the era, this new stand actually seemed to improve the atmosphere at Windsor Park. Unlike the old Spion Kop the new West Stand (as nobody ever called it) had a roof that improved the ground's acoustics. The new enclosed feel helped Northern Ireland fans create the sort of positive atmosphere that had often eluded the 90-year-old ground.

The first roar of the new Kop arrived in the 60th minute when Hughes latched onto a pass from Blackpool's James Quinn before sweeping the ball home. Oliver Bierhoff's incredible six-minute hat-trick may have given the European Champions a 3-1 win but Hughes's goal had started, or at least reinvented, the cult of the Kop.

20 February 2002 — Northern Ireland 0 Cyprus 0

Unfortunately the optimism of that balmy August evening didn't last for long. Windsor Park, home of Ireland's most successful club Linfield, is situated in the south of the city. The ground is surrounded by a sprawl of terraced streets, in what is traditionally a working class Protestant area. The snooker player Alex Higgins and the singer Ruby Murray grew up in the stadium's shadow.

Linfield's support is predominantly drawn from the Unionist community and the ground has been referred to as a 'cold house' for Nationalists. At both Linfield and Northern Ireland games, it was not uncommon to hear sectarian songs emanating from the old Spion Kop.

While the new stand brought new hope, some old attitudes remained. In February 2001, the Celtic midfielder Neil Lennon played for Northern Ireland at Windsor Park against Norway. While Norway ran out 4-0 winners, it was Lennon's reception that made the headlines. While the majority of Windsor Park got behind the midfielder, a sizeable minority of the home support booed Lennon's every touch. Many Northern Ireland fans support Celtic's Glasgow rivals Rangers, two clubs divided by the same sectarian tensions that have plagued Belfast for generations. For the Lurgan-born and Catholic-raised Lennon, it was a traumatic experience. The manager Sammy McIlroy substituted him at half-time. Not for the first time in history, Northern Irish football was left shamed.

That wasn't the end of the sordid sectarian affair. In August 2002 Lennon was set to captain Northern Ireland against Cyprus, in a friendly match at Windsor Park. On the day of the match, the Loyalist Volunteer Force sent a death threat to Lennon via a Belfast newsroom. Understandably, Lennon decided to pull out of the game and he subsequently retired from international football. The game went ahead, finishing 0-0 with the new Kop half full. The reputation of international football in Northern Ireland had reached a particularly low ebb.

18 February 2004 — Northern Ireland 1 Norway 4

In the two years that followed Neil Lennon's departure from the international scene, a curious divide developed between the Northern Ireland team and their supporters.

On the field, the much-maligned team had hit their nadir. One appalling performance followed another as the Ulstermen established themselves as genuine international minnows. Famously, Northern Ireland went 13 games without scoring a goal.

In the stands, something of a noisy revolution was taking place. The Lennon incident served as something of a wake-up call for both Northern Ireland fans and the Irish Football Association. It would be disingenuous to suggest sectarianism at Windsor Park was eradicated overnight but a new counter-culture developed in the years that followed the Cyprus game. The self-styled Green & White Army introduced a raft of new songs that focused on supporting the team while also challenging the popularity of loyalist songs. The ironic chant of "We're not Brazil, we're Northern Ireland" became the Kop's calling card, as blue Rangers scarves gave way to comedy green wigs. It was positively naff, but at least it was positive. It was a grass-roots, supporter-driven movement that sought to change attitudes with a uniquely Northern Irish brand of zaniness.

When Norway visited Belfast in February 2004 it had been almost three years since Northern Ireland had won a match and two since they had scored a goal. It was perhaps no surprise then that the Norwegians were 3-0 up at half-time in Lawrie Sanchez's first game as manager.

However, the game's major talking point arrived in the 57th minute. Keith Gillespie flighted over a wonderful cross from the right flank, which was met by the head of David Healy. His header crept past Thomas Myhre and into the net in front of the Kop. Normally a consolation goal in an international friendly would be met with a muted response, but Healy's ninth goal for Northern Ireland was celebrated like a last gasp World Cup winner. It's little wonder. The goal ended a 1299-minute wait that had stretched over 13 games and two years. The celebrations were so wild that some Northern Ireland fans missed Norway's fourth goal that arrived less than a minute after the restart.

More significantly, it saw David Healy crowned as the new king of the Kop.

To some, Healy is a journeyman Football League striker who enjoyed moderate success with the likes of Preston North End and Leeds United. To Northern Ireland fans, Healy is something of a saint. His 36 international goals in 96 appearances over 13 years made him a national hero.

He was no flat-track bully, either. He registered goals against England, Spain and Germany. Nor was he a penalty box poacher. He beat Peter Schmeichel from 30 yards and lobbed Iker Casillas from 20. George Best might be the greatest player to come from Northern Ireland, but David Healy was Northern Ireland's greatest ever player.

7 September 2005 - Northern Ireland 1 England 0

By the time England's golden generation rolled into Belfast, Northern Ireland had gone some way to repairing their reputation on the international scene.

Healy's drought-ending goal against Norway was followed a month later by the Ulstermen's first win in 16 games, with the Preston striker scoring the only goal in a 1-0 friendly win over Estonia. Four days before the game against Sven-Göran Eriksson's England a 2-0 win over Azerbaijan with goals from Stuart Elliott and Warren Feeney gave Northern Ireland their first competitive win since 2001.

Despite that success, Lawrie Sanchez's men were overwhelming underdogs and with good reason. England had just defeated Wales 1-0 at the Millennium Stadium with a squad full of world-class stars such as David Beckham, Steven Gerrard, Frank Lampard, Michael Owen and Wayne Rooney. With hindsight it's easy to dismiss Eriksson's team as over-hyped, but with that roster they had to be considered contenders for the following summer's World Cup in Germany.

By comparison, Northern Ireland were a team of journeymen. Only the Aston Villa duo of Steven Davis and Aaron Hughes and the Birmingham City pair of Maik Taylor and Damien Johnson played in the Premier League.

Windsor Park was a far cry from the spacious modernity the Welsh had afforded England four days previously. The old-fashioned ground held less than 15,000, but it generated an atmosphere that few international grounds in Europe could rival. The 4,000 fans in the Kop stand created a powerful and intimidating atmosphere that unquestionably played a part in this unlikely victory.

The first guttural roar of the Kop was heard inside the first five seconds. From kick-off, England rolled the ball back to the feet of the left-back Ashley Cole. Before the Arsenal defender could move the ball on he was grabbed and wrestled to the ground by the former Willem II striker James Quinn, in a move that could best be described as unorthodox. On the face of things, it was a ridiculous challenge to make but it set the tone for the Kop and the night ahead.

The Kop's defining moment arrived in the 74th minute, with the game scoreless. The England goalkeeper Paul Robinson hooked a high clearance into the air, only to see it drop inside the centre circle. The quick-thinking Steve Davis controlled the ball before strolling forward unopposed. With no England player within five yards, Davis stood still before clipping the ball over the heads of the defence and into the path of David Healy. Cole and Jamie Carragher had pushed up in an attempt to play Healy offside, but Rio Ferdinand and Luke Young stood their ground, leaving Northern Ireland's record goalscorer in

acres of space. Healy took one touch with his instep, allowing the ball to bounce inside the area, before rifling a shot towards goal. Robinson got a hand to the ball, but he couldn't stop the thunderous shot from finding the far corner of the net. The Kop erupted.

Healy jumped in the air like a little boy celebrating an imaginary cup final winner in his back garden. It may as well have been Healy's cup final. It may as well have been Healy's back garden. The noise, emotion and colour that poured forward from the Kop is something no one who witnessed it will ever forget.

Northern Ireland held on to win 1-0. In the grand scheme of the World Cup, it meant nothing. The Ulstermen finished fourth in the group while England went on to reach the quarter-finals, but it altered the perceptions of the Northern Ireland team within Northern Ireland.

For years, Northern Ireland fans had to hide their colours or explain their reasons for actively supporting their national team.

The victory was greeted with universal praise, as politicians and celebrities who had previously considered the Northern Ireland team toxic, queued up to heap praise upon Healy and his teammates. BBC Northern Ireland cleared the schedules to show a full re-run of the match just four hours after the full-time whistle. There were newspaper supplements, DVDs, mugs and wall murals.

Four years after the Neil Lennon debacle, it was once again socially acceptable to be a Northern Ireland fan.

6 September 2005 - Northern Ireland 3 Spain 2

If the victory over England changed football in Northern Ireland, then you could perhaps argue that the victory over Spain changed world football.

Luis Aragonés's Spain side arrived in Belfast off the back of a World Cup campaign that started brightly before they lost to France in the second round in Hanover. Although the Spaniards hadn't yet become the all-conquering force they would develop into, their starting line-up was dotted with star names such as Raúl, Fernando Torres, Xabi Alonso, and Carles Puyol. They started their campaign with a 4-0 win over Liechtenstein, while Northern Ireland were humbled 3-0 at Windsor Park by Iceland.

Sanchez drastically altered his team, selecting the teenagers Jonny Evans and Kyle Lafferty, but it wasn't enough to stop Xavi and David Villa scoring two fine goals either side of a close-range David Healy equaliser.

It looked as if Spain were on their way to another three points, but Sammy Clingan and David Healy had other ideas. Spain prepared for a typical 'Irish' set-piece as the Ulstermen filled the penalty box for a free-kick just in front of the Kop. But rather than clipping the ball into the area, Clingan choose to side-foot the ball along the ground for Healy, who smashed it through a crowded six-yard box and into the net, with just under half an hour to play. How Spain fell for such an obvious bluff is anyone's guess.

But the best was still to come. With 10 minutes left, the substitute goalkeeper Maik Taylor launched a long kick into the Spanish half. Michel Salgado allowed the ball to bounce, which let Healy slip in behind him. Healy spotted that Casillas was five yards off his line and quickly produced a sublime lob from just outside the area to complete his hat-trick. It was an outrageous piece of skill from the Leeds United striker, who once again celebrated in front of the Kop, 364 days after his famous goal against England.

More was to come from Healy and Northern Ireland. The striker ultimately hit 13 goals in Euro 2008 qualifying including another hat-trick away to Liechtenstein and a fine brace at Windsor Park over Sweden. Northern Ireland also managed Windsor wins over Latvia and Denmark, while claiming draws in Copenhagen and Stockholm. Unfortunately they failed to qualify, finishing third in the group after frustrating defeats in Riga and Reykjavik.

Perhaps the ramifications of this result were felt more deeply in Spain. Raúl hit the post in the dying minutes at Windsor Park. It turned out to be his last game for his country, an unfitting end for one of Spain's greatest talents. After another defeat to Sweden a month later Aragonés was forced into making a number of drastic changes. It wasn't long before Andrés Iniesta, David Silva, Cesc Fàbregas, Marcos Senna and Joan Capdevila were introduced to the starting side. All five would play a crucial role in Spain's eventual Euro 2008 success with Aragonés developing a system that saw Senna protect Xavi (and Iniesta) from the sort of rough-house treatment he received at Windsor Park. It echoed the system Barcelona used that saw Edmilson deployed in the protective role. Sergio Busquets would eventually redefine the position for both club and country.

That success allowed the new manager Vicente del Bosque to develop what arguably became the greatest international team of all time, lifting the 2010 World Cup and Euro 2012. Their form of dominant possession-based football that both protected their defence and wore out their opponents became the most discussed and mimicked style in a generation.

Perhaps if Healy hadn't scored that outrageous lob in front of the Kop, Aragonés wouldn't have axed Raúl and altered his system. Perhaps he wouldn't have found the formula that Del Bosque eventually developed. Perhaps Spain wouldn't have won the World Cup in South Africa. Perhaps possession football wouldn't have come to dominate the world game. Perhaps.

14 November 2012 - Northern Ireland 1 Azerbaijan 1

Six years after his hat-trick against Spain, David Healy was a shadow of his former self. Injury-thwarted stints at Fulham, Sunderland and Rangers had eventually led Healy to a deal with the League One club Bury. Even at international level Healy's form had subsided, and he scored just two more goals after his record-breaking Euro 2008 campaign.

Northern Ireland hadn't fared much better. There were impressive victories under Nigel Worthington over the likes of Poland and Slovenia and new man Michael O'Neill had guided the Ulstermen to a 1-1 draw with Portugal in

Porto, but there was little else for the Kop to be cheerful about.

In their last home game Northern Ireland had sunk to an embarrassing 1-1 draw with Luxembourg while they trailed Azerbaijan by a goal as the game rolled into stoppage time. As a last throw of the dice O'Neill replaced defender Craig Cathcart in the 82nd minute with a rather more rotund version of David Healy.

In the sixth minute of stoppage time, Northern Ireland were awarded a free-kick just outside the area, in front of the Kop. There was only one possible outcome. Healy stepped up and side-footed the free-kick past both the wall and the goalkeeper.

It was an equaliser but it was also a final goodbye. This was Healy's encore and everyone on the Kop knew it. It was a horrible performance in horrible conditions, but it was worth every last second just to hear another joyous rendition of "Healy! Healy!".

29 March 2015 - Northern Ireland 2 Finland 1

While no one expected David Healy's international career to go on forever, most expected the stand he made his own to remain in place for generations to come.

Not least the architects of the revamped Windsor Park. In 2012 the Irish Football Association unveiled government-sponsored plans to update Northern Ireland's national stadium. The decrepit South Stand would join the old Railway Stand in the history books, while the 1980s North Stand and the 1990s West

Stand (the Kop) would be incorporated into the new design. The finished article would be a modern 18,000 all-seater stadium that was designed to retain the charm of the old Windsor Park while improving spectator facilities.

Although the Kop would be refurbished it would remain an integral part of the rechristened National Stadium. Or at least that was plan until March of this year, when Mixu Paatelainen's Finland came to Belfast for a Euro 2016 qualifier.

Since Healy's retirement, his old strike partner Kyle Lafferty had done his best to fill his boots. After the Enniskillen-born forward left a bankrupt Rangers in 2012 his club career had turned into an unusual European adventure with stints at Sion, Palermo, Norwich City and Çaykur Rizespor. While Lafferty has always proclaimed his love for his country, his international career had been fraught with frustration. Injuries, disappointing displays and a daft red card against Portugal had made him an unpopular figure with sections of the Green & White Army.

The manager Michael O'Neill's faith in the 6'4" forward was finally repaid in Budapest last September, when the striker scored a late winner in a 2-1 win over Hungary. In October, Lafferty netted again as the Ulstermen beat the Faroe Islands 2-0 at Windsor Park. Four days later the former Burnley striker tore the Greek defence apart, scoring the second goal in a 2-0 win over Claudio Ranieri's men in Athens. At the age of 27, some nine years after his debut, Lafferty was finally fulfilling his early promise.

November's 2-0 defeat to Romania in Bucharest did little to dampen the Kop's enthusiasm for the Finland game and Lafferty was given a rapturous response upon his return home. The love-in was cemented in the 33rd minute when Lafferty scored a marvellous 15-yard volley to give Northern Ireland the lead in front of the Kop. He hit his second of the game and his fifth goal of the campaign six minutes later when he scored a towering header reminiscent of Healy's drought-ending goal against Norway.

Just as 11 years previously, the Kop rocked in celebration, chanting the name of their country's new hero. But this time there was no need for self-deprecation or irony. Northern Ireland fans really did have something to celebrate. With 12 points from their opening five games the Ulstermen are within touching distance of qualifying for their first major championships since Mexico '86.

It was something of a shame that Beret Sadik scored an injury-time consolation goal for Finland, because unbeknown to the 4,000 Northern Ireland fans behind it was the last international goal the 'new Kop' would ever witness.

Less than 48 hours after the Green & White Army celebrated a glorious 2-1 victory over Finland, the Kop was sealed off after huge cracks appeared at the back of the old stand, with one corner of the 18-year old edifice seemingly sinking into the ground. Within a month the IFA confirmed everyone's worst fears. The most famous stand in Northern Irish sport was to be demolished immediately.

It left Northern Ireland fans wondering what exactly caused the Kop to collapse and who was at fault. Worse still, were the fans at Northern Ireland v Finland put in danger? It could take years before we get a definitive answer to those vital questions.

In the meantime, June's game against Romania will go ahead at Windsor Park, with the Kop's refugees rehoused in the new East Stand. In the long term, the IFA hope that a third new stand will be at the west end of the ground as part of the redevelopment, but whether the third incarnation of the Kop can recapture the magic of the stand that witnessed all those David Healy goals is doubtful.

18 years is a short lifespan for a modern stand, but the Kop packed a rich store of memories into its two decades. Thousands of Linfield fans witnessed nine league title wins from the Kop, while fans of clubs such as Cliftonville, Crusaders, Ballymena United and Larne will all have

fond memories of watching their teams in cup final action from the West Stand.

But much like its favourite son David Healy, the Kop made its name at international level. Not only did it look down upon famous victories over England, Spain, Sweden, Denmark, Poland, Russia and Finland, but it also the hosted a shift in attitudes.

While the war against sectarianism in football is far from over, the Green & White Army won its most significant battle on the Kop. Huge strides forward have been made, with Northern Ireland games at Windsor Park now almost entirely free of the blatant sectarianism the dogged the nineties.

The legacy of the Kop is one of positivity, an attitude which is often difficult to achieve in Belfast. The cult of the Kop will long outlive the stand itself. Ⓑ

Blizzard Books

Erbstein: The triumph and tragedy of football's forgotten pioneer

Dominic Bliss

Before the Shopping Centre

How crowd violence brought an end to the existence of Belfast Celtic

By Conor Heffernan

Founded in 1891, at a time of political upheaval in both the North and South of Ireland, Belfast Celtic, the 'Grand Old Team', were far more than a football club.

For more than 50 years, the team was a beacon of hope in a religiously divided land. Supported primarily by the Catholics of the Falls Road, and wearing the same green-and-white hoops as Celtic of Glasgow, on which it was based, the club stood out for fielding players of both religious denominations in a world in which your religion often dictated your employer, team, colleagues and friends.

What's more, Belfast Celtic were successful in doing it.

During its lifespan, the Club won 14 league titles, 8 Irish Cups, 11 City Cups and a host of other tournaments. It was, in the words of the Belfast Celtic Society, "a leading light in Irish football", gaining the admiration of football fans on both sides of the religious divide in Northern Ireland.

Sadly it was the same religious divisions that the club hoped to overcome that effectively led to its demise when sectarian violence erupted during an important league match.

Act I: Religion, Rivalry and Revenge

"When we had nothing, we had Belfast Celtic, then we had everything."

Belfast Celtic historian Bill McKavanagh

In December 1948, Belfast Celtic lined up for a vital league game away against their fierce rivals Linfield at Windsor Park. Located in a predominantly Protestant area of Belfast, Linfield, unlike their rivals, were famed for their uniformity. Only Protestants played for Linfield, only Protestants managed the players and the fans who passed through the turnstiles to support them were predominantly Protestant. Unsurprisingly given the nature of Northern Irish society during these years, encounters between the two sides were often marked by sectarian disputes. From Belfast Celtic's first encounter with Linfield in the early 1900s, games had been marred by disorder and violence between the fans.

Adding fuel to the fire in 1948 was the matter of that year's league title.

Linfield were top of the table, three points ahead of Celtic and looking strong contenders for the title. A win over the Grand Old Team would effectively clinch the League, whereas a Celtic win would re-open the title race. The opening minutes of the match reflected what was at stake. Tackles flew in late, elbows slyly struck opponents in the back and every break of the ball was hotly contested. Cheers from the crowd amplified at every clash, urging the players to give more. It wasn't long before such intensity resulted in injury.

Midway through the first half, a 50-50 challenge between Celtic's Jimmy Jones and Linfield defender Bob Bryson resulted in Bryson being stretchered off the field. The agony visible on Bryson's face did little to quell the anger of the Linfield fans, who responded by charging toward the Celtic supporters in the away stand in the hope of exacting revenge. Following several minutes of unrest, the Royal Ulster Constabulary marched into the stands, batons aloft, resulting in an uneasy calm eventually descending across the stands.

Bryson's injury reduced Linfield to 10 men and it was little surprise that Celtic were soon on the front foot. Compounding Linfield's misery, their goalkeeper Alex Russell was soon forced from the field following a head-on collision while saving a shot. When the referee Norman Boal brought an end to the first half, Linfield entered the tunnel with only nine fit players.

There were further skirmishes between rival fans at half-time when Linfield's secretary, Joe Mackey, inexplicably announced over the Tannoy that Bryson's leg had been broken thanks to Jimmy Jones's tackle. "Mackey was guilty of inciting the crowd for more or less laying the blame on me for Bryson's injury," said Jones years later.

Jones had every right to feel aggrieved as, in the event, Bryson's injury was not as serious as was first thought. However, Mackey's half-time pronouncement made Jones even more of a target for the home crowd. When the teams returned onto the pitch for the second half, it was clear tempers hadn't calmed. Even with nine men, Linfield, willed on by the roars from the crowd, launched wave after wave of attacks against Celtic. Passions boiled over and midway through the second half, Boal sent off Celtic's Paddy Bonnar and Linfield's Albert Currie following a clash between the two.

The decision to reduce Linfield to eight players sparked further fighting on the terraces, as a sense that they were being wronged gripped the Linfield faithful. Once more baton-wielding police moved in and restored the peace.

Despite the chaos in the stands, the game went on. While both teams continued to press in the second half, it looked as though the game had tipped Celtic's way when, 10 minutes from full-time, they were awarded a penalty after Jackie Denver had been hacked down by Jimmy McCune. As Harry Walker stepped up to take the kick, an eerie silence fell across Windsor Park. It was soon penetrated by the cheers from the Celtic supporters as Walker slotted the ball home. A Celtic win would have reduced Linfield's lead at the top of the table to a single point.

When Linfield's Isaac McDowell burst down the wing with only four minutes remaining, heartbeats began to quicken. Jinking around the desperate tackles from the Celtic defenders, McDowell floated a cross into the box which was met by the boot of Linfield's Billy Simpson. As the ball flashed into the net, home fans poured onto the pitch in jubilation. Songs echoed through the stadium as a parade began on the sidelines. Such innocence was not to last.

As more and more fans entered the field, a small section of Linfield supporters began to target Celtic players. Verbal taunts soon turned to threats, which then turned to physicality. For the third time, the police were forced to employ their batons. The remaining four minutes of the game were played in an atmosphere of danger.

When the final whistle blew, Linfield fans once more spilled onto the pitch and resumed their targeting of Celtic players. This time the police force was slow to respond.

Sensing an opportunity to exact mob justice, a group of 30 Linfield fans charged toward Jimmy Jones. In a desperate attempt to avoid the crowd, Jones rushed towards the safety of the dressing-room but was intercepted by the mob. Manhandled by the supporters, Jones was dragged over the parapet into the terraces below the main stand. Punches and kicks began to rain down on Jones's body.

When a policeman warned the attackers, "If you don't stop hitting him, I'll use my baton!", he too was assaulted. On the other side of the field, Jones's parents watched in horror as Linfield fans began jumping on their son's legs. Commenting on the attack in 1989, Jones still remembered that "a fella jumped off

a wall onto me leg." He had every reason to recall the incident vividly. The attack left Jones with a broken leg and was only ended when a friend, Sean McCann, somehow managed to retrieve him from the attack.

Jones wasn't the only Celtic player who found himself at the mercy of the mob. As the rest of the Belfast Celtic players ran towards the dressing-room, the goalkeeper Kevin McAlinden and the defender Robin Lawler were caught by the oncoming crowd and left seriously injured.

In the dressing-room, the Celtic players frantically began to grab any shovel, broom or makeshift weapon they could find, in anticipation of an oncoming attack. When they learned of Jones's fate, they had to be restrained by the club's directors from re-entering the battle zone. Their anger soon turned to despair when Jones's limp body was carried in by McCann.

When the Celtic chairman Austin Donnelly came in soon afterward, he could barely contain his anger. The normally austere Donnelly told the players, "We can't let you boys put up with the likes of that..."

Unbeknown to the players, Donnelly intended to stick to his word.

Act II: Ending an Institution

"Some people believe football is a matter of life and death, I am very disappointed with that attitude. I can assure you it is much, much more important than that".

Bill Shankly

Disgusted by the ferocity of the violence exhibited in the Linfield match, Celtic's directors called an emergency meeting on the night of the game. There, the directors took the fateful decision to with-draw Celtic from the League once the 1948-49 season had finished.

An air of resignation hung in the room. They were putting an end to an institution, a club that, as the legendary Celtic trainer Michael McGuigan once said, was a part of the community, part of the lives of every man, woman and child living on the Falls Road.

The directors would have been well aware that it wasn't the first time such an action had been taken by Celtic. Between 1912 and 1917 the club had taken similar steps as sectarian violence had increased in the face of demands for Home Rule and, subsequently, independence from the southern part of the country. Likewise from 1920 to 1924 the club chose to remain inactive following a flurry of gunshots during a cup game during Ireland's War of Independence

Outside of the Belfast Celtic boardroom, the responses to the Linfield violence echoed the complicated world of Northern Irish politics. Catholic supporters raged against the inability of the police force to protect the Celtic squad while retorts from the other side argued that the police had done their best. The often-ignored middle ground cited the thuggish behaviour of a small minority.

The conversation about who was to blame extended far beyond the footballing world. Football acted as a microcosm of the greater societal trends in the North. For nationalists, the Linfield attacks were seen as symbolic of the greater discrimination Catholics faced on a daily basis. When the North's footballing body, the IFA, eventually closed Linfield's home ground for a month and fined them as punishment, Catholic politicians such as Eddie McAteer brought the matter to the parliament at Stormont in a bid to gain further retribution.

Angered at the reluctance of Protestant politicians to ascribe blame to the police, McAteer, perhaps unwisely, remarked in the Government Chamber that the police were too fond of using their batons on political opponents, but not Linfield supporters. Amidst the uproar and hubbub from the ruling party members, it became clear that justice would not be forthcoming for Celtic.

Celtic's first game after the Linfield debacle saw them put 10 goals past Distillery, with Johnny Campbell, Jimmy Jones's replacement, scoring six. Any celebration among the Celtic fans soon became muted as it became clear that something was occurring behind the scenes.

Although the Board's decision to withdraw the team from the league had been made in secrecy, evidence of their decision quickly began to trickle out. The morning following the Distillery game, the nationalist newspaper the *Irish News*, reported that Celtic's Paddy Bonnar was in talks with West Bromwich Albion. Fans were re-assured that such talks were tentative, but they were warned by the paper that more was likely to follow on the transfer front with several key players earmarked for moves abroad.

The paper's prophecies came true in March when Robin Lawler and Johnny Campbell were sold to Fulham for a knockdown price. Writing in the *Irish News*, Ben Madigan summed up the confusion of the Celtic faithful: "The quick-fire transfer of Robin Lawler and Johnny Campbell to Fulham in the London Club's bid for promotion against the challenge of West Brom and Spurs has left the soccer world guessing. Your guess is as good as mine as to whether Celtic will carry on in Irish League football."

Two weeks after Madigan's article, Celtic's full-back Tom Ahearne was sold to Luton Town. In less than a month, three of Celtic's core had been offloaded without any explanation to the fans. The remainder of the season would see Madigan continually lament the actions of the Celtic board, accompanied by various guesses as to their motives.

Madigan was a well-respected journalist who often had the inside scoop on the internal dealings of Belfast Celtic. His inability to decipher what was going on troubled fans.

On April 16, Belfast Celtic informed the Irish Football Association that they would be unable to fulfil reserve games for the remainder of the season due to "congestion and an upcoming tour of the USA". Journalists and fans alike suspected that there was more to the story.

On April 21 their suspicions were confirmed when the *Northern Whig* broke the news that Celtic's directors had issued a formal letter of resignation to the IFA. When confronted by reporters about the future of Belfast Celtic, the Celtic chairman Austin Donnelly grimly told the press, "We have gone from the Irish League".

The remaining weeks of the season saw Celtic lag behind Linfield, who eventually clinched that year's title. It mattered little to fans, who were much more concerned about whether the club would survive another year. Before Belfast Celtic embarked on a summer tour of the USA, fans were informed that the board would review the decision to withdraw from the League following the tour.

While the Belfast Celtic players and directors enjoyed a warm reception from US audiences, fans at home anxiously awaited news of the club's future. Madigan's reports in the *Irish News* began to descend into more and more outlandish conspiracy theories. Arguments were put forward that Celtic's resignation was a display of brinkmanship from the club. It was posited that the IFA would beg the Grand Old Team to return to the league as they had reportedly done in 1924. The fact that the IFA had accepted Celtic's resignation, albeit with great sympathy, did little to stop Madigan's theories from gaining traction.

Four decades after Celtic's withdrawal, the former player Paddy Bonnar told reporters that internecine fights among the board were to blame for the club's decisions. Others would cite supposed financial issues. Nowadays members of the Belfast Celtic society are unequivocal that the Club's decision was down to the failure of the IFA to guarantee the safety of Celtic players.

When Celtic returned from their summer tour, any hope of them rethinking their withdrawal from the league was dashed. Within a week of their return, the *Irish News* was reporting that Paddy Bonnar, Harry Walker and Charlie Curry had all accepted moves elsewhere. They were soon followed by George Hazlett and others. By late June, it became clear that Celtic wouldn't be returning to the Irish League.

When the 1949-50 season kicked off, it did so without Belfast Celtic.

Act III: Gone but not forgotten

"Belfast Celtic will be missed..."

> Belfast Telegraph, 1949-50
> Season Preview

While the directors' decision to withdraw the club from football had been a difficult one, the club historian Bill McKavanagh says, "There was total support from the supporters at the time."

That was not to say that fans were not upset by the decision. Reflecting on the demise of Belfast Celtic in the late 1980s, the Celtic fan Jimmy Overend recalled his sadness: "It was like a black cloud coming down, as if there was nothing to live for or look forward to on a Saturday. It's a grief which never went away."

Overend wasn't alone in his despair. When Ulster TV commissioned a documentary on Belfast Celtic in 1989, interviews from former fans revealed how the club had given fans a belief in the future, something that the people of the Falls Road could be proud of. Since the early 1900s, Celtic fans had always publicised the importance of the

Grand Old Team. In 1901 a fan known as Crossbar wrote a verse that summed up the club's place in the community

"Out of seeming nothing;
Out of shadow and gloom;
Out of a hollowed vacuum
Came something to keep us in tune.
Something to interest and please us;
Something we call our own;
Something we almost worship;
Loving beyond control.
Boys by practice and training;
Diligently keeping fit;
Men by planning and scheming
Built it bit by bit.
Loyally working together;
Faithful to their scheme;
Out of little or nothing
Came the champion Celtic team."

So how did fans cope? Denial.

McKavanagh believed that Celtic fans comforted themselves with the idea that Celtic's withdrawal was simply a temporary measure. Withdrawal was seen as a tactic in a game of brinkmanship with the IFA. After all, the club had withdrawn and come back twice before in its history over that very matter. How were the fans to know that this time history wouldn't repeat itself? Rumours began to emerge that the club was seeking to join the football league in the Republic of Ireland, an option that was quickly dismissed by the FAI, the governing body in the South.

While the Celtic fans waited in limbo, the players began to forge new careers across the British Isles. Some remained in Northern Ireland, while others joined the likes of the former Belfast Celtic legend Charlie Tully, in moving across the Irish Sea.

By the 1950s, it appeared fans of the former Belfast Celtic were left with two choices: to renounce their allegiance to Celtic and support a new club, or to become neutral spectators. It was a decision that few football fans want to take. As time passed however, former Belfast Celtic supporters began to flock to nearby clubs to get their weekly fix. Others began to undertake regular pilgrimages to Glasgow to support Celtic or, in later decades, make the 60-mile journey to Derry City or Coleraine. A minority dropped their interest in football altogether.

As the players and fans moved on, Celtic Park, or Paradise as it was affectionately known, continued to stand just off the Falls Road, a powerful and poignant reminder of past glories.

It continued to function as a greyhound stadium run by the former Celtic manager and Liverpool legend Elisha Scott. During his time with the club, Scott won 10 league titles and oversaw the development of players like Charlie Tully. For 10 years Scott would look on as dogs ran alongside the grass where he had tasted both victory and defeat, or at games between junior football teams who had rented the pitch. It was a far cry from the heyday of the 1920s, when Belfast Celtic had won four League titles on the trot.

Three years after Celtic's dissolution, hope briefly flickered.

In aid of De La Salle Boys Home in County Down, a Belfast Celtic XI, under the name Newry FC, took on Celtic at Celtic Park in 1952. An unsurprisingly emotional affair, the game featured the former Belfast Celtic star Charlie Tully leading out the Glasgow team to face off against Belfast. Tully's career had begun at Belfast Celtic under Elisha Scott. To return to Paradise after everything that had happened was overwhelming.

While Celtic of Glasgow would eventually win the game 3-2, the result mattered little to the fans. The chatter and jokes among the supporters felt like tribute to times past. For 90 minutes, fans of the Grand Old Team were offered the rare opportunity to step back to a time when Belfast Celtic were the Kings of the Falls Road.

Towards the end of the game, Belfast Celtic fans in the home stand unfurled a large banner pleading with their former team: "Will ye no come back again?"

Soon after the crowd broke into singing of the well-known ballad,

"Will ye no come back again?
Will ye no come back again?
Better lo'ed ye canna be;
Will ye no come back again?"

They wouldn't. Two years went by before a benefit game for the former Manchester City inside-left Peter Doherty would see the Grand Old Team reassemble once more, again to play Celtic. In 1960, Belfast Celtic played its final game, a testimonial against Coleraine.

As the Troubles developed in the late 1960s, Belfast Celtic faded further into the memory. By then the big rivalry in Northern Irish football was between Linfield and Glentoran – or their Scottish equivalents, Celtic and Rangers. Indeed, it is often remarked that those

Belfast Celtic fans who moved to support the Glasgow version did so with the zeal of converts. Throughout the Troubles, former Belfast Celtic fans travelled to Glasgow, first on cattle boats and later by ferries. Whenever the ferries didn't run, it wasn't unheard of for fans to hire fishing vessels to make it to Glasgow.

The 1980s saw the end of greyhound racing at Celtic Park and eventually the stadium was sold to property developers. Paradise was bulldozed and replaced with a shopping centre. The decision caused uproar among the club's veterans, with several former players refusing to enter the shopping centre as a matter of principle, even after a small plaque dedicated to the club was installed.

The construction of the shopping centre did serve to stoke the embers of the Grand Old Team. In 1989, a lavish reunion was held for former players at the Threepenny Bit, King's Hall in Belfast. The occasion was documented by Ulster TV and helped pass on the memory of Belfast Celtic to a new generation. In 2003 a handful of committed fans established the Belfast Celtic Society as a tribute and, in 2010, secured the opening of a club museum in the shopping centre over Celtic Park.

While the club may no longer grace the field, the Society has ensured that the memory of the Grand Old Team will last. It is a fitting tribute to a team that for 50 years provided joy to the people of the Falls Road. 🅱

94

Theory

"The whole thing is random and erratic."

The Man who Built White Ships

Stanko Poklepović, the oldest coach in Europe, and the importance of spiral impostations

By Alex Holiga

The road meanders through a succession of small neighbourhoods, intermittently featuring bleak housing projects, ramshackle industrial architecture and nondescript modern glass-and-steel business buildings; you hardly notice any of Split's supposedly Mediterranean features until you get to the centre. But by that time, you will have seen at least a dozen of murals, all with the same theme: Hajduk, the city's main football club, is massive here.

From the Bellevue, which hasn't changed all that much from 1936 when it was the best hotel in town – Edward VIII and Wallis Simpson famously dined there on the eve of the abdication crisis – a walk of less that half an hour takes you to Poljud Stadium. You go through a confusing labyrinth of narrow, cobbled streets to the old Hajduk ground, Stari Plac, now just a fenced meadow squeezed on a street corner and used by RK Nada, the local rugby union club; you turn left and, as the urban landscape gradually turns more contemporary, arrive at the venue.

Built for the 1979 Mediterranean Games with a then-futuristic roof structure resembling a sea shell, the Poljud was counted among the most beautiful stadiums in Europe. Now visibly neglected and reduced to 60% of its original 55,000-capacity, it's still by far the best in the country, but has only hosted one competitive national team match in the last 18 years. That's the way things are in centralist Croatia, where the capital, Zagreb, gets all the good stuff.

Not far from Poljud, there's a tavern called *Kod starog mornara* (The Old Mariner's). It's a beautiful morning in Split and Stanko 'Špaco' Poklepović is there on the terrace, soaking up late winter sun. Everything about him is distinctly old school: the clothes, the jokes, the way he charms the waitress when ordering a *viljamovka* – the local pear brandy – at 11am. But he's keen to show he hasn't lost touch with modern football and its ways. "I've always been in it, to the maximum," he says. "I may have been out of work for four years, but interpreting football has remained my obsession. I know exactly what needs to be done, I'm familiar with every corner here and aware of the club's orientation towards the future. I don't find any of it difficult."

At 77, Poklepović was the oldest professional football manager working in Europe, until he was sacked in April.

He took over when his predecessor, Igor Tudor – 40 years younger than him and previously a defender for Croatia and Juventus, who played in the 2003

Champions League final against AC Milan – suddenly resigned in February, having been in charge since 2013. The squad was in disarray, weakened by the sales of three important players in the winter transfer window, but included two of Hajduk's most valuable assets: their pair of talented teenagers, Andrija Balić and Nikola Vlašić. Both were born 60 years after their new manager, at a time when he was already considering retirement. This is Poklepović's fourth stint at the club, but he's only here until the summer, when Hajduk are expected to appoint a more long-term solution. And he's only the oldest gaffer in Europe because Ćiro Blažević, 80, who led Croatia to third place at the 1998 World Cup, abruptly left his post at NK Zadar in December.

Špaco is a showman, always making sure to provide the press with headline material. He often makes jokes – sometimes saucy – about his players, himself and his peers ("Igor Štimac is stronger than me. He's a mature man who can do everything, even sexually – which I can't anymore," he said about his former player, who has taken over from Blažević at NK Zadar). They love him for it, but, as a result, he's seldom taken seriously when he does say anything serious, so he treats journalists with suspicion. If you're only in it for the latest anecdote or catchphrase, Špaco will oblige, but if you'd rather have a meaningful conversation, you first need to convince him you're genuinely interested in what he has to say.

"So I suppose you want to know about spiral impostation, am I right?" he asks, taking a small sip of his brandy, and the question feels like a test. He's referring to the unusual term he used a few days earlier to describe his side's on-pitch shape, baffling and amusing reporters in equal measure.

"Yes, but I'm also curious about your more general views on football as well as your playing philosophy," I answer. He seems satisfied with that and, without much further ado, begins his exposition.

"Football is a game of balance. Throughout history, coaches have been trying to win games by inventing and applying different strategies to counter-balance the opponent's play. That interaction, setting up your defence to oppose the other team's attack and vice versa, is what always drove football forward. That's also how formations evolved, because each action was followed by a reaction. First you had the W-M system, which can also be described as 3-4-3; when coaches realised that three forwards were too much for the three-man defence to handle, the system evolved into 4-3-3 and 4-4-2 and various modern formations. But the formation is not tactics. It's only a medium you use to develop team play. In the 1950s, Hajduk had Bernard Vukas, who was one of the best players in the world at the time. However, back then players were allowed a lot of space and time on the ball. Eventually, teams started using specialists whose only job was to mark Vukas. If he knelt down to tie his shoelaces, that player would kneel down next to him; if Vukas decided to go to the toilet in the middle of the match, his marker would follow him there. Things like that took man-marking to new heights, as it was clear that even a world-class player becomes much less effective if he's denied that space and time.

"By the 1970's, when I first came to Hajduk as an assistant to my lifelong friend Tomislav Ivić, we had each player strictly marking his opposing number, except for the libero, who was the corrector. Then we introduced pressing, which can have three different targets: space, man and the ball. Pressing on the ball, which is also called *gegen-*pressing, appeared last and it's still very prominent today. But pressing can be counter-productive if you're also using man-marking, so zonal defence gradually became more widespread. Zonal marking, which is the foundation for all modern formations, has its specific geometry, because you have to cover the whole pitch. Today, that zone has developed some new properties, which can no longer be described as elements of play. They are, in fact, features of modern football and there are three main ones…"

He suddenly stops. Allowing the underlying suspicion he developed over time to resurface, he asks, "Is this what you wanted me to talk about? I hope I'm not going too fast for you to follow, because up until now all this was just the basics." I assure him it's exactly what I hoped for and he turns to Hajduk press officer, who sits there with us. The man is all ears as well. *Šjor* ('Mister' in local dialect) Špaco gives us a broad smile, takes another sip and continues.

"As a manager, I'm primarily interested in the technology of team performance. It is also my job to develop a modern football expression for my team, because you cannot expect to beat anyone if your style of play is not up to date. I've stayed in touch with current trends and came up with this theory on three main features of modern football, which I named rhythm, concentration and re-formation. All the good teams have a recognisable rhythm, which is essential for the way they play. You need to train your players into a state where they do everything in the team rhythm. When you achieve that automatism, you gradually accelerate it, because you need to play very fast today. Then there's concentration, which means getting to the focus of the play. Often you see the greatest concentration of players around the ball area, but it's not like when little kids play and they all chase the ball because their notion of space isn't yet developed. This is organised concentration, with the intention of stifling the opponent's passing options, which is a prerequisite for pressing. As players grow up, they develop this intuitive understanding of space with regards to the ball and other players. But concentration is asking them to do something which may feel counter-intuitive, to leave their position and descend into the epicentre of play. You can't rely on instinct anymore, it must be put into the service of the collective; the players need to think and know what they're doing.

"The third feature follows concentration, and that's re-formation. It refers to transition, both defensive and attacking, the way of quickly re-establishing shape after concentrating, which is really hard. You need to devise patterns of movement and look to break the opponent's formation in half, because you want to leave them in a situation where they must defend with as few players behind the ball as possible. This is where you use specific elements acquired through practice, such as what

I call the 'team dribbling' — and by that I mean confusing and deceiving the other team, getting them to where my team wants them to be."

Poklepović has refused to categorise his team's formation, saying it's asymmetrical and escapes the classical definition. So, in that context, I pop the 'spiral impostation' question. What is it?

"Instead of using parallel lines, I position my players like this [he uses glasses, cups and various other objects on the table to demonstrate his point]: you see, it's a curve, a spiral. One wide player is always higher than the other, or he always stays by the line while the other is more inside, not really a winger... You do this across the entire formation. If applied properly, nothing, not even a bird, can pass through the spiral! But that's primarily a defensive tactic, aimed at closing spaces more efficiently. It's something temporary, before you can develop your team's proper play. Although the spiral is still more universal than the *pirija*, which is basically a one-time thing..."

Pirija is, of course, another tactic invented and named by Špaco himself. The aim is to block the opponent's flanks high up and divert most of their play to the narrowing corridor through the middle of the pitch. Hence the name: *pirija* ("funnel" in local dialect). The idiosyncratic terms Špaco uses bring to mind the biggest Hajduk icon of all time, Luka Kaliterna. A goalkeeper in the very first Hajduk team back in 1911 (his brother, Fabjan, co-founded the club), as well as their first domestic

manager twelve years later, after a dozen Czechoslovakian and Austrian[1] gaffers, Kaliterna was a major influence for generations of other managers and known for his many sayings, such as, "The play, not the player, scores goals," and "See everything, look at nothing."

Poklepović, who spent his entire playing career at RNK Split, was coming through the youth ranks in the 1950s, when Kaliterna led them to two promotions in four years and reached the Yugoslav top division with the city's lesser club. He played under him again on two later occasions. How influential was Kaliterna for him, I dare to ask.

"Massively! He was ahead of his time. His coaching methods, many things he taught us, are still relevant today. I remember he always used to say that we need to act like a sponge: clench when we're defending and release when we're attacking. There was no one else like him."

Among RNK Split players from those years were four men that later went on to become very successful managers. There was Ante Mladinić, who coached Yugoslavia national team and won the league with Partizan Belgrade in 1978; Mirko Jozić, world champion with Yugoslavia's Under-20 side in 1987, a Copa Libertadores winner with Colo-Colo in 1991 and later Croatia manager. There was, of course, Poklepović, decorated with four honours in Croatia (with Hajduk and NK Osijek) and two in Iran (with Persepolis). But the one who topped them all was Tomislav Ivić,

---

[1] *Technically, the first five were Austro-Hungarian.*

who won league and cup titles in six different countries – with Hajduk, Ajax, Anderlecht, Panathinaikos, Porto and Atlético Madrid. Poklepović first played with him, then under him at RNK. In 1973, he joined Ivić at Hajduk, as his assistant and youth coach.

"Those were the days… The papers called me the 'Builder of White Ships', because I worked with so many youngsters who became stars in that white Hajduk shirt," he says, giving in to nostalgia for the first and only time during the interview. The team won two consecutive league titles, in 1974 and 1975, with Ivić in charge. "He was intense. He had this hot, peppery temper that other coaches lacked, but also possessed a unique creative fluid. Ivić knew exactly what he was doing, always! We were extremely compatible."

But as Ivić left for Ajax to replace Rinus Michels – and immediately won them the Dutch title, their first in four years – Poklepović stayed. He was hoping to succeed his friend, but wasn't given a chance. Ivić returned in 1978 and rehired him, they won the league again and reached the European Cup quarter-final in 1980, then he left again – this time for Anderlecht, winning the title in his first season there as well. Hajduk passed on Poklepović one more time and it was only in 1984 that they finally appointed him. And although Hajduk played attractive, attacking football, came close to winning the league and eliminated the likes of Metz, Torino and Dnipro in Europe, he was fired in March 1986 after a dispute with the club leadership over his star player, Blaž Slišković. "He was a top player, but a bohemian," Poklepović said. "Once he did something really stupid and I wanted to throw him out

of the team, but chairman intervened because the club wanted to sell him that summer. So I had to go."

His career path took him to smaller clubs in Yugoslavia as well as to places like Cyprus, Iran and Hungary. In 1992 Poklepović won his first piece of silverware, the inaugural Croatian league, back with Hajduk Split. But Špaco never stayed anywhere for more than a year or two. Some say that was because of his restless spirit, others claim he hasn't been able to communicate his ideas to players with authority because of his facetious nature. It may also be true that he doesn't get along well with powers that be, never hesitating to express his opinion on just about everything. That certainly proved correct during his short-lived tenure as Croatia manager, before the nation was admitted to Fifa in 1993.

Franjo Tuđman, the country's authoritarian first president, was a man with a keen interest in football. Upon his intervention, Dinamo Zagreb changed their 'Soviet' name in 1991 – first to HAŠK Građanski, combining and claiming the heritage of two most successful pre-Second World War Zagreb clubs, then to Croatia Zagreb. (The name Dinamo was brought back in early 2000, shortly after his death.)

"I once told him he didn't know anything about football," Poklepović claims. "Ooh, he didn't like that one bit. He preferred to be surrounded by people who would never contradict him, like Ćiro Blažević." Of course, Blažević was also a Dinamo man and a member of Tuđman's political party, HDZ, so the president saw him as more suitable for the job…

The more we talk about the past, the grumpier Poklepović becomes, revealing the internal struggle that must have troubled him for many years. Here is a man who clearly thinks his work has never been appreciated enough and yet he tries to keep critics on his side. I walk with him to the press conference, which turns out to be very different to usual. He fumes at reporters for 15 minutes about not being "positive enough" and not giving his players the "support they need". He leaves visibly upset, mumbling outrageous curses and without so much as nodding his head as he passes by.

At 77, Špaco still feels he has something to prove but is aware of how little chance he has to do so. Even as we spoke, it has later emerged, Hajduk were interviewing candidates to replace him from next season, regardless of how he did. And it's by no means easy to achieve anything when his two best players are 17-year-old kids, the half-built "white ships" which he would never get to steer once they're at least close to being finished. The whole situation is a constant reminder that, after a long and meandering journey, this Old Mariner's managerial career was running on borrowed time; a metaphor for mortality.

The Whisky Option

Malcolm Allison's time at Sporting was brief but fans remember him fondly

By Simon Curtis

The atmosphere in the malodorous wood-panelled room was clunky and uneasy. A twist of blue smoke drifted slowly from the end of a cigar resting on an ashtray in the middle of the table. Only the sound of a group of children playing football in the street below broke the silence. By the ashtray, dead centre of the table, as if the space had been measured before the objects were set down, lay a single sheet of paper and an unopened bottle of Scotch. João Rocha, the high-profile president of Sporting Clube de Portugal, smoothed his hands over his bald head and, turning to his interlocutor without as much as a smile, said, "I'm afraid it's one or the other, Malcolm."

Legend has it that Malcolm Allison's next move was to lean forward, pick up the bottle and leave the room, the stadium and the club. His time leading Portugal's famous green and white hoops, brief and glamorously successful, was over in one simple, dramatic Dartford Gunslinger gesture.

To try to understand what might lead Allison to such headstrong actions at the age of 50, we must travel back from the narrow alleyways of early eighties Lisbon to the dank pebbled streets of East London in the fifties. It is a journey which will uncover the flamboyant and seemingly shallow and flash Londoner as a man way ahead of his time, a gifted centre-half and mentor to a young Bobby Moore, who was destined to become an indisciplined but extravagantly gifted coach and one who would eventually be the catalyst for the stellar managerial career of one of the modern game's biggest names.

The glory years of Malcolm Allison's Manchester City tenure are well-trodden, the gory years that followed in an ill-thought-out second spell in charge equally familiar, but the sometimes bleak, sometimes vivacious end to his coaching career represented by the three jobs he held in Portugal make a fascinating postscript to the undulating story of a man who found himself operating in a time warp, where all around him struggled to keep up.

Allison played most of his career for West Ham United at a time when the club was building a grand reputation for being a finishing school of aesthetics in English football. The team would later provide Geoff Hurst, Bobby Moore and Martin Peters for England's 1966 World Cup-winning squad and, later still, under the astute guidance of Ron Greenwood and John Lyall, become known as the West Ham Academy, a homely place where a decent Trevor Brooking pass through midfield was just as likely to gain roars of approval as a bullet header from Clyde Best or a crunching 30-yard drive from Billy Bonds. They may have gained a reputation as a bit of a soft touch to the northern teams, but West Ham United's eagerness to play the game *in the right way* was never dimmed by the catcalls.

Allison, then a burly central defender and the assertive mouthpiece of the team, began to influence the manager Ted Fenton's tactics at West Ham as early as the the 1950s, despite a somewhat frosty relationship between the two men. The journalist and former Arsenal player Bernard Joy later remarked that West Ham's leaning towards attractive football was designed in part at least to help the locals escape briefly from the drabness of their everyday lives. For this they had Malcolm Allison to thank.

Allison's teammate Mike Grice said at the time, "Before the weekend, three team sheets would go up for match days. Malcolm would look at them all, take them down and go and see Ted Fenton. When they went up again afterwards, they had invariably changed. After a while we all knew what to expect. Ted would post the team, then Malcolm would go and persuade him to change it."

Spending long hours after training in Cassettari's, a small Italian-owned café around the corner from Upton Park, Allison, along with his teammates Noel Cantwell, Phil Woosnam, Frank O'Farrell and John Bond, would spend their time moving salt and pepper pots around the tables, extolling the virtues of fearless attacking football. All would go on to put Allison's coaching philosophies into practice in their own managerial careers. "As such, what happened at the Boleyn Ground in the fifties can be understood as a kind of revolution, a series of culture changing events, that included worker (player) control...," said the author Brian Belton. "There was, as John Cartwright [a West Ham youth player who later became England Under-21 manager] described it, a form of communism at the club. The players really ruled it. In short, the dictatorship of the football proletariat."

Tuberculosis put a premature end to Allison's playing career, but, by the time he arrived at Manchester City in 1965, he was becoming 'Big Mal', the larger-than-life womaniser and champagne connoisseur. A sizeable Havana cigar was never far from his lips, an expensively cut sheepskin coat slung around his giant shoulders, but beneath that brash exterior lay an articulate and innovative football brain. From tactics to match preparation, from diet to the weight and design of the strip, nothing escaped his close attention.

City would undergo a complete revolution, from second-tier no-hopers, playing to crowds as low as 8,000, to European trophy winners and league champions within three years. Allison, under the watchful gaze of the general manager Joe Mercer, engineered the brightest attacking machine English football had seen since the Tottenham double-winning side of 1961. Allison took his inspiration from the great Hungary side of the early fifties and allowed a collection of technically gifted players to take wing. That side, born out of the thick snow of the game that came to be known as 'The Ballet on Ice', in which Bill Nicholson's star-spangled Spurs side was taken apart on a treacherously slippery surface in Manchester in 1967, heralded three magical years of robust and artful attacking football.

With Allison insisting to the television cameras that "it's a simple game and we try to keep it simple", he built his side around the rock-solid defending of Mike Doyle and George Heslop, the tireless midfield prompting of Colin Bell and Alan Oakes and an attacking trident of Francis Lee, Neil Young and Mike Summerbee that was constantly fed from the wings by the impish Tony Coleman. Allison's philosophy of quick, neat, one-touch passing to feet would bring a league title that season, followed by a League Cup and an FA Cup and a European Cup Winners' Cup in a run un-matched in the club's history.

Allison's influence does not stop there, however. Leaving City in 1973, after a misunderstanding with Mercer about managerial structure and succession, and with the great side that they had built beginning to crumble, Allison began a trek through English football, coaching at Crystal Palace and Plymouth Argyle, before leaving England altogether and becoming, in 1981, the last man to coach Sporting to the Portuguese League and Cup double for 30 years.

João Rocha gave Allison a budget for new signings. Among his top-quality reinforcements for the season ahead were the Hungarian goalkeeper Ferenc Mészáros, the defender António Oliveira, António Manuel Nogueira and up-and-coming youngsters like Carlos Xavier and Mário Jorge.

The 1981-82 championship started with a sunny 2-2 draw between Sporting and Belenenses at a packed Estádio José Alvalade. Despite the draw, the crowd registered with pleasure that the team was playing a brand of innovative attacking football. Sporting won their next five games, with the triple-headed attack of Rui Jordão, Oliveira and Manuel Fernandes immediately demonstrating the form that would make them feared. Sporting went 21 games before finally being defeated, by Boavista.

Sportinguistas also became aware of Allison's brusque sense of humour as the team brushed aside Red Boys of Luxembourg in the Uefa Cup. Asked by a reporter why Sporting's defence had been jittery, the coach replied, "The defence played badly? What did they have to defend? Red Boys had an attack?"

The next European game was particularly attractive to Allison, as his team was given the opportunity to take him back to England and show his compatriots what they were missing. Allison always loved proving his critics wrong and, somewhere deep inside him, he wanted to hear noises of acceptance from the country that had turned its back on his talent. Sporting's opponents were Laurie McMenemy's exciting Southampton side, featuring the likes of Kevin Keegan, Alan Ball, Mick Channon and David Armstrong. At the Dell, Allison's Sporting were magnificent, running out 4-2 winners and allowing Allison the opportunity to bask in the glory by taking a slow walk along the touchline at the end of the game to receive the applause of the locals.

Sporting beat Rio Ave 7-1 in the game that clinched the championship, with Rui Jordão scoring five of the goals. Sporting finished two points ahead of Benfica in the end, taking their foot off the accelerator after sealing the title, but still lost only three times all season. They also reached the Cup final, in which they faced Sporting Braga. As Allison walked out before the big crowd at Jamor with his customary fedora and cigar, he was upstaged by the Braga coach Quinito, who appeared immediately behind him wearing a tuxedo for the occasion. But on the pitch Allison's men undressed Braga completely with a sure-footed 4-0 win to clinch the club's fifth double.

Despite his success in the first year at Alvalade, Allison left the club at the beginning of the following season, with rumours suggesting that Rocha could not stand the attention his coach was getting from the fans and, more importantly, the local and national media. António Oliveira said, "It was a deeply unjust process that was unleashed on Mr Allison. An agent was preparing the smooth arrival of Jozef Vengloš and managed to invent stories about the relationship between Allison and President Rocha." Oliveira ended up as the immediate beneficiary of the fall-out, replacing the departing Englishman as player-manager while Vengloš's contract was negotiated.

The story of Rocha, Mal and the bottle of whisky adds drama to an already smouldering scenario. Tales of Allison drinking and womanising on the club's

pre-season jaunt to Romania may also have contributed to his departure. What is certainly true was the impossibility of Big Mal remaining Big Mal with *Grande João* in the same building. Allison is said to have been last seen leaving the ground with an armful of papers and his newly acquired bottle of Scotch. The fact that he had produced a swashbuckling winning side the like of which green and white fans would not witness for another 18 years (when the club finally brought home another league title under László Bölöni) held little sway with Rocha.

Sporting was Allison's last big football success. Flops, failures and truncated stays followed at Middlesbrough, Kuwait and Bristol Rovers. "Malcolm was a man who enjoyed life to the full and wanted to transmit the joy of working in the industry of football to all of us players and staff," said Oliveira.

Allison — with time and the ravages of the good life swiftly catching up with him — still had time to alight at a football outpost called Setúbal. He had wondered about his damaged reputation in football after hitting so many bum notes in the British press, but in Portugal he was revered as a coaching giant and, as he exited the airport in Lisbon, he was mobbed by well-wishers who remembered what he had done for Sporting.

Even to this day, he remains popular. On a recent taxi ride from Lisbon airport, I hazarded the usual football conversations with the driver and on mentioning Malcolm Allison, almost caused the man to drive across the middle of the Rotunda do Relógio, the manic roundabout situated outside the airport. "Malcolm Allison, the great Mister" apparently still held the affections of Sportinguistas everywhere.

Vitória de Setúbal were down on their luck, slumbering in the second division when the new coach breezed in under a cloud of cigar smoke one morning. In a quiet town of sardine grills and Atlantic sunshine Allison began to be rebuild. He brought half of his Sporting heroes the 35 kilometres south from Lisbon. The captain Manuel Fernandes, the goalscorer Jordão, the centre-back Eurico and the midfielders Ademar and Zezinho all arrived, as did the scruffy keeper Ferenc Mészáros.

Soon Allison had Vitória on the way to promotion. It was around this time, in mid-1987, that Vitória's goalkeeping coach began to take his son along to training sessions. His son was a Physical Education student in Lisbon and, at 24, was keen to learn from interesting and innovative teachers. He was fascinated and soon became a permanent fixture at squad training. The goalkeeping coach was called Felix Mourinho.

Felix had been a stalwart goalkeeper for Vitória and had kept goal for them in the inaugural game at the Estádio do Bonfim. He later turned out for CF Belenenses and managed Rio Ave. José Mourinho has been spoken of as a disciple of many of the great coaches he worked with, but it was while watching Allison's unique brand of tactical innovation and free thinking that he gained his first insights into the world of football management and tactics.

Roger Spry was Allison's conditioning coach at Setúbal and had the young José as his assistant. He said, "In one sense he [Allison] was a fraud in that he was this flamboyant character to the media and the public, but in private he was quiet and one of the most knowledgeable coaches I have worked with. I have worked with some of the best managers in the business, including José Mourinho and Arsène Wenger, and I would put Malcolm in that category. He really was that good. He was a luminary and a visionary and a teacher. Mourinho worked with Malcolm and me at Vitória de Setúbal and I can see Malcolm's influence on José. I can see Malcolm in 90% of the things that he does. Malcolm would make every player under him believe he was the best in the world in their position. José is the same."

Allison's spell in Setúbal also revealed another side of life to a man who had been brought up in London and had lived with the trappings of the champagne life ever since. He found peace living in a beautiful farmstead tucked into the rolling splendour of the Arrábida hills, a ridge of mountains separating the Atlantic Ocean from the rich pastures around Palmela and Setúbal. There, content to drink glasses of the sparkling *vinho verde* and enjoy the delights of clams in white wine and grilled sea bream, Allison was said to have reached peace with himself. His partner Lynn accompanied him and they enjoyed a bucolic lifestyle.

Having got Vitória into the top flight, it all went sour again for Allison, as the club struggled to finish eighth the following season. The coach picked up a seven-week touchline ban for abusing a referee and began to fall foul of the fans too, who booed him in a late-season game loss at home to Salgueiros. With the club's president keeping half an eye on Manuel Fernandes, Allison's Sporting and Vitória captain, who was readying himself for a first step into football management, the axe fell once more.

Allison's reaction was to move to the Algarve, where the president of Farense, Fernando Barata, offered him a job. António Boronha, a colleague of Barata's, remembers Allison's stay there well. "Every Monday we would have lunch with him," he said, "an expansive period, spent talking about the good things in life, at a restaurant called 'Green' in honour of his continuing affection for Sporting."

Boronha would become president after Barata and struck up a friendship with Allison as the coach drifted towards the end of his managerial career among the fishing shacks and cobbled streets of Faro. "I would often enjoy spending a couple of hours with Mal, going over the previous day's match," he explained. "Always in good spirit, always humorous, always in a fine mood, despite it being a bad season for us.

"We ended up being relegated and Malcolm left under a cloud after a home defeat by Braga with the total indignation of the fans ringing in his ears. He had played our central defender, a Brazilian called Luisão, up front. Fernando Barata left with him in the end. Paco Fortes followed as trainer and I, three months later, as President."

For Allison, it was the beginning of the end. The maverick trainer, whose stay in Portugal mirrored the highs and lows of his managerial career elsewhere, had only the bottle ahead of him. **B**

Messi and the Machine

Could playing video games be shaping the present generation of footballers?

By Richard Fitzpatrick

Barcelona's 3-1 victory over Manchester United in the 2011 Champions League final was probably the high point of Pep Guardiola's reign at the Camp Nou. Afterwards, the team flew from London back to Barcelona. While his teammates celebrated on the plane, giddily drinking and singing, Lionel Messi sat in his seat fiddling on a PlayStation. He may well have been playing himself playing virtual football.

It is well known how popular video games are among professional footballers. They're a useful distraction during careers that have long periods of downtime spent on aeroplanes, in training camps and foreign hotels. As well as helping with idleness, they can diffuse stress. Andrea Pirlo, who reckons PlayStation to be the world's best invention after the wheel, passed the hours before winning the 2006 World Cup final with Italy playing video games and sleeping.

There is anecdotal evidence that players find video games useful for study. Neymar says he adopted moves from football video games and assimilated them into his play with an old teammate at Santos, Ganso. Bafétimbi Gomis, the Swansea City striker, used Football Manager as a research tool before joining the club this summer from France, boning up on his future teammates' attributes.

Gaming, of course, is essentially a sedentary pastime, but it is possible that the skills required to play video games might be useful for nurturing certain parts of footballers' bodies and brains, according to a paper published in 2013 by Professor Jocelyn Faubert, a psychophysicist at the University of Montreal.

Faubert trained 308 observers, including 51 English Premier League players, as part of a motion perception study, which tested the ability of professional footballers, ice hockey players and rugby union players from France's Top 14 league against two other test groups — elite amateurs, including athletes from Europe's Olympic training centre, and 33 university students who weren't athletes.

Faubert wanted to find out what makes sportspeople special. He devised a computer game, a type of graphical simulation machine, called a NeuroTracker. It has no end goal. No story. No sporting context. Players don't have to find a treasure or kill people along the way. They have to index a number of spheres floating in 3D space, which means they have to track them mentally. Each task goes on for about six to eight seconds. If players are logging well, the device speeds up and if they log badly it slows down. The exercise lasts for 15 minutes at the most. What Faubert discovered was interesting. Professional footballers scored better than university students and top amateur athletes.

"I kind of expected they would be better at the start," says Faubert. "I designed the task so it would focus on the mechanisms that I thought were necessary for good reading of the play and so on, but what really blew me away is that they learnt so much faster for this task that really had no specific sports element. There's movement, but then there's movement in real life, too.

"Their brain is really wired in certain ways – it's plastic, as we say. Their ability to adapt quickly to something like this is a form of intelligence that's not measurable by IQ or mathematical skills. To get to the top in sport, you have to have extra mental ability. That's why it's extraordinary when we watch players in the field, and we say, 'Oh, my God, how did he see that coming? How did he process that?' It's a certain type of intelligence."

There are several curious findings in Faubert's perception study besides the fact that a professional footballer can "hyper-focus" better than an undergraduate student. He discovered people scored better sitting down than standing up. This indicates a link between balance, which is a hallmark of the best footballers, and cognitive ability.

Faubert cites a scientific paper that shows high-level athletes have increased cortical thickness in certain areas of their brains when compared with test groups. One of these chunkier areas in the athlete's brain is the superior temporal sulcus (STS).

The STS is used by people for two critical functions – for joint attention, where a person guides the gaze of another person, like the way a mother might draw a toddler's attention to a colouring book, or a footballer might instinctively alert a teammate to a moment of danger near their goalmouth, and for biological motion perception. This is the capacity, for example, to recognise jagged human movements when they're shown as a few dots jumping around or, in the case of a frenetic football match, to anticipate an opponent's movements.

Faubert also references a study that found athletes might be able to process crowd scenes, like a busy pedestrian crossing, faster than non-athletes, and draws the comparison with a goalkeeper rushing out to gather a cross in a crowded box.

The conclusion he draws from the NeuroTracker, which has been used as a training device by Manchester United, is that it can arguably improve players' concentration during a game.

"We show by cause and effect. We separated the soccer players into three groups. We did the NeuroTracker training and measured (pre and post) their ability to do passing and decision-making on the pitch, and they improved while the other groups did not improve."

Is it possible to train a footballer's brain? Professor Ian Robertson, a neuroscientist at Trinity College, Dublin and the author of *The Winner Effect: How Power Affects Your Brain*, makes the point that the brain is like a muscle. Use it or lose it. If you sit on the couch for too long passively watching television, say, or you don't make demands on the brain, it atrophies – the connections in the brain reduce, which leads to a loss of cognitive function. Alternatively, playing a video game can be stimulating.

"The evidence is that the brain circuits people exercise when they are playing demanding perceptual motor skills games actually improve the function that you require to play them," says Robertson. "I know that if you play games like *Medal of Honor*, for instance, then your capacity for spatial thinking improves.

"*Medal of Honor* is a game about shooting, but you have to navigate yourself through a three-dimensional environment. You have to do computations in your brain to work out where you are in this building that you can only see part of, which is important because you see another figure coming with a gun so you have to be able to do the computation about when that person is going to come around the corner and shoot you. Do you want to survive in the game? These are incredibly complex computations and they improve that aspect of your thinking – your ability to think spatially.

"Similarly, your speed of perceptual motor coordination will improve. To the extent, for example, that soccer involves fast-moving computations of where you are in space in relation to other people, and in making very fine-grained perceptual discriminations, then it is theoretically possible that your spatial awareness as a soccer player might be improved by playing that kind of video game. We know, for instance, that surgeons who play a lot of video games, which make demands on their perceptual motor system, perform better and have better accuracy; they show slightly better surgical technique."

Faubert concurs with Robertson's thinking. He explains that a footballer's working memory is used in the same manner for playing video games as it is for making decisions on a football pitch – the ability to focus intensely, to track multiple elements, to anticipate things that are out of sight and that come back into sight, to make calculations and predictions. That innate ability of football's finest playmakers to read a game, to end up in the right place at the right time, is a function of good visual memory.

"The video games that have shown some transfer," says Faubert, "are mostly shooter-type video games. Games where you're a soldier or something killing beasts, entities are coming from different directions, and you have to focus on your task and at the same time you could be struck by something else on the side or behind you. You can't just focus on the centre; you have to distribute your attention. I know that I saw a tank two minutes ago that is probably closer to me. Your brain is working. It's manipulating these things online and that is where there could be common circuits in the actual game of soccer where play action is dealing with all of these events coming from different directions – your teammates, your opponents, the ball."

Picture for a second one of the most famous tackles in football history. On 7 June 1970, England played Brazil under blazing noonday sun in Guadalajara, Mexico. The reigning world champions faced the winners of the previous World Cup. In the second half, Carlos Alberto hoofed the ball skywards from his box. Jairzinho trapped the clearance by the touchline, close to the halfway line, and bore down on England's goal. Bobby Moore and Brian Labone were the only two outfield defenders left guarding England's half of the pitch.

Moore had to judge the distance between himself, Labone, the oncoming Jairzinho and the position of his own goal. Should he shepherd Jairzinho away from goal or infield towards Labone? He had to seize up Jairzinho's body language. Would the Brazilian feint and try to send him the wrong way? Would Jairzinho pass left to his onrushing teammate, Tostão? Might he try a wall pass? Should Moore feign a tackle? Should he wait and give Alan Mullery, who was tracking back from midfield, enough time to make an interception? Moore had to juggle all these permutations in his head while back-pedalling furiously towards his own goal. Just as Jairzinho entered England's box, Moore pounced and stole the ball. Crisis averted.

"It is very similar to what you would have to do in a video game," says David G Kirschen, an optometrist at UCLA's medical school, "where you see the play developing and you have a couple of choices and you have to react, to do something. In this case, you have to push a button. From the visual perspective, the gamer and the soccer player are both looking at something, which allows them to become visually aware, and they make a decision for a motor action based on what they are seeing."

Kirschen and his colleague Daniel M Laby, who works as an ophthalmologist,

studied US Olympians from the 2008 Beijing Games. They discovered that some visual functions are more important than others. Archers' binocular vision – the way their two eyes work together – is very poor. Why? Because they only use one eye. Boxers' vision is poorest of any group tested, which follows since their targets are big and close-up.

Kirschen and Laby found that soccer players, who track flying objects at a distance, scored well on contrast sensitivity, which is a feature of action-based video games such as *Call of Duty*. Contrast sensitivity is the ability to pick a target out of a background – for instance, the ability quickly to identify a ball, which might have multiple colours similar to the opposition team's jerseys, which is rolling on the green grass or flying in the air amidst the flashing lights of pitch-side advertising hoardings. "If you have poor vision, your contrast sensitivity goes down," says Kirschen.

One of the defining traits of elite athletes is their excellent eyesight – with a few notable exceptions like the blurred vision Paul Scholes suffered during his Manchester United career. For example, in a four-year study of 387 players from the LA Dodgers baseball franchise, about 2% of its players registered vision below 20/9, which is the theoretical upper limit of the human eye. In 30 years studying people's eyesight, Kirschen has only come across a handful of non-athletes with 20/9 vision.

It is not that top athletes have superior reaction times to the rest of the population, as David Epstein noted in his book, *The Sports Gene: What Makes* the Perfect Athlete, it's that they have better eyesight than the average Joe. Good vision helps them better to pick up on visual clues so they can make better decisions, like choosing the right instance to pinch a ball from the feet of the marauding Jairzinho. Sir Clive Woodward, who coached England's rugby union players to a World Cup win in 2003 and who, in his role as the British Olympic Association's director of elite performance, employed a visual skills expert for Britain's Olympic team, put it succinctly: "nothing happens in sport until the eye tells the body what to do."

The danger with playing video games, however, is that they can take over your life. Zlatan Ibrahimović has written in his autobiography that he could go 10 hours at a stretch playing football video games. He had an anonymous gamertag online. So does Messi. There were times when Ibrahimović played with Internazionale that he'd arrive goggle-eyed at training after only two or three hours of sleep. His fingers used to dance over the controls of his Xbox. It was like a fever. "I couldn't stop," he said, "and I'd often sit with [his son] little Maxi on my lap and play." He has since replaced the hobby with hunting. He puts his years of gaming frenzy down to an addictive personality.

David James, who played 53 times in goal for England, got in a pickle in 1997 when he mentioned during a newspaper interview that his obsession with playing video games was affecting his concentration. He said the night before he let in three goals while playing for Liverpool against Newcastle United he had been up late hammering away on his PlayStation.

"I'm a very competitive person," he says. "For example, there was a game called *Final Fantasy*, and the rumour was that someone had completed all three CDs in 60 hours of game play so that was like a red rag to a bull – I just dedicated myself to try to beat that target."

James, who is player-manager with Kerala Blasters FC in India, hasn't bought a video game in over a decade. Since 2000, he's "traded an acute focus" on gaming for an interest in sports psychology. He says the problem was that he ate up time in the hours before a match playing video games like *Final Fantasy* and *Tekken* (he used to find football games unrealistic: "if anything they were annoying") instead of bracing himself for the job in hand.

"I remember I had a conversation with Colin Jackson, the Olympic athlete, back in the 90s and he said his coach banned him from playing on consoles before competition because of the nervous energy that it took out of you. That's the thing – anything done in excess, I would argue, is detrimental to performance. There are so many key factors – awareness, reflexes, responsiveness, especially in football, which are a massive part of the game. If you're numbing all those senses in overuse – and I would go as far as to include reading books, to a point – you can lose yourself.

"I've learnt through sports psychology, you have to spend an appropriate amount of time focusing on the task ahead, doing imagery work. None of my managers banned consoles. Today, it's interesting because consoles have been overtaken by phone apps that are very addictive, the likes of *Candy Crush, Bubble Explode*, which players can get lost in."

James makes a distinction between addiction and obsession. "With an addiction, you could argue that you don't have a choice. As someone who smoked for 15 years, and found it very difficult to get off the habit, that was an addiction. When I wasn't doing it I was in a bad mood and yearning for nicotine. I knew I was addicted to cigarettes whereas I was obsessive about video games until I got another focus."

James reckons that top-class footballers share the same obsessive drive that defines train-spotters and stalkers. How normal is it to kick a football a thousand times a day? He had a hunch, for example, that David Beckham was an obsessive when the winger first joined the England training camp, staying about after training endlessly to practise his kicking. It was no surprise when he later discovered Becks, who would arrange his Pepsi cans so they faced the same way in his fridge door, admitted to having Obsessive Compulsive Disorder.

"I don't think elite athletes get there by being normal – that obsessive nature to be able to commit yourself to so many hours of dedication beyond the norm. Even within the football fraternity, there is a level of normality with addiction, competitiveness. You'll find the same environments with video games as you would with other leisure pursuits. If you get two footballers playing golf it becomes a competition. Is it golf they're addicted to or the competition? I'm not sure.

"The problem we have as sportsmen, especially if you're involved in things like the English Premier League and international matches, when you've got athletes that are at the top end of the spectrum, you have to be obsessive. Normal people can't cope with the amount of focus required and the long hours of preparation and rehearsal in order to get to the top of the pile. The danger is that when someone obsessive about things like myself puts that focus on video games – or loads of other things in my life that I give the utmost attention to – instead of football."

It is a question of balance. Douglas Gentile, an associate professor at Iowa State University's Department of Psychology, likes to quote an old line from the conductor Leopold Stokowski: "If I don't practise for one day, I notice it; if I don't practise for two days, the audience notices." If used sensibly, though, there are aspects about playing video games, especially action-based ones, which recommend themselves to professional footballers.

Does playing video games help to make Messi a better footballer? It could be that gaming – apart from being a preferred leisure pursuit – becomes an integral part of footballers' training-and-fitness regime; another counter-intuitive way to get an edge like doing yoga or ballet, one which appeals to their obsessive, competitive nature and draws on keen eyesight, spatial awareness and a greater ability to "hyper-focus". The game has come a long way since Fred Pentland, one of football's revolutionary thinkers at the start of the last century, used to school his players at Athletic of Bilbao on how best to tie their bootlaces. Ⓑ

Not at All Costs

Paul Tisdale has not only revolutionised how Exeter City play, but how they think

By George Caulkin

There is the usual flotsam of this unusual life: pages of scouting reports, a whiteboard with fixtures scrawled on it, empty mugs and full bottles, a framed poster of Wembley, old copies of *Rothmans Football Yearbook*, mobile phones throbbing on the desk. On the shelves, two things request attention, a thicket of *Roy of the Rovers* annuals and the *Oxford English Dictionary*.

This is the Cat and Fiddle, Exeter City's training ground and, like its name, a sense of difference is not difficult to discern. The prefab buildings where the youth team train were rescued and reconditioned by supporters. In the kitchen, Jenny and Anita are volunteers, trust members and season-ticket holders, who say, "they don't just teach players football here, they teach them manners."

Existence in League Two can be haphazard, reliant on dedication and twisted by fortune, and it is rare to find a club – at any level – guided by principle as Exeter are. There has to be practicality because they are a cash-flow business, unable to spend what they do not earn, but it is shaped by a philosophy which upends most of what we know.

In the office he shares with Paul Tisdale, the manager, among the annuals, reports and phones, Steve Perryman explains that philosophy by way of anecdote. He is comfortable like that, a football man telling football stories and somehow familiar because of it, even if his words lead in an unexpected direction. He speaks like a football man, a man of Tottenham Hotspur – a record 854 appearances – but he is voicing a quiet subversion. It is how they do it here.

His title at Exeter is Director of Football, but even that is not straightforward. "I'm supposed to be between Tis and the board, but his character, style and organisation means he's direct into them. I'm a director with a small d and I'd prefer to be called the manager's aide. Not a mentor, not an assistant, but an aide." Tisdale calls Perryman an "ally – we see it the same way," and their working environment is tight, close.

At the end of his playing career – two FA Cups, two League Cups, two Uefa Cups, one England cap – Perryman set forth into management. He assisted Ossie Ardiles at Spurs and then traveled with him to Japan before striking out on his own, spending five years with Shimizu S-Pulse. He came home and sought work, helping out at Exeter – he was paid expenses and nothing more – before returning to Japan and Kashiwa Reysol.

By the time he took his present role, back in 2003, his outlook had changed for good. "I'd been to Japan and seen what respect is," Perryman says. "Respect in the sense of 'you're the manager and we'll follow you', both from the players' point of view and from those above, too. Everyone says you go abroad and get a new surge of energy and that's right; everything was fresh.

"I'd been driving around the North Circular Road for 20 years, seeing the same cars, the same traffic, the same faces and same lights... You don't know how much it wears you down. Then you're in a new country and the traffic is probably 100 times worse, but there's a Toyota you've never seen before, a different office block over there, two people bowing as low as you can get and it's all new, it's all great.

"I came back with this huge energy, so why waste it, but I was never going to work again for a businessman who, because of his money, could tell me what to think about football. I could listen to Alan Sugar all day long about business, but he wasn't going to tell me about football and he didn't like being told that. I'd got out of that pit. Realistically, I wasn't going to get a job. I did go for a couple of interviews, but I talked myself out of it. 'Okay, so what's the money?' X. 'Okay, well X doesn't entitle you to expect me to lie for you'.

"I said at one interview 'what sort of club are you?' They asked me what I meant. 'Well, for instance, do you want to produce your own players?'

"'Oh yeah, we want some of that.'

"'Do you want to be part of the community, grow your support?'

"'Yeah, we want some of that, too.'

"'Okay — and think about this one — do you want to win at all costs?'

"'Well, we want to win.'

"'We'll take that as read — everybody wants to win. Are you win at all costs?'

"'We want to win.'

"'I know that. I want to win. But how are you going to win? If your centre-forward does an obvious dive in the 92nd minute and wins a penalty that's totally undeserved, are you happy, sad, angry or do you not give a shit?

"'We want to win.'

"'Well, in that case, I think you're a win at all costs club. I've got no problem with that, but I'm not your man.'"

Tisdale, Perryman says, is not that man, either. "We want players listening to tactical messages, the technical messages and the disciplinary messages. But I'd find it very hard if I had to listen to a manager saying, 'Go down in the box, run the ball to the corner flag.' We think that teams who overuse the phrase 'game management' are not right. You see it here; teams are extra positive, go a goal ahead, retreat onto the back foot and we take the initiative — who is most likely to win?

"This is a whole bigger subject, but people spend more time teaching anti-football than they do football. Tis teaches football. He doesn't want players running the ball to the corner flag, he doesn't want kidding or diving. It's not like a daily message – it's an environment. Not everybody gets it."

A couple of hours earlier; still morning, but the Centre Spot Bar at St James Park is already heaving and Tisdale is gripping a pool cue. Outside, there is a noticeboard, with details of meetings, dates, games, and above it in black letters reads a defining statement, 'We Own Our Football Club.' In reception, Clinton Morrison, the former Republic of Ireland striker, now 35, was chittering away and he said hello. "You're here to see the manager? Intelligent man. Really clever."

On a makeshift stage in the bar, Tisdale is not playing but pointing, using his cue as a prop. Observed by Perryman, who chips in with the odd comment, and Julian Tagg, the vice-chairman (as the sign suggests, the club is owned by a Supporters' Trust), he introduces the journalist interloper at the back of the room and then works through a DVD presentation of Exeter's last match, running through clips, keeping the message light. "Be ready to anticipate," he says and then, later, "Be connected and you'll win more than you lose."

Communication is a big thing at Exeter – more of that later – and Tisdale asks his players to describe their style. A few arms go up. 'Fluid,' says one. 'Tempo,' says another. 'Connected,' chimes a third. So much of football is about these mental drills and repetitions, the basics and routines. "Compete, tidy, set, support, forward, forward running," Tisdale says. "Do all that and we'll be a hell of a team."

He deploys his own version of their style: "kinetic, to use a posh word."

Tisdale drives back to the Cat and Fiddle. He had left home at 6.20am, stopping at a service station for coffee and to complete his presentation, arriving at the training ground for 8.30. "A whirlwind since then," he says; he has been trying to sign a player on loan, which is a luxury here. Last summer, they were placed under a transfer embargo after borrowing £100,000 from the Professional Footballers' Association to cover running costs, obliging Tisdale, who is 42, to re-register as a player.

That must have been a strange experience for a man whose relationship with the sport is not traditional. A midfielder, who rose through the ranks at Southampton, he acknowledges that he "never fulfilled any kind of potential," and when he is asked one of those standard, time-buying, button-pushing questions, where you assume the answer will be one thing and it turns out to be another, his answer is so stark it takes the breath away. Did he enjoy being a footballer? "No."

Football is arbitrary, he says: you work, you practise, you improve your frailties and hone your talents and then, at the end of it all, the bloke in the dug-out either fancies you or does not. He found that experience jarring. "The whole thing is random and erratic. If you're a person who is considered and pragmatic and likes to quantify things – I've got that sort of mind – not only is it hard to fathom, but it's also quite unsettling not being able to quantify that x leads to y leads to z.

"There's no process you can look at. You'd think it would be get fitter, improve your left foot, do this and it just takes care of itself. It doesn't. The whole industry is so subjective. And then, if you're on the outside of it, it's very easy to hit a spiral of lack of fitness, lack of confidence, lack of continuity, lack of that process so you can plot it, so you have players who slip through the net. It's very erratic.

"A lot of it made no sense to me. Moving on from Southampton, I realised I'd been coached to play a certain way and then arriving at another club it was like a completely different sport. It was that clear. There's not only a technical and physical set of variables, but it's also a culture and that's the intangible bit. How do you cope with all that? I found that period of my life very unsettling. I'm not blaming anyone, that's just what it was like.

"What you don't realise on the outside is that every club has its own dynamic. Everything can be perfect for you – the club, the geography and the culture – and then the manager changes and he's got a different opinion. You just can't plot, unless you're Ryan Giggs and you're going to make it wherever you go. A lot of the time it's pot luck, it's a lottery and then that duty of care, that feeling of treating people correctly is last on the list because it's all about winning on Saturday."

In retrospect, it was the wrong career. "At the age of 15, 16, I was already in the clutches of Southampton," he says. "No one asked if I wanted to do it, I was just in it. My father [who was in the Admiralty; Tisdale was born in Valletta, Malta], took me places and he's assuming I want

to be a footballer. I didn't want to be a footballer but, crikey... he never asked me, he assumed and I just assumed it's what I'd do and I'm playing for England Schools and why not?"

Tisdale was also an opening batsman (and is now a member of the MCC). "I would have done far better as a cricketer, I've got no doubt about that, now I look back," he says. "I would have been far better at it and it's purely cultural." Why? "The environment, the people you're with. No matter how many sports psychology books you read there's an innate environment you're in that either brings out the confidence in you or doesn't.

"For someone who has an inquiring or considered mind, a sport where there are more quantifiable things than not would suit me. Plus the type of people you mix with. I was a more confident individual in that dressing-room, I was able to quantify the sport and what I needed to do to improve, because you score runs, you get wickets. It's a simpler way of quantifying your success. Football is so subjective; there are so many variables.

"I prefer management ten times more. I have my own destiny in my own hands – to a degree, not completely – and I've got control. I had no control as a player whatsoever. I was quiet, I was introverted, I wanted to find some answers within the coaching and feedback to find out what I was supposed to be doing and there was very little. Did I enjoy it? It's a great lifestyle, but it's a very stressful lifestyle if you have a considered mind. I see so many young footballers with the same issue."

Yet Tisdale is now the subjective one, the arbitrary one. "You can't please everyone," he says. "You can only pick 11 players, but all I can do is the best for them, empathise with players and make the process simpler for them. These chaps want to be footballers, it's their industry and hopefully I'm giving them the environment to get the best out of themselves. Communication is probably the biggest tool you've got; nine out of ten times it's communication. Most footballers deal really well with good information, even if they're not getting the answers they want."

Tisdale is not a football man; not in the same way that Perryman is. He would never talk about the sport being a drug and management an addict's balm. Perhaps he is not consumed by it in that emotive sense. "It's my industry," he says. "It's what I know best. That's quite a deep question. I don't really know. I love what I do. I love the sport. The sport and the industry are very different and I'm creating my own way of being in the industry and enjoying it.

"I wasn't so successful as a player that I got that huge rush from it. You get these huge spikes of adrenaline once or twice a week and who knows what that does to you. The truth is I won't know until I've not had it. I really enjoy the Monday to Friday and then Saturday is the business. For me, it's all about the Monday to Friday, the environment, the team, a constant focus on developing and building. You can't take your eye off the ball for Saturday, but it's not all about that."

He stumbled back into the game, home in Bath, where his parents were from, the playing side of things winding down. After loan spells, a move to Bristol City, a loan at Exeter, a "brilliant" year in Greece

with Panionios, struggling with a back injury, he would go to the university to use the gym. They were about to start a football programme and the director of sport walked past him one day – he was doing sit-ups – and asked him if fancied being coach.

"I liked the idea of the empty office, no players, no name for the team, no equipment, nothing," he says. "Nothing apart from, 'I want you to start a football programme here,' like an American Uni thing, enter a league and see what you can do. I liked that; having had no control for the previous 10 years, I then had everything. I came up with the name 'Team Bath'. It was mine, I'd created it."

There were four promotions, an appearance in the first round proper of the FA Cup.

He met Perryman through friends and was invited for an interview at Exeter in 2006. A man noted for his sartorial elegance, he arrived wearing shorts. "Only because I'd been on holiday," he says. "I didn't have time to go home. I didn't really want to leave the university anyway. Now I'm thinking back, it does sound very odd, but at the time it felt perfectly natural. Why drive for an hour just to put on a pair of trousers only to drive for an hour back? Now I look at it, I think 'what was I doing?'"

Whatever it was, it worked. Tisdale has been in place for nine years, building, analysing, creating, nurturing an environment, and is the second longest-serving league manager behind Arsène Wenger. In his first season, Exeter reached the Conference play-off final. In his second, they were promoted.

They climbed to League One, secured their status and then finished eighth in 2011, equalling the highest placing in their history.

There have been opportunities to leave, for Southampton and Swansea City, among others, but the timing or circumstances have not been right. "I've asked myself, 'Why did I start doing this?' And it wasn't because of football, it was because I wanted a place where I could be myself and create an environment.

"It's been said of me that I'm not ambitious enough, but it's not about the bigger budget, the bigger league – bigger is not better. And when I've had those opportunities, they were at a time when I'd committed to the people here. I'd given my word. It works both ways. When I've had a chance to move and not gone, it's as much about the fact I've not wanted to move. You look after each other. You're on the same team. I would put it like this – I see it as working with Exeter, not for Exeter. Ambition – how do you define it?"

Tisdale has taken training, eaten lunch in the canteen (cooked and served by Jenny and Anita), which doubles up as a gym, and had treatment on a fractured metatarsal (his comeback was brief, aborted when he trod on a stone while running). There is a meeting with his staff, five men in a room and a run-through of their next opponents, studying their set-piece routines, film from their latest match. They mull over selection, push through a list of transfer targets.

The sale of Matt Grimes to Swansea in January, for a reported fee of £1.75m, has given Exeter some leeway, but the margins remain narrow. "Financially, Exeter would be a mid-Conference team," Tisdale says. "The top 10 teams in the Conference outbid us on players. It's not an even race from day one, so it's hard to judge how successful we are.

"We've got no debt, we're financially viable, players enjoy it here and we're healthy. Is that a success? It's part of what we do and what I think is important here. I'm a complex individual and this is a complex intellectual challenge down here, but ultimately, at 5.55pm on a Saturday, everyone judges you on whether you're good or bad. You have to cope with all that."

Tisdale describes himself as a "managed pessimist". He does not approach matches "as if everything is going to be all right. I have to go through all the problems and issues and work it all out, where the risks are, cover those, go through it all. I'm not a reckless optimist." Preparation is key and yet if that sounds like a dry view of football, then it is entirely misplaced, because there is a purity to Tisdale's vision.

"It's frightening what you see," he says. "You hear managers saying, 'Right, okay, manage the game' – that's come into the vocabulary. You're a goal up – game management. It's sort of code for squeezing the boundaries, taking it into cheating in some areas. It's code, I think, used terminology. Managers say, 'Kill the game for the last 10 minutes'. Well, that's what you're doing. You're killing the game. People pay to watch 90 minutes, not 80. It's not to say I'm a romantic. I want my team to be practical and disciplined and reduce errors in those situations. It's how you do it and I want my team to do it in a proper way."

Tisdale says 'proper' a lot and it is not a verbal tick. Where does it originate from? "My grandmother? My family? I don't know," he says. "I like things done correctly. I'm very English. Respectful, being considerate of others. It just makes sense to me, not cheating, not cutting corners. Proper. I went to boarding school, grammar school. I played cricket and it's like nicking the ball down the leg side and then walking. That's the best way I can describe it."

(An aside: when they were still in League One, Exeter played Huddersfield Town. They had to win to avoid relegation and with eight minutes left, Tisdale's team scored. With the clock ticking down, the ball drifted out of play next to the dug-out for a Huddersfield throw-in. In this situation, most – all – managers would find a way to waste time, knock the ball away, let it run, or hold it and not let go. Tisdale picked it up and gave it to the opposition full-back, who took a quick throw. What on earth was he thinking? "I was saying to my team that we're good enough," he says. "The ball should be in play. You've got to know what you are.")

A strong non-conformist streak stretches to Tisdale's apparel and he will often be found in tweed, cravat and flat cap, the definition of a country gent on a catwalk better known for its nylon and stuffed suits. It is a legacy of one of the most enduring relationships in his life, which began when he strolled into a Ted Baker shop in Covent Garden with Ken Monkou and Graeme Le Saux, his teammates at Southampton, and met Ray Kelvin, the clothing company's founder.

"Ray was a larger than life character and he must have seen something in me because we very quickly became best friends and now I'm an ambassador for Ted Baker. It's a brand that suits me; slightly eccentric, English, proper, do things right. He's taken an interest in me, he's my advisor, my mentor. I'm very lucky. You're at the mercy of the people you meet in life – good parents, bad parents, good school, bad school – and it's a lottery. He's a person I've been very fortunate to meet."

His match-day attire is another Exeter quirk. "It's business day," he says. "It's making a conscious decision to step up for business. It's looking the part, looking your best because it's about raising standards for the game, representing your team and feeling that you're out there in front of them. I always stand, I never sit, because it's the tone you set.

"I walk to the technical area and I've got the best shoes, the best silk scarf, the best shirt, waistcoat and tweed jacket and I'm going to stand there for the whole game. It just represents something. I can't do a lot on the touchline apart from make my substitutions, but I'm not afraid to stand there with a deerstalker on. I'm not afraid to stand there with a cravat on. I don't wear a cravat at home, but there comes a point where you've got to stand up and say, 'We're having this'. It's my way of convincing the players."

At Team Bath, he encountered and was influenced by other sports, other coaches; Kelvin is a businessman. Tisdale sees all those skills as transferable. "I love the intellectual challenge of playing against an opposition," he says. "I call it Top Trumps. If everyone has a team playing 4-4-2 then it's just about having better players. So you look for strengths and weaknesses and it's why my teams always play unconventional shapes and systems. I'm trying to find space, stop them and highlight my one or two key players. When you're compromised by finances, you've got to get the best of the players you've got."

Tisdale is the last to leave the Cat and Fiddle. He locks the front gate. This is part of it, the routine, the nitty gritty, the mundane, the reality of football at this level, but he, Perryman and Exeter also prove there is room for the unexpected, for difference. At his first fans' forum at the club, he was told by a supporter that he had no passion, that he stood by the side of the pitch bereft of emotion. Where was his anger, his energy?

"But how could I think if I was screaming?" he says. "If I'm going to ask you to solve a really difficult conundrum, try doing it while shouting as loudly as you can. It's not easy. Do I tick the boxes? I don't know. I'm not bothered. It's not just about being a football manager. The biggest thing I'll get from my time at Exeter will be the people I work with, the relationships, the feeling of building a team and doing something the right way.

"You can't be right all the time. Someone will have a grievance with you at some point. It's impossible not to upset someone in this position. Stereotypes, clichés, I don't know. I'm certainly not the norm, but I'm not out there trying to be risqué or unconventional. I have to remember why I started this. There are plenty of frustrations at the club through its limitations, but it's about knowing how you are. We know what we stand for. There's no one way of winning." **B**

Wrestling with the All-Blacks

How Declan Edge is trying to make New Zealand take football seriously

By Charlie Eccleshare

Although a giant in some sports, New Zealand is undoubtedly a footballing minnow. It sits in the other sports powerhouse-football weakling category that used to describe the USA and Australia until they embraced soccer and began to make an impression at World Cups.

New Zealand had the distinction of being the only undefeated team at the 2010 World Cup but failed to qualify for Brazil 2014 and have only reached the finals twice, without recording a victory.

It's hardly surprising New Zealand struggles to compete at football's top level, when you consider that its national team went a year without playing a match between June 2004 and May 2005. The regularity of the team's fixtures has at least improved – around seven matches a season over the last nine years – even if the national team has not really kicked on since the 2010 success.

Something is stirring there, though, and one person who is trying to change New Zealand footballers' mentality is Declan Edge, the Director of Football at the prestigious Olé Academy in Porirua on the country's North Island. Edge is a stubborn, opinionated, divisive ex-player who coached his son and three of his son's friends all the way from the Waikato Under-13 side to being signed

by professional clubs. And he insists he's only just getting started.

In 2006, Declan Edge didn't trust anyone else to nurture his 12-year-old son Harry so left his job as a financial planner to focus on the youth team at the Hamilton-based club Waikato FC that included Harry, Ryan Thomas, Declan's nephew Jesse Edge and Tyler Boyd. Thomas and the two Edges now play in Europe and Boyd is at A-League side Wellington Phoenix.

Thomas, a 20-year-old winger is already a key player for the Dutch Eredivisie side PEC Zwolle, and scored twice in their 5-1 hammering of Ajax in the Dutch Cup final last April. Harry Edge, 20, plays for Zwolle's Under-21s as an attacking midfielder, while his first cousin Jesse Edge, 20, is a centre-back for Vicenza in Serie B.

Declan's disciples are joined on the continent by other young, ambitious Kiwis. These include the West Ham centre-back Winston Reid, 26; Bill Tuiloma, 20, a defender at Marseille; the striker Chris Wood, 23, at Ipswich on loan from Leicester; the Burnley midfielder Cameron Howieson, 20; the Ipswich defender Tommy Smith, 25, and Marco Rojas, 23, a winger at FC Thun on loan from Stuttgart.

Declan Edge also played a part in Wood and Rojas's development, having coached them at senior level for Waikato FC, while Wellington Phoenix midfielder Jason Hicks is another Kiwi international who worked with Edge at Waikato.

That list might suggest New Zealand football is in decent shape, but Declan Edge disagrees. Or at least he believes that New Zealand is producing good players in spite of itself. He is highly critical of the New Zealand football system and stresses that the country has no concept of how to produce good players.

As a former footballer with 42 All Whites caps and a club career that included spells at Notts County and Shrewsbury Town, he has no doubt that he does. "Four players who are pros come from one Under-13 team that I coached," Edge said. "At that time I looked around New Zealand and Australia to see where they could learn the game, but nobody was doing it properly so I did it myself.

"New Zealand football is in chaos. It has no investment, no system to produce young players, so it just keeps its fingers crossed, replaces a few board members occasionally and hopes to get better. If I can produce these guys from one little team with no money and everyone in the country trying to stop me, why can't the rest of them do something?"

Edge relishes explaining how his Under-13 team produced so many good players. His son Harry has been told by his father he won't be available for All Whites selection for a couple of years lest it affects his club career.

Does he have a choice? "He does what he's told."

As well as being unflinchingly forthright, Edge is determined not to repeat the mistakes he's observed others making. "I question everyone and everything," Declan Edge says. "I have never been friends with anyone in New Zealand football because I am different. I would always do the opposite of what everyone was doing because to be innovative and to be a leader, you need to stretch boundaries.

"My players are all very technical and when they are very young, we work on technique and mentality first - size and power come later. With Harry, Jesse, Ryan and Tyler, we trained twice a day and taught them that to make it as a top-level athlete you need to have put in at least 10,000 hours of practice.

"From the outside it looked brutal. I could be vicious with them, but I did that knowing it was for the best. And to date, I've made no mistakes. I was simply reminding them that if you want to play in the European leagues, you have to be tough. Real tough.

"The New Zealand football association tried to stop me from coaching, but I knew what I was doing – if my kids were going to get moves to Europe, they needed to be desperate for it."

A major part of Edge's philosophy is promising players early on that if they put in the work, they will definitely make it as a professional footballer. This approach defies the conventional wisdom that you should not put children under too much pressure.

Edge disagrees: "You have to make deals with players, you have to promise them that they will become a professional. The young player has to know at about 12 or 13 that he's going to be a pro. Guaranteed.

We got in big trouble with the New Zealand football authorities because they said 'you can't guarantee them anything'.

"There was a myth that only a chosen few could make it, but the people saying that don't realise how easy it is to become a professional footballer, and we told the players that.

"I said: 'Trust me, you'll see when you make it that there aren't many good footballers. Every coach around the world is looking for better players.'

"With kids, once you show them there's something to aim for, they'll work 100% towards that. It's demotivating if the coach says only a few of them will make it."

The obvious counterpoint to Edge's philosophy is that, aside from the issue that not every aspiring footballer can make it, children will be even more crushed by failing to become a professional if they had been guaranteed it. "If that happens, it's because they didn't work hard enough," is the coach's response.

Talking to Edge, it's easy to imagine why he quickly became the scourge of New Zealand football. As well as his aggressive and sometimes dogmatic approach, he openly admits results are irrelevant to him, as his focus is always on the performance and what's been learned.

His employers have often viewed this approach – aimed at developing players in the long-term at the expense of picking up short-term gains – with suspicion. Enforcing this philosophy has led to Edge being sacked from numerous managerial jobs, such as at Melville United (a side in the Northern Region winter league) after they were relegated in 2012 and at Waikato FC later that same year.

"It's all about the marshmallow effect[1]," Edge explains, "where you accept short-term losses for the long-term benefit. For instance, Jesse Edge was always bigger and stronger than the other kids. But I never allowed him to use his power and pace in matches because I knew once he got to the top level, everyone would be just as big and as strong. So I forced him to work on other sides of the game.

"All through the age groups at Waikato, we lost most weeks because as soon as we won a couple of games, I'd move the players up an age group.

"I've been sacked many times, but I'm not in the business of winning games. I'm in the business of creating players good enough to go to Europe."

Thomas experienced first-hand what it was like playing for Edge's youth sides and recalls: "We hardly won a game. We hated losing all the time but it was fun to have possession and just play."

Declan's nephew Jesse also played in the losing Waikato junior teams and looks back fondly on his time there. He said, "No one was tougher than Declan but he was always very honest.

[1] *The marshmallow experiment was conducted at Stanford University in the 1960s and 1970s and showed that children who could master self-control and appreciate the value of delayed gratification were much more likely to be successful.*

"I didn't find it particularly strict, he just prepared us for going abroad, and it made moving to Vicenza much easier."

Jesse Edge admits that losing all the time could be frustrating, but it was helpful in the long-term. "We would lose 5-0 or 6-0 a lot," he said, "but that would partly happen because we would try things like playing it out from the back, and I'm glad I was forced to work on other aspects of my game."

Declan Edge has been Olé Academy's Director of Football since he was sacked as Waikato manager at the end of 2012, whereupon he took Thomas and most of the club's best players with him. Olé are famed for playing a possession-based style of football (Edge claims he has got his teams playing between 700 and 800 passes per match at all age groups) and the outspoken coach now has the facilities and investment to produce even more players. Already more than 30 alumni are at foreign clubs or at US universities with a view to becoming professional through the MLS (as former All Whites captain Ryan Nelsen did).

Perhaps the most important aspect of the academy for Edge is that it puts his players on an even footing with their foreign counterparts by providing them with international standard facilities. Olé provides state-of-the-art gyms, nutritionists and dieticians, and all players are tracked by GPS, fitted with heart monitors and receive detailed video analysis.

If the players can take advantage of this and emerge before 2018 then the Kiwis could be in a position finally to make an impact at a World Cup. And Edge says, "I've got three or four players at the academy now who are going to be even better than Ryan, Harry and Jesse."

Olé is not alone in nurturing young Kiwi talent – alternatives include the Wynrs Academy, which acted as a finishing school for the likes of Rojas and Wood, and the Asia Pacific Football Academy, which has links with Chelsea and whose alumni include Tuiloma, Howieson and Alex Rufer, an 18-year-old at Wellington Phoenix who is the nephew of the 1982 World Cup player Wynton Rufer.

Jesse Edge feels that with a lot of young players coming through, the next few years could be a seminal period in New Zealand football, especially with the country hosting the 2015 Under-20 World Cup where 24 nations are competing.

"The Under-20 World Cup is very important for New Zealand football," he said. "We're aiming to get to the last eight, which we've never done. And then it's all about 2018 in Russia. I think we'll qualify – we've got lots of good young players in strong leagues."

Jesse, who has 14 caps for the Under-20 side, also feels that the Kiwis' success at the 2010 World Cup had an effect on young players. "It was a big eye opener and got a lot more kids into the sport," he said. "To remain unbeaten against countries like Italy and Paraguay showed New Zealand can compete."

In many ways, though, the football-obsessed Jesse Edge is the exception to the rule in New Zealand where most young sportsmen aspire to play for the All Blacks, the all-conquering rugby union team. Jesse Edge believes football is no longer seen as a sport solely for those who couldn't make it in rugby. He says: "At school, football used to be seen as a bit of a girls' sport – you were soft if you played football; hard if you play rugby. But it's changing and a lot of young people are getting involved in football."

Jesse still believes there's much work to be done though in how New Zealand football is run and he looks enviously at Australia. "The way the youth system is set up there is a different class to New Zealand," he said. "You can't compare. The facilities, youth development programmes and infrastructure are so much better.

"A big part of it is investment, but there also needs to be people at the top pushing for better coaching of young players. We want to test ourselves against the best in the world and beat them, and we need a system in place that supports us."

Jesse Edge's fearlessness about playing the bigger footballing nations would please his uncle. Something that infuriates Declan Edge about New Zealand football, which he wants to change, is the inferiority complex many of the players have. "All the stuff about a football tradition is a myth," he argues. "I read about 'footballing hotbeds' with lots of talented players, but football doesn't care where you come from.

"We do a lot of brain work and we tell the kids aged 11 or 12 that where they're from is irrelevant. There is no reason New Zealand can't be successful."

The New Zealand FA for their part have attempted to help the Under-20 team at the World Cup by organising a number of matches for the young All Whites.

Last June, Jesse Edge was one of eight overseas-based players who joined up with the Under-20 squad to participate in the Panda Cup International Tournament in China. The Kiwis lost to Croatia and China

but drew 0-0 with Brazil. They then flew to Doha in September and beat Morocco 3-1 after losing to Chile and Qatar.

At senior level, Englishman Anthony Hudson was appointed the All Whites manager in August 2014. Three years ago, when he left a coaching job at Tottenham to manage Newport County (in England's fifth tier at time), the then Spurs boss Harry Redknapp likened Hudson to a "young José Mourinho".

Though Declan Edge's priority is not the New Zealand national team ("I couldn't give a shit about that"), he is aware that partly due to the players he has produced and is producing there is the potential for the All Whites to improve. "There's a big New Zealand football story going on at the moment," he says. "Ryan Thomas will make a big difference to the national team – he is going to be a global superstar, mark my words."

Spending time with Edge, you feel at times invigorated and at times a little sceptical. Fundamentally, though, you are left hugely curious as to where his project will be in a few years' time. He could be speaking proudly of the Edges and Thomas emerging as key players for European clubs and that he has plenty more kids now playing in Europe.

Or he could have been sacked multiple times again. Or both.

Whichever way, the success of his protégés will almost certainly have a big impact on whether New Zealand has emerged as a credible footballing nation in time for the 2018 World Cup. Declan Edge simply says: "This project, this journey we're on, it's only just getting started." Ⓑ

128

Polemic

"brave", "proud" and "cruel."

Against Sanitised Football

Can fans fight back against clubs who seek to ignore their history for bland branding?

By Alexander Shea

It is awful, jarring, the equivalent of a scraping fishbone stuck in a football fan's gullet.

It is a cringe-worthy television advert produced by Qatar Airways, starring the players of Barcelona.

If the advert did not exist, it would have to be invented. For there is no other existing piece of media that better encapsulates the worldview of football in the neo-liberal age. It is 40 seconds of distilled ideology at its purest.

The advert begins by zooming in on a mystical Neverland-like 'FC Barcelona island' – an island taking the form and colours of the *blaugrana* crest. On this island, Lionel Messi and co arrive at a glass behemoth of an airport. It is one of those hyper-modernist airports, a transparent, shimmering structure of flowing glass so universal in its blandness that it could belong to any country – the sort of airport you would insert into your modernist utopia in *Sim City*.

Messi and the gang, seemingly alone in the airport, roll up to the check-in desk in their rock-star gear. Behind the players lies a void of squeaky clean airport marble, like a hospital for rich people. It is notable how the 105,000 fans who attend each home game have been

erased from this fantasy. "Don't worry", the advert implicitly suggests, "there are no fans in this shiny airport wonderland. You are alone, safe from the masses." Messi et al are relaxed: phew, they can get away from the roar of the crowd.

And all of this with Samsung suitcases.

Let us just say that Craig Calhoun, the London School of Economics' sociologist who has called globalisation the ideology of "wealthy frequent fliers", would have a field day... The Barça players clearly belong to a deracinated, transnational elite.

Now on board a Qatar Airways plane, the players jet across the world, making stops in Paris, Tokyo and Miami. At each location they enter party mode, rejoicing in a World Cup-like carnivalesque atmosphere in which everyone dances along smiling and in which each time there is a noticeable lack of football.

I wonder what Barcelona's *socios*, the members of the club, made of the advert. Of all clubs in European football, Barcelona has always been identified as a bastion of identity politics, its footballing kernel inseparable from its left-wing collectivist politics forged during the Spanish Civil War. Particularly as the club has such a strong historical connection with anarchist political philosophy, I think Barcelona's socios might feel uncomfortable swallowing their Qatari medicine.

The club, as Sir Bobby Robson put it when in charge of the team, is "the invisible army of Catalonia", displacing its (claimed) political nationalism and anti-Madrid sentiment into sporting battle. So intense are the emotions stimulated by the club that the board is having to expand the cemetery adjacent to their stadium, so that more fans can rest in perpetuity next to their 'home'.

How depressing it is to see the club allow its image to be manipulated so vulgarly in the pursuit of profit. Barcelona is supposed to *mean something*, to be a shared emotional space in which a chronology rooting back to the 1930s is evoked and celebrated. It is not supposed to be a commercialist utopia we can all fly to.

In an age in which the largest football clubs, such as Barcelona, Real Madrid or Bayern Munich resemble transnational corporations by commodifying their 'brand' in international markets, a sea-change has taken place in clubs' identities. Football clubs are sanitising their self-images, removing emphasis from the political narratives that previously gave their teams meaning.

Football has never been just about football. When 11 players take the field for your side, they become the embodiment of the 'imagined community'. As the political scientist Benedict Anderson argued, in large societies in which we will never meet the vast majority of those who claim the same identity as us – a Frenchman from Paris cannot meet all his fellow Frenchmen – a sense of community is produced not by face-to-face interaction, but in a collective imaginary in which all members imagine themselves as a single community. This imagined community is reaffirmed in a shared chronology of the nation, with events such as 1789, 1848, 1914 or 1968 providing a common narrative of identity.

In a postmodern society in which we all have plural identities – I am a Tottenham Hotspur supporter, a Radiohead devotee, a university student, a middle-class boy from a working-class family, a Brit raised in Brussels – there are no longer hold-all identity frames like 'class', 'religion' or the dichotomy of 'civilisation' v 'barbarism' that act as nodal points for our identities. We no longer live with shared experiences: not all kids now go to Butlins on holiday or undergo military training together.

Football matches on television, or in person at the stadium, thus offer one of the sole devoted time slots in which society is experiencing the same event at the same time. In the latest World Cup, 88.4% of Dutch people watched their national team's victory against Chile. 82.1% of Belgians watched their national team beat South Korea. 81.3% of Greeks saw their team defeat Côte d'Ivoire.

It's a lot easier to imagine and invest emotionally in 11 men as the embodiment of our nation than it is to rationalise abstractly that that bloke from 300 miles away, whom we will never meet, is also a member of the 'we'. The psychological dynamics of football stadiums result in clubs becoming lightning rods for charged political identities. With the alienation of industrialist society, in which the division of labour means that we compartmentalise our 'professional' and 'personal' lives and rarely find ourselves together in a substantial grouping of our colleagues, football stadiums offer a unique social function.

They become an emotive space, in which the crowd can take on a singular voice in their chants - a process that the psychologist Gustave Le Bon called the 'de-individuation' of society. As Le Bon showed, when individuals are in groups, they lose their inhibitions and are more willing to flout social norms. As a result, football stadiums provide a seemingly enchanted space in which the norms of the current political order can be suspended, and furthermore, resisted.

When Lechia Gdansk played Juventus in the 1983 European Cup Winners' Cup in Gdansk, football became the site of ideological transformation. With the president General Jaruzelski having banned Solidarność, the Polish anti-Communist ship workers' movement, 16 months prior to the game, the match took on significance when it was announced that Lech Wałęsa, who had recently been released from jail, would attend. The leader of Solidarność and the subject of a smear campaign by Jaruzelski, Wałęsa maintained a real fear that he would be booed by a crowd won over by regime propaganda, an act that would have represented the symbolic death of Solidarność.

Instead, as the game reached half time, a cry of "Solidarność! Solidarność! Solidarność!" reverberated around the stadium. As the home team manager Jerzy Jastrzębowski recalls, "We were in the dressing-room at half-time when we heard it and it sent shivers down our spines, the whole ground singing 'Solidarność'." State television was so concerned about the ramifications of the chanting on public opinion that it delayed the broadcasting of the second half for six minutes. When the game finally came back on, it was broadcast without sound. The symbolic authority of the regime had been compromised; all of Poland could see that workers had turned against the workers' party.

Similarly, the Parc des Princes of Paris Saint-Germain, until its recent purging by PSG's Qatari owners, was a symbolic battleground between the Left and Right of Paris. Situated at one end of the stadium, the Kop of Boulogne, the Boulogne Boys promoted a Fascist, overtly racist ideology in which their *tifosi* paid homage to the iconography of the 1930s. At the other end, in the Virage Auteuil, left-wing workers and immigrants fan groups provided an alternative. In 2010, after a racist attack by the Boulogne Boys on the Supras Auteuil, a member of the latter killed Yann L, a Boulogne ultra. In response, the new ownership disbanded both groups, but then took the further step of preventing any fans from choosing to sit next to groups of others. Instead, a new ticketing system was introduced which randomised seating allocation. Ticket prices were ramped up and the ownership admitted that it was implementing a strategy of 'fan gentrification' whereby it was trying to attract wealthier fans. As one club spokesman put it, the club was attempting to replace hard-core supporters with 'fan customers.'

Trying to separate football clubs from their histories is wrong. We cannot sanitise football clubs, removing them from the meanings that their communities have invested in them, before branding them as 'global products' to be sold via merchandise. I am reminded here of the Argentinian political theorist Ernesto Laclau's theory of the role of the 'empty signifier' in neoliberal capitalism. Laclau argued that in order to amplify their market appeal, brands would 'empty' themselves of their controversial significations, their political roots, and market themselves using bland, catch-all terms with which anyone could associate.

When Barcelona markets itself abroad as *mes que un club*, because it shows 'solidarity' and the value of 'passion', one has to resist the temptation to yawn. Any fan in the world could project their own commitments onto such phrases and be a Barcelona fan. The brilliance of the marketing strategy is that the words solidarity and passion essentially mean nothing; who can object to such principles? It is the same reasoning as when Barack Obama ran on the mantra of 'change' in 2008. Change? Okay. But *which* change?

There are two logics of football fandom that are at war in the modern game, and regrettably, I think the wrong one is winning the battle. These two logics are those of (1) football as event, carnival v (2) football as emotional investment; a debate that has been defined by French theorists as the clash between *plaisir* and *jouissance*.

Football as an event or as plaisir refers to a model of World-Cup like fandom, in ascendance today, in which fans celebrate each match as some Dionysian event of utopian happiness. Fans, sporting face paint, dancing side by side and doing Mexican waves revel in the now, everyone having a great time. Football becomes a site of consumption: indistinguishable from going to the cinema or a nightclub with the point being to consume 'happiness' via beverages, merchandise and gleeful dancing.

There is nothing inherently objectionable about the model. Apart from the fact that it is:

a) incredibly conservative as it uses a mass event in the manner the state wishes us to: to enjoy ourselves, consume and forget issues of political contention. No example is better than this than the 2014 World Cup in Brazil, in which the government was more than happy to ignore social protests, placing emphasis instead on the euphoric imagery of fans dancing side by side while getting drunk on the Copacabana.

b) quite frankly, really boring after five minutes. Where is the meaning in a dramatic narrative in which everyone gets on? Does Switzerland versus Switzerland get your juices flowing?

The second model of fandom is that of football as emotional investment or *jouissance*, the latter loosely translated as taking pleasure from suffering. This is not meant in some sadomasochistic, Nietzschean sense but rather in a more quotidian context. Any hard-core football fan will tell you that a goal scored in the 94th minute of a nail-biting, frustrating game leads to greater emotional arousal than a goal scored after 10 minutes. It is because pleasure that is produced as a result of suffering (of 93 minutes of internally whispering to ourselves that a draw would not be that bad, of self-talk) acts as a release from tension, providing an infinitely more aroused 'high' than a straightforward win. We 'get off' on suffering a little bit; it is the reason why cyclists both relish and dread the uphill climb.

Being a football fan is about being ready to suffer. To be ready to get soaked, and secretly enjoy it, on a Tuesday night away at Carlisle United. It is a perverse sense of enjoyment that arouses people; faced with the repetition and banality of everyday life, is it not understandable that people enjoy the absurd?

For these devoted, suffering fans, football is the serious life, not some game to be consumed like a soft drink at the weekend. It is the realm where emotions are produced, emotions which are not triggered by the everyday routine. Is it particularly surprising that the emotions awakened, the sense of community produced by being part of the collective, leads to political affiliations? These are people living what is a thickly layered emotional experience.

In similar terms, we cannot remove the fan from his social context. If a football club is situated in an industrial workers' town, as it is in Donetsk to give one example, it would be an act of violence to demand that fans separate

their social identity from their support for the club. Indeed, Shakhtar is such a pertinent example because the billionaire owner Rinat Akhmetov has demanded precisely that, to the mass protest of fans (even before the club was forced to – temporarily, hopefully – relocate because of the conflict in eastern Ukraine).

To pick on a theme first detailed by David Winner, football needs Darth Vaders. We need to have certain clubs that we love to hate. They provide a historical richness that we need to give our lives meaning. Otherwise football will become a soulless rationalism in which rootless clubs, transnational Manchester Uniteds, play against each other.

Clubs that deploy Fascist iconography should be banned from doing so, only because such symbols carry such latent representational force, associated as they are with the traumas of the 1940s. They should be banned because not to do so would be to contravene the European Convention on Human Rights, representing a traumatic threat to a black or Jewish player's psyche on the football pitch.

Nevertheless if fans of a particular club wish to self-identify with the neo-fascist movement, we cannot stop them. A recent movement in European and US philosophy, neo-fascism renounces the genocidal ideology of the 1940s, but nevertheless promotes an aesthetic of masculinity and self-discipline. It is self-contradictory and holds a latent, if not overt, racism in my view.

But we cannot have our cake and eat it too. If we allow Livorno to display Communist icons despite the genocides perpetrated by Stalin, can we object to Roma fans promoting a censored version of Fascism? If football fans want to celebrate the Nietzschean triumph of the will and an ideal of masculinity separate from racist ideology, that is their prerogative as autonomous individuals, as long as they do not endorse discriminatory policies. We have to remember that much of Fascist ideology was originally not explicitly racist, but rather a philosophy drawing on Romanticism's love of the homeland. This is a fine, fine line and one that I think the tensions of neo-fascism will inevitably cross. But we cannot try fans in advance or judge them guilty by association.

Besides, can we expect football fans not to be attracted by such an ideology when much of football subscribes to a Fascist aesthetic? Cristiano Ronaldo is inadvertently a supreme representative of Fascist masculinity: he is overwhelmingly individualist in his play, refers constantly to the strength of his will in rendering him the player that he is and flaunts his sculptured body like it is a public exhibit. Not to mention the awkward fact that he seems enamoured by the purity represented by Madrid's all-white shirt.

To return briefly to the Qatar Airways advert, no other metaphor could express the alienating nature of modern football to the local fan than the mystical Barcelona Island of the advert. It de-territorialises football completely, a fantastical utopia chopping off the roots of Barcelona's history. It implies that to reach Barcelona land, you have to travel on Qatar Airways, rather than, say, actually visiting the club or studying its history.

It says something about how disillusioned I was that I positively enjoyed this next video that was recommended to me. It is the perfect contrast to the sanitised Qatar Airways utopia.

It is called *The Last Argument*, an anti-'modern football' manifesto uploaded on YouTube by Dynamo Kyiv ultras in 2011.

It is the footballing equivalent of Friedrich Nietzsche, like watching football fans' testament to *Thus Spoke Zarathustra*. Nietzsche famously wrote of his fear of the coming of the 'last man', a man no longer willing to take any risks or invest himself emotionally in any goal, a man wary of life, waiting to die. Dynamo Kyiv fans' decision to entitle their video *The Last Argument* takes on a deeper meaning in this context. Where Qatar Airways brushes off history, Dynamo Kyiv fans actively embrace it. They self-consciously are placing themselves within an ideological narrative.

The argument of the hour-long video is crude, raw and discomforting. But it is appealing nevertheless, for all the same reasons that Nietzsche remains a seminal philosopher today.

The video begins with a man standing, head tucked downward, on a metro platform waiting for the train. The train arrives. He gets in. The train then sets off again, becoming a blur as it accelerates. A narrator voices over the action: "Do you live? Or do you only think that you live? Nowadays life is like a recurring dream. Monday, in the morning you go to work, in the evening you watch TV before having a dull orgasm before you go to sleep... They tell you that this is how you live life: to consume more it is necessary to work more."

These guys have clearly read Nietzsche as well as Marx's theory of alienation, using the modernist symbolism of the metro to represent the oppressiveness of industrial society. It is pop philosophy but it hits home. Whereas modernism is worshipped by Qatar Airways, it is demonised by Dynamo fans.

The leaders of the various Ukrainian ultra groups then revert to a common discourse. Football is about emotions. Emotions that you cannot experience in other areas of life. Emotions that are like an explosion. You cannot abstract a people from their politics; you cannot turn an active footballing public into a passive football audience.

Troublingly, the ultras endorse pre-arranged punch-ups with fans of other clubs in determined, remote locations. This is disgusting, reifying as it does archaic notions of masculinity and honour through violence. This reflects the dual heritage of the counter-Enlightenment as represented best by Nietzsche: railing against the rationalist philosophy of the French *lumières*, counter-Enlightenment philosophers stressed not only the primacy of emotions but also implicitly endorsed violence. While I am of the opinion that humans need to have some medium in their life where they can channel

aggression, through playing football, boxing or whatever, it is not desirable that such anger is expressed through mass beatings.

Nevertheless, even if expressed in inappropriate terms, their clubs truly mean something to them. The team is a pocket of anti-establishment ideology, a critical site of resistance to the dominance of the every day. There is a romanticism about Dynamo that you will not find on Barcelona Island. I know which side I will be gunning for.

Which is why I am calling for football clubs to reclaim their identities, as particular and local as they may be. This could be done by publishing less airbrushed histories of their clubs – a lesson Real Madrid's directors would be wise to learn after producing the mother of all whitewashings – naming stands in the honour of their supporters, reserving seats for working-class fans, refusing to taint their match-day shirt with gambling sponsorship, providing fans with a stake in their club or advertising themselves internationally as the team of left-wing progressives. It will not make money, but it will mean something.

For at the moment clubs are moving towards becoming rootless, even soulless entities. Entities obsessed with money rather than meaning. Entities that know the cost of everything but the value of nothing. Ⓑ

The Trials of Baghdad Bob

Can Roberto Martínez restore his reputation after a season of wilful blinkeredness?

By Paul Brown

You remember Mohammed Saeed al-Sahhaf, don't you?

Little guy with specs, green army uniform, black beret. All the rage during the Iraq war. Talked a good game, though most of it was nonsense, totally divorced from reality. He was the Iraqi Information Minister during the 2003 invasion, but soon became known as Comical Ali. Or Baghdad Bob.

His outrageous announcements were legendary. US troops were "committing suicide by the hundreds on the gates of Baghdad" he told the TV cameras, with the sound of gunfire getting ever closer to his compound...

Maybe the comparison is unfair, but there were times last season when Roberto Martínez seemed to channel this ridiculous caricature of a man. In the same way Baghdad Bob would try to convince you there were no tanks in his city even when you could see them all over it on the news, Martínez would try to convince you that his side had shown incredible character and belief, even though they'd just conceded six times at home.

"We always looked a threat going forward... The margins are very small," he said, after Everton lost 5-2 in Ukraine to a rampant Dynamo Kyiv side.

A season of such promise almost ended in the most abject of failures, Everton flirting with relegation on the 30th anniversary of the most successful campaign in the club's history. The boys of 85 had long been shaking their heads in collective disbelief at some of the things Martínez was saying in public by the time Dynamo finally destroyed Everton's last slim chance of rescuing some pride with a rare piece of silverware. For a while there was the real possibility that Martínez would do what he had at Wigan — win a trophy (in their case the FA Cup) and get relegated doing it.

But to go down would have been unthinkable for Everton. No other club has spent as long in the top flight of English football, and they had never been relegated from the Premier League.

Even under Mike Walker.

Eventually they scrambled their way to safety, but the danger that Martínez would end up presiding over the biggest ever turnaround in club fortunes was clear and present for a long, long time.

His first season had been magnificent, ending in a record Premier League points tally which in most other years would have been enough to qualify for the

Champions League. Chelsea, Arsenal and Manchester United had all limped away from Goodison Park defeated, Bryan Oviedo had scored their first winner at Old Trafford in 21 years. The buzz was back. Martínez was the new Messiah. The anti-Moyes. The man who understood the School of Science and was bringing back the glory days.

Fast forward a few months and the same fans hailing him as the best thing since Howard Kendall were calling for his head, wags on Twitter had replaced his image on the billboard outside Goodison with a picture of Mr Bean, and pundits and commentators were branding him stubborn, naive and foolish.

Where did it all go wrong?

Picture the scene. January 2015, south London.

Everton have just won (unconvincingly) for only the second time in 14 games. Mighty Selhurst Park has been conquered and Martínez is addressing the national press – in a corridor outside the toilets. A season full of promise had descended into dark and dangerous territory, early talk of a top-four finish long since replaced by anxious whispers about the drop.

But you wouldn't have known it from his sunny demeanour as he tried to convince us that no, he wasn't relieved to have finally won a game and no, relegation was not on his mind at all. What Martínez did say was interesting, though. "Obviously if I'd started believing in all the things I read last year I'd have been too

big-headed even to speak to my wife," he said. "And this year I'd be cutting my veins when I walk into the house."

There is some truth in that. Too many people got too carried away with Martínez in his debut season. Some were even touting him as the next manager of Barcelona. Now, his critics were multiplying every day and the ferocity of their attacks was growing too.

But that little comment got me thinking. 'Suicidal' was how Martinez and his tactics have been described many times before. But there was one particular game that stands out.

Anfield. It's always Anfield, isn't it? The name alone is enough to make any decent Evertonian shudder. Almost exactly a year to the day before that win at Selhurst Park, Everton went into the Mersey derby riding high on a wave of Martínez-fuelled optimism.

They left with the bubble well and truly burst. A thrilling 1-1 draw at Arsenal early in December had suggested Everton really could play the Martínez way anywhere. That they could dominate even the best teams in the country on their own patch, pass them off the pitch and match them ball for ball, man for man.

It was a fool's dream.

Three goals down in a whirlwind 35 minutes at Anfield and it soon became clear that the Martínez model would have to be modified.

Suicidal. That's how the pundits described his tactics that day, and it's hard to argue with them. Trying to press high and dominate possession against the best fast-break team in the country, with both your full-backs pushing on at the same time was a recipe for disaster, and so it proved.

That 4-0 thumping showed the rest of the Premier League how to beat Everton. It may have taken them until the following season to start doing it. But that was the beginning of the end. "Too exposed, too naive," Martínez said in a rare moment of honesty after Everton's biggest derby defeat since 1982. But it took him a long time to fix it because that is exactly how his side started the following season.

By the time Everton returned to Anfield last September he had figured it out, playing three holding midfielders instead of the usual two and scraping a 1-1 draw after a last-gasp thunderbolt from the unlikely hero Phil Jagielka. But only after his team started the season by conceding ten goals in three games – including so many so quickly to Chelsea in a bizarre 6-3 hammering at Goodison on August 30 that you almost lost count.

Their form was patchy for weeks afterwards, not helped by a growing injury list made worse by the rigours of the Europa League, where victories came more easily because teams had not yet worked Everton out. But the pressure really grew during a woeful run of seven defeats in nine games between November 30 and January 1, when the shoehorning of an ageing Gareth Barry into a makeshift back three for a 2-0 defeat at Hull was perhaps the most mystifying tactical decision of the whole campaign.

The most common criticism of Martínez is that he is too stubborn. That he refuses to change the way his side plays. Look at Brendan Rodgers, they say. He changed tactics, formation and personnel and revived Liverpool's fortunes (briefly). But this is unfair. Forget the fact that Rodgers has more options because he has vastly more money to spend and look at the facts.

If anything, Martinez changed things even more than Rodgers did last season – he just failed to produce the same results.

Playing three holding midfielders away from home at bigger clubs and surrendering possession was a pragmatic but necessary move, and one that would have been totally alien to him in the past. But experiments with Barry in a back three, Leighton Baines in midfield, Kevin Mirallas up front and Steven Naismith as a false nine were all either limited success stories or unmitigated disasters.

He was also about to employ as big a change in his pass-first philosophy as you could possibly imagine for a man so intent on possession football. Against West Ham in the FA Cup his defenders began launching it long. No more slow, patient build-up play. This was direct football. But it went largely unnoticed.

Romelu Lukaku, who scored a late equaliser that day, would go on to suggest the players had begged for a more direct style and that he was benefiting from it, though Martínez denied it. They employed the same tactics at Upton Park in the replay, when they outplayed their opponents to score twice with ten men after Aiden

McGeady was sent off, only to cough up an extra-time equaliser and lose 9-8 on penalties.

By then Baghdad Bob was in full effect. The typical Martínez press conference after the latest defeat would be littered with words like "brave", "proud" and "cruel".

When I saw him at Selhurst standing outside those toilets, I couldn't help wondering whether down the pan was exactly where Everton's season, and their manager's career, were heading. In the end it didn't come to that. And Martínez will get time to prove that his debut season at Goodison was no fluke and that he's not just a coat-but-no-knickers manager.

It won't be easy though. Those who loved him for his relentless optimism now ridicule him for his seeming inability to face facts.

The smart grey suits seem a little less classy. The brogues have lost their polish.

The belief is gone.

Will the city fall? Never, Sir. There are no tanks in the city and the infidels are surrendering in their hundreds. Soon you will see a glorious victory.

Let's hope so.

140

Fiction

"I want to get it back. And if
I don't get it back, I intend to
exact retribution."

The Tackle

John Brodie, the former winger turned detective, returns to hunt down some stolen medals

By David Ashton

Hughie Johnstone was a small man, legs a touch bowed, coughing into his hankie — a wet cough that caused my girl Rosalind to frown. She was a nurse at the Royal Infirmary and Greenock, the town in which we were both born, specialised in rain. The damp air could have been cut up and sold to the desert sheikhs but here it just produced pulmonary ailments and a quick trip to the cemetery.

The hankie was carefully folded and stowed away neatly. Hughie was a fastidious soul; to look at him you'd never guess that he had ruled a Morton midfield like the Kaiser for a long skilful era. The big clubs had come and dangled the jerseys — one Royal blue, one green and white hoops — but the wee man would not be budged and the management knew better than to force the issue until he nodded his assent. Elsewise they would have been lynched from the nearest lamp post like Mussolini.

Rangers it was eventually. He might have been heading towards the twilight of his career but even in the half-dark he took them to a couple of league championships and three cups. The wee man was a hero. Even the Celtic fans showed respect. There are few heroes now. To be such a person you have to care for something more than your life. I am not one of these men.

My name is John Brodie. Vulcan had a limp and so do I. His was caused by an angry Jupiter, mine by a right-back who broke my leg in pieces and, with that tackle, ended a part of my life. After that I went to hell. Down to the very depths. With Rosalind's help I was finding my way back out again but it was touch and go. Always touch and go.

"I was at the same school as your father," Hughie remarked, breaking into what had become, without me knowing it, a long silence.

"He never said."

"Andy was two years up on me. Played a wee bit on the wing, jist the one trick though. He was mair intae the politicks."

My father had been a Clydeside Communist. He died of cancer and his last words were, "The only good thing about this bugger. It gets the Tories as well."

"They tell me you investigate things," said Hughie.

"He sticks his nose in and gets battered for his pains," Rosalind remarked pertly, then stood up and shrugged on her coat. "I'm away to my work."

Hughie and I watched her head for the door. The raincoat was tightly belted to her waist and flared above the knee of her seamed black stockings. It was not an unpleasant sight.

"Help yourself to another cup of tea, Mister Johnstone," she called back. "John will never remember. His head is full of gaps."

Door closed. The lady gone. I poured Hughie out a fresh brew to prove how wrong Rosalind could be on occasions, making sure the strainer was well positioned – unlike the present Morton defence – before answering the wee man.

"I uncovered a bribery case. A bookie. Rigged bets. To do with a football match."

"I heard about that."

"Word got round. Folk come to me. Small cases mostly."

Hughie took out a spectacle case, carefully removed the glasses and put them on. His eyes through the magnified lens were, behind the folds of skin, veined but bright blue. "Such as?" he asked.

"My last enquiry was the dual disappearance of Ming the Merciless and Joey the budgie." I took a deep breath. "Ming was the beloved tomcat and Joey the equally adored budgie of two neighbours of mine in the next tenement. I ascertained that Joey was in

the habit of being let out his cage to sun himself on the back window ledge."

"That wouldnae take long in Greenock," observed Hughie.

"The bird never flew away though perhaps he did this time because he was gone. But then, through diligent questioning, I discovered that the other neighbour had left her window propped open on an empty box of black magic to let some air into the kitchen. Ming must have squeezed through and made a lunge. I found them both below, behind the midden bins. Dead on arrival. Mortal embrace."

"Like a winger and a full back, eh?"

I had told this idiotic story so that Hughie would be under no illusions as regards my investigative ability but I could see from the flinty look in his eyes that he hadn't bought the body swerve. After all he was without doubt one of the hardest men to slide a ball past in Scottish football. His sense of anticipation was uncanny and he rarely fouled. You only commit such an act when you're not there - out of position. My whole life, I have occupied that space.

"Rosalind said ye got a battering?"

"The bookie's hard men."

"Did the boot go in?"

"Had its moments."

Silence. From somewhere beneath, there was a noise from the Willow Bar, which lay directly below my floral lino; a loud laugh followed by the crack of dominoes hitting a tabletop indicated that someone had just laid the double six. I had moved down here from the attic room at the top to get nearer the action. Hughie fished in his cup with a spoon, came up with one stray tea leaf I had missed and gazed at me steadfastly. He was going nowhere.

"All right," I sighed. "What can I do for you Mister Johnstone?"

"Someone has stolen property of mine," Hughie said quietly. "I want to get it back. And if I don't get it back, I intend to exact retribution."

This time the silence was profound. Nothing from the bar below. The whole of Greenock – mute.

When Hughie had come back from Rangers to spend the final two years of his career with Morton, he was slow, could still see a pass, but the legs were gone. In a game against St Mirren, bitter rivals, a hooligan bunch of Paisley cloggers, one tough nut kicked the wee man up in the air – wanted to make a name for himself, seen too many cowboy films about the fastest gun.

Hughie picked himself out of the mud – the rain was belting down – and the crowd fell quiet at the witnessed humiliation - in time past he would have left the tough nut kicking air. Towards the end of the game, Morton were awarded a free-kick. About thirty-five yards out. Hughie indicated he would take it. The rest of the team shrugged their shoulders – he was not heavy booted, it was a long way out, but he was captain. The leather sphere, as they say, was like a cannonball, sodden with the downpour. I was about ten at the time. My father had

cupped his coat round my head to save me from the worst, and I could barely make out the figures through the stair rods slanting down.

The tough nut was right in the middle of the defensive wall. Hughie hit the ball and the ball hit the man. It broke his nose, dislocated his jaw, gave him two keekers and put him into hospital for three weeks. The game was a draw.

So when Hughie said he was going to exact retribution, he was not kidding.

I took out a Woolworth's pad of paper that had a pencil attached to the side and looked down at the blank page. "And what is the name of this dirty rotten thief, Mr Johnstone?"

"Barry. Barry Wilson."

I wrote it down in block capitals. This was bad. This was *very* bad.

The story Hughie told me was as follows. All of his mementoes he kept at home in a neat wee pre-fab up in Gibshill. That particular scheme was bandit country, delivering the post at Christmas was like Wells Fargo surrounded by Geronimo's Apaches. I had done it one year to earn some spondulicks in the company of Sid, a cheery Englishman who drove a red postie van, and every day we were bombarded by a hail of stones, razor sharp tin cans and home-made arrows from the unseen tribal warriors.

Nevertheless Hughie's pre-fabricated dwelling was untouched, his reputation saw to that – had the man not played for the Scottish League XI against their English equivalent alongside the great Matt Busby? They got beat 3-1, but Hughie had put one sliding block on Stanley Matthews that was still debated in the pubs with salt and pepper pots taking the part of both men.

But the wee man did not take such respect for granted. He snibbed the windows and locked the door when leaving, dribbled a tennis ball with some of the hellish midget ruffians that were gathering missiles for the next postal delivery and left all in good order.

So – there came a day, yesterday in fact, when he returned, opened the door, and immediately saw a pale rectangular patch of wallpaper where a glass case had hung on the wall.

"It was my medal case," he said quietly.

"All gone?"

"All gone."

"How many?"

"Fifteen. From when I was in the juniors, top o' second division with Morton, Scottish Cup final with the Huns and the Hampden Game."

I noticed his hands were now clenched. White-knuckled. Delicate stuff. "Tell me the circumstances, please?"

To this rather po-faced enquiry that disguised a rising panic within, Hughie replied in formal tones, nodding his head slightly as if ticking off the facts. "It is well known up the Gibby that I leave the house every Wednesday afternoon."

"Bowling green?"

"My brother's widow, Mary. Tea and ginger biscuits."

Now it was my turn to nod. Widows are a responsibility. "So your movements would be known?"

"Right enough. This time o' the year, it's well dark afore I get back."

"Any sign of a break-in?" A shake of the head. "So, they had keys?"

The eyes darkened over as if a thought was troubling him. Then he replied. "They had *something*."

Now we had come to the bit that I had been dreading – the cause of my inner panic – this was not a back green job. How come Hughie had laid this theft at Barry Wilson's door?

This is how come.

One of the baleful midgets had been sent to get the family tea from the local fish and chip shop. No fish just chips. *Toma's* it was called and run by Big Fat Toma – in fact a relatively small man but fat right enough, who sported a big scar down the side of his face because he had once run with The Cheeky Forty, a gang of hoodlums that had fought running battles with the police and Canadian sailors during the war. The rancid smell from his chip fat could stop a Sherman Firefly in its tracks but the price was cheap and Toma sometimes threw in a pickled onion if the mood took him.

It was raining of course and the boy hurried to get the twice-saturated chips back home but en route noticed a big black limousine parked in the gloom on a side street.

Big black limousines did not belong in the Gibby.

As he watched, a figure ran from Hughie's house to the car. A door slammed and it took off. The boy mentioned it to his father who dragged him to the wee man the next morning when word got round that sacrilege had been committed.

The running figure was not identified but the boy's eyes, though smarting with the vinegar coming off said chips, functioned enough for him to make out a licence plate in the lamplight.

Personalised. Easy to remember. *BW – 303030*. The initials were obvious and the number had its own significance.

"Why would Barry Wilson want your medals, Hughie?"

"He offered to buy them. I don't like the man."

"Where was this?"

"Cappielow. He invited me as a guest. The directors' box. I should have stuck tae the terracing. Where I belong." I had been writing some of this down on the Woolworth's pad. The biro started smudging all over my fingers. I hoped it was not an omen. "It was after the game. We won 4-3 but the defence was rubbish. I told him so." Hughie twisted in his chair abruptly as if he had heard something. "Have ye noticed how small his eyes are – Wilson?"

"I don't know the man up close."

"Like a snake. Or a weasel. Some kind o' rodent. It was then he made his offer – all smiles. When I said I was keeping what I had earned, it was not for sale and never would be – it was like – a different person. The smile was gone."

The wee man sat there like a piece of granite and I shook my head – something was buzzing around inside it like a midgie on the prowl. " Why would he desire your medals?"

"He said he wanted them tae hing on the wall at Cappielow, in the board room. But I knew better. He wanted them for himself."

"Why?"

"He has none of his own."

There might be some profound psychological truth behind that remark, but Hughie's face was simplicity itself. I wiped a smudge of biro onto the pad from my thumb. "Why don't you just – go and face him out about this?"

"I have no proof – a wee boy in the rain. He'd jist laugh."

"Barry Wilson may well just laugh at me."

Hughie's head snapped up and those bright blue eyes burned in. He reached into his pocket, took out a small purse, extracted a clean five pound note and laid it down. "You're an investigator," he said. "Away and investigate."

With that, he put his specs back in the case, coughed into his hankie, a precise discharge, and left. I sat there and regarded the Woolworth's pad. Scrawled sentences to do with chips in the rain but the block capitals could not be avoided. Like the full-back who cut me down.

"BARRY WILSON," they said, and no matter how much I squinted, the letters would not change. Hughie's declaration echoed through my mind in similar fashion. "*I intend to exact retribution.*"

Alec Mangan was always ahead of the game. First at school to smoke, first to get found cheating at three-card brag, first to get his girlfriend pregnant – in other words a born journalist. His face was puffy, eyes sliding sideways like a goalie in the mud, and he nursed the whisky I had bought him like a newborn infant.

He worked as a reporter for the local *Greenock Telegraph* but had connections into the Glasgow papers – put it this way, Alec sniffed at corruption like a pig does truffles. Not to uncover it, necessarily, he could always be bought off, but the smell *attracted* him.

Jimmy Lapsley, the barman at the Willow, frowned over – he was a decent soul and a great friend of my father who had been domino champion and his partner in the doubles – Jimmy had also witnessed me near drink myself to death in the bad old days and forever worried that I might return to evil habits.

But I had a chaste half pint before me, not a dram in sight. On the case, eh?

Alec sucked in a lungful of his Lucky Strike – he was deeply influenced by the likes of Frank Sinatra – and blew out a perfect smoke ring. A bit wasted

in the Willow Bar; the place was quiet in the early evening and had that strange familiar and forlorn emptiness – beer and cigarette fumes mingled with the faint trace of morning Brasso and the furniture polish that Jimmy used so diligently to keep the place shining. He was an officer in the Boy's Brigade.

"Barry Wilson, eh?" Alec pronounced through another lungful, "Quite a boy. Quite a boy."

I knew no more the man than the rest of Greenock which was that about three years ago, Morton were in a moribund state and Wilson had turned up out of the blue, taken over the finance, had become chairman, sacked the manager – who admittedly was next to useless – assumed the dual role, got an experienced trainer in and then found the money to buy some half-decent players – especially in attack. Barry liked to attack.

Three-nil was his preferred score-line. *BW 303030.*

He had also pulled off some stunts that offended the purists such as having Miss Glasgow kick off the first ball of the new season in her bathie costume – thank God there was a blink of sun that day otherwise the poor girl would have frozen to death – and hired a barrage balloon that floated over Cappielow for selected home games with the slogan *BARRY'S BOYS RULE – OK?*

Like or lump him, he got folk through the turnstiles and Morton teetered uneasily in the top half of the Second Division – a lot better than the lower depths where they were usually marooned – but – and there's aye a *but* – the team had so far won nothing and rumours of financial skulduggery followed Barry around like a bad aftershave. These he brushed off like so much fluff from his black mohair suit. A pure white shirt set off his all-year tan. Quite a boy.

Alec's shrewd, treacherous eyes measured me up. "How come you're interested in Mr Wilson?"

"Just curiosity."

His glass was empty and I signalled Jimmy to set up another. A gloomy shake of the head and the barman did as requested. He was, in fact, as near as damn it, teetotal. I limped to the bar, paid, looked at the pale hunched figure in the mirror that was myself, came back and planked the glass before my informant. A meditative sip, then Alec dished the dirt.

"Nobody can lay a glove on our Barry. They say it's all borrowed money, the ground put up as a guarantee, seat o' the pants stuff, but nobody knows."

"Where does he come from?"

"The planet Zog. A man of mystery. They say he's got connections to some of the big boys in Glasgow. Gangsters. Life takers. They say."

"*They?*"

Alec raised one nicotine-stained finger and tapped the side of his nose – he then reached out and poked me in the sternum with the same digit. "One thing. He has two heavy-duty merchants who never leave his side. Maybe when he

goes to the lavvy, but that's about it. It's no' so much the size – it's the look in their eye. If you're thinking of going up against Barry – I would strongly advise the opposite."

"I've been kicked by hard men before."

"Wouldnae be a kick, John. It would be a knife through butter."

For a moment there was a weird glint of compassion in Alec's eyes, then he threw back his dram, stubbed out his Lucky Strike and grinned like a shark. "But let me know. I'll rustle up a headline. *Washed-up ex-footballer found hanging on butcher's hook.*"

Only Alec's little joke but for some reason the barb went deep. A strange thing about pain – it resides in so many places. Sometimes in a twisted broken bone that will never quite heal or in the pathways of the heart that seem so full of bloody potholes.

But for me it is pictures in the mind. I was a young winger, a Junior game, full of promise – the man against me going in the opposite direction, ashes in his boots and mouth.

Now that I look back on it, I realise I must have danced past him once too often – when you're young, other people don't register. This time he did.

A savage tackle. A sickening crack. I never played again. My left leg is twisted. Rosalind insists that in certain positions it can be quite arousing but the woman's just being kind.

I hit the booze bad for a long time and the dependence still waits for me crouching like a beast in the corner, but I manage to walk a very thin line. I can still hear that crack though.

"John?" Jimmy's voice broke into my reverie — Alec Mangan had gone, promising to phone a few pals in Glasgow in case some scandal might have surfaced recently. His reporter's nose was twitching and he knew I was up to something. I kept Hughie well out of it but implied that there was a certain bit of "exploration" to be encompassed. Fancy words. Alec sniffed and lit up another fag. I promised that if anything newsworthy transpired he would be the first to know and he seemed, for the moment, satisfied with that. "I have two meat pies left over frae this morning," the barman continued solemnly. "Do you and Rosalind want them for your tea?"

"I intend to make spaghetti, Jimmy. There might be a certain clash of cultures."

He nodded acceptance of such culinary mores. "Ye want a game of dominoes then?" Jimmy was forever trying to lure me into the contest in the hope of resurrecting the championship-winning team that he'd had with my father.

"I have some thinking to do, I'm afraid."

Thinking was *good*. Jimmy was happy with that. As he held a glass up to the light to give it a final swipe, I saw behind him on the wall where all the Morton souvenirs were arranged, a photo of the second-division winning side with Hughie sat right in the middle of the front row. In his hands was a large cup and round his neck was a ribbon with the medal dangling.

I looked down at my hardly touched half-pint — what was it I had just said about thinking?

Rosalind Connor hoovered up the last strand of pasta clean as a whistle. The sauce was, to be honest, mince with another hat on, but her father was an Irish doctor and they had never got on — he was a potato fanatic so anything that stood up against the spud was fine by her.

He was also a heavy drinker, had died of liver malfunction, and I wondered sometimes which man she was trying to save.

One thing for sure — she had green eyes, a wicked smile with slightly large teeth that must have left a few love bites in their time, and a figure, in that starched sloping uniform, to rouse many an ailing patient from his sick-bed.

I had, while she scoffed in like a trooper, nurses being forever hungry, told her the tale of *The Case of the Missing Medals*. Not quite *The Maltese Falcon* but you never can tell.

My reading matter had shifted recently from Chandler to Dashiell Hammett who had the same hard-boiled sultry dames with blond hair and blood-red lipstick. But his heroes seemed to suffer more pain than Chandler's.

Rosalind leant back, sipped at her Barr's Irn Bru and fixed me with those green eyes. "So what's the plan?"

"Two-pronged. One is I find out all I can about Barry Wilson, the other is that I go to see him and ask it straight. Even if he denies, he may reveal something."

"I like the first one better."

"How come?"

"If you pitch up – he'll know who you are."

"Unless I am heavily disguised."

"And if what that shitty wee nyaff Alec Mangan says [nurses swear a lot] is anywhere near the truth – you could end up where I work."

"Correct."

I tried to arrange my features into the guileless façade of a man who would never stick his head into the lion's jaws but she shot me a look of disbelief and slugged back the Irn Bru.

"I have an early shift tomorrow – the Kidney Ward, a bundle of laughs – I need to wash off the muck and get to my scratcher. Pronto."

"Can I come?"

She smiled despite misgivings. "It's the least I can do. After all – you made the tea."

And so to bed. But our sweet slumbers were interrupted by a midnight hammering on the door. I stumbled out of the sheets while Rosalind cursed, shoved into my stripy pyjamas and fumbled my way to open up a crack.

A tousle-headed boy with a big square face and hair like a divot gazed back at me. "It's my Uncle Hughie," he gasped hoarsely. "Done in."

Rosalind was right in that a person connected to this affair might land in hospital but it wasn't myself. I followed divot head, Malkie Johnstone by name, as he informed me, down to the Royal – leaving my sleeping partner muttering about the Kidney Ward.

The boy was near incoherent but as we grubbed our way along in the dark streets, I managed to get out of him where the doing-in had taken place. Cathcart Street, which is a long way from Gibbshill – what the hell was Hughie doing in that neck of the woods? I asked the boy who hung his head and mumbled something that sounded like, "Ma mammy'll tell ye." He seemed an awkward strange soul and communication was not his first port of call – so I stopped asking questions and moved as fast as my gammy leg would allow. I had thrown a raincoat over my pyjamas and stuck on a pair of old shoes so I looked like some distant relative of Long John Silver as I limped along.

I was known at the Royal through Rosalind and got smuggled in past the dragon of a matron to where Hughie lay in a small side ward. A worried looking woman was seated beside the bed – she had a round face that seemed better suited to smiling - and looked up as we came in.

Hughie was pale and winced every time he moved, but did not appear too badly damaged. The skin was drawn tight across his cheekbones but no blood or bruises to be seen. His hair was plastered flat like a wee boy going to his first dance.

"What happened to you?" I asked, as Malkie moved behind what I took to be his mammy.

"Just came out the close. Bang. Two men."

"I heard the shout," the woman said. "Malcolm and I ran down."

"Jist as well," Hughie muttered.

"Recognise them?" I continued.

"Too dark. Too quick."

"Size even?"

"Bigger than me. That wouldnae be hard."

His lips twisted in a painful smile as he introduced me to the woman, Mary Johnstone, widow of his brother Robert, and mother of Malkie.

Her words tumbled out in a stream. "We'd just had mince and tatties, Hugh was for the bus for the Gibby, we aye eat tardy because Malcom's at the football practice so we have to wait on him but that's not my fault."

"Nothing is your fault, Mary." Hughie's comment, fondly if painfully uttered, did nothing to assuage Mary's sense of guilt — she shot out sentences like a water pump.

As far as I could follow from the scrambled syntax and occasional digressions — as well as Wednesday tea and ginger biscuits, Hughie visited for a Friday supper — not fish, they were good Protestants — mince and tatties, which had been his brother Bob's favourite, good lean mince, mind you, from

Soutar's the butcher. Malcolm had indoor practice with his team so came back late, often with a bruise or two, he played centre-forward and that's a terrible place for getting knocked about, they all ate together and of course this night had talked of nothing else but the disgraceful theft of Hugh's medals, what kind of bad people were in the world and where was the justice? Look at poor Bob who had drowned in an accident at Largs. And then the attack at the bottom of their own close — after money no doubt. Whit a world.

Mary stopped abruptly as if someone had pulled the plug. She turned to look at the man on the bed. For a moment her lip trembled, then she straightened up and I glimpsed a different woman with a decent kind heart. "Well, you men will have things to talk about," she said quietly. "Men always do. Come on, Malcolm. You have your work in the morning."

She stood up, leant over Hughie, patted at him awkwardly, and left followed by her silent son. Malkie managed a nod. The door closed. The wee man and I looked at each other until he finally spoke. "He's an apprentice cooper, Malcolm. Like his father. Good with his hands."

I had sensed more than one undercurrent during all this but families are often so — a labyrinth — if I have a couple of years to spare on occasion, I'll ask Rosalind about her own. For the moment I had some other fish to fry.

"How bad are you?"

"Cracked ribs. Strapped up. Two. I've had worse."

"You think it was Wilson's men?"

"I wouldnae know."

"Why send for me then?"

"Ye live close by."

"Hughie, I've had sufficient of the one-liners. I'm tired, I've been pulled out of my bed and unless you have something more to tell me I'm going back there. You can have a nice wee rest and I will see you in the morning. Now – do you have something to tell me?"

I was beginning to have a feeling that some game was being played that involved me being kept in a state of ignorance. Hughie however did not look impressed by my incisive declaration and a flinty look settled on his face.

"Ye're gey full of puff for a man that's carrying my fiver."

"Already spent it. Wine, women and song."

"Now who's got the one-liners?"

Our eyes met for the first time that night. The fierce blue in his was diminished. Clouded. By pain or was something else troubling him? Hughie nodded as if he had made some decision. "The Forsythe brothers. Pals tae you?"

"Big Neilly is for sure. Shug and Jaffa just come along for the ride." I had a flash in my mind of the three of them – good-natured Neanderthals until aroused – battering the hell out of the bookies' hard men who had been battering hell out of me. "They helped me out of a predicament."

"Ask them – tae keep an eye open on Mary and Malcolm, eh? For a few days."

"Why would Mary and Malcolm be involved?"

"Jist – ask Big Neilly. I'll pay good money!"

A pleading note had crept into his voice and it was more upsetting than if he had screamed the roof down. What was he hiding? What the hell was going on? "All right," I replied. "I'll have a word. But they'll be conspicuous."

"Bigger the better." An approaching ambulance wailed outside in the silence.

"Anything else you want to tell me?"

For a moment Hughie looked as if he might say something but then he started coughing and reached for his hankie. From its depths the words came – thick and muffled.

"Away and investigate. That's yer job."

It was a claggy Saturday morning. Morton reserves versus Dumbarton of the same ilk. The first team had been knocked out of the Scottish Cup, which was playing that weekend so this was the bill of fare at Cappielow – needless to say, no barrage balloons. About 120 hardy souls, 10 of whom were from Dumbarton, watched a dispiriting collection of trialists and old gunslingers boot the ball to and fro.

One of the boys reminded me disturbingly of myself – clever on the ball, fast, but too careless. Good but perhaps not quite good enough. A winger of course.

I watched for a while, gathered up my nerve and then made my way round the back to where the offices had their position. Alec Mangan had supplied me with a card that purported to make me a reporter from the *Greenock Telegraph* seeking an interview with Barry Wilson. Naturally if there were any problems arising he would deny it utterly.

The best thing about Alec was that you could always trust him to be untrustworthy.

The "office" was a large room where three young girls sat typing and answering various correspondence. Two of then were obviously bored stiff, dreaming of dances at Cragburn Pavilion where Prince Charming chewed gum and showed a nifty turn of foot but the third, whose name tag on the desk announced Senga Baxter, hunched seriously over the Remington, horn-rimmed glasses gleaming. A plain wee soul, sharp-featured, but she was the only one who looked up.

I had rung and bluffed my way to an appointment, obviously with one of the other girls because Senga did not look impressed by either the card I showed her or myself. I did not blame her – there's something about me that suggests I am rarely to be what I claim.

"Martin Scobie?" she pronounced dubiously – a name I had written on the card and was already beginning to regret. "Ye'll have to wait a minute."

She then walked towards a door that had the words *CHAIRMAN WILSON* in large letters and I noticed that her back view was as uncompromising as the front. After a moment, having

disappeared through the door, she reappeared, stepped to the side, gestured a trifle impatiently and in I went to the lion's den.

A man stood looking out of a large CinemaScope type window that stretched almost the length of the wall and overlooked the Cappielow pitch. "Shoot for God's sake!" he shouted, as far down below the trialist I had noted, hesitated, then dabbed the ball daintily towards a non-existent centre-forward. A defender hoofed it into the sky, the referee blew for half-time and the man shook his mop of blond hair in disgust. "If that's the future, we're fucked."

He turned and smiled at me. "I'll have to remedy that my friend!"

Barry Wilson. Stocky, immaculate, tanned face, light brown eyes but Hughie was right – small in size and a little too close together, but nobody's perfect. We introduced ourselves, tea and biscuits were waiting on a side table, I produced a better class writing pad than the Woolworth's one and we had a pleasant chat about Morton, his hopes for the team, how football was in the dark ages as regards selling it to a new audience. Miss Glasgow and the barrage balloon were only the beginning – Barry wanted an all singing, all dancing show.

"Between you and me, Martin," said he. "Football should be better than sex!"

"That wouldn't be hard in Greenock," I ventured.

Barry roared with laughter but all the time his eyes (small or not) had been measuring me up while I did the same to him. I couldn't identify his accent, faint traces of Glasgow perhaps but – "Are you thinking about something, Martin?"

"I was trying to place your accent," I answered, honestly for once – you can always try being honest once in a blue moon.

"I am from all over the place. Universal, that's Barry Wilson!" He laughed again but I sensed he was losing interest – his gaze flicked to the window where the two teams were creeping back onto the field. Now or never.

"I expect you heard about the tragedy of a valued servant?" I put to him in newspaper speak.

"Tragedy?"

"Hughie Johnstone. His medals stolen, a vicious assault that left him lying within an inch of his life at the Royal Infirmary."

I had deliberately over-exaggerated the circumstance just to see the result. If Barry was connected he'd know from his goons that the assault had been short-lived. Sure enough, he blinked for a second before replying. "That's terrible. An inch of his life?"

"So the rumour goes." He'd check of course and find out otherwise but for the moment I had him on the back foot. "D'you think they're connected?"

"What?"

"The theft and the vicious attack."

"How would I know?"

"I'll put that down as no comment." I was beginning to enjoy myself in Ming the Merciless mode. "It is also rumoured that you offered to buy these medals."

"What?"

"And that Hughie refused."

"I – merely suggested to him that he could loan them to the club, to hang in the board room – at no time did I offer money."

"Is that because of the financial situation?" This was dealt from the bottom of the pack and stopped Barry dead. "It is also rumoured that the well's running dry."

His hand shot out to a nearby desk and pressed a buzzer. "I think it's time you left," he said tightly – smile gone, eyes like slits. The hair was still blond but the tan had paled.

"Oh but I've got a load more interlocutions –" The door flew open and two men stood there – Bill and Ben the flowerpot men they were not. As Alec Mangan had foretold, it was their very stillness that conveyed the menace. Both had broad flat impassive faces. I now remembered that Ming the Merciless had ended up a corpse behind the midden bins.

The notebook was wrenched from my hands and given to Barry. Much good it would do him – the "shorthand" I had written was hieroglyphic nonsense. That thought comforted me as I was hustled ignominiously out through the office. Senga looked up once more and her thin lips twisted in either derision or sympathy – difficult to tell.

I was booted out from a side door of the stadium. Bill and Ben had not altered expression or said a word. The kick crunched up between my legs and the pain was considerable though, thank the lord, it missed the crown jewels by a fraction.

The door slammed shut as I lay on the street looking at the dog ends in the gutter. A subdued shout came from within the stadium. Morton had just scored. I hoped it was the trialist.

A fine drizzle descended in swirling layers over the Broomhill football pitch as two amateur teams got stuck into one another. The centre-forward of one side was Malkie Johnstone – he'd had a severe haircut since I last saw him and it made his head look even squarer.

Hughie stood among the spectators and shook his head as Malkie tenaciously shielded the ball from two of the opposition. "He's should have got rid of it tae the winger but he doesnae think quick enough." The ball was booted off Malkie's toe and the winger, who bore a keen resemblance to a smooth-haired dachshund, spat in disgust at such neglect.

I had returned to the hospital to find that the wee man had discharged himself and left me a note that I could find him at the Broomie. He held himself somewhat stiffly but then so did I. As we watched the game I filled him in on what had happened.

"So – whit's the next step?" he asked, before calling out. "Wing, Malcolm. Gie the ball tae the winger!"

The boy looked up and his jaw dropped – he obviously had not known Hughie was watching – then he automatically hoofed the ball towards the dachshund who scuttled to the corner flag and hammered in a cross. Malkie hardly rose off the ground but the ball somehow skited off his head and ended up in the net.

Amid all the celebrations he looked once more towards Hughie – there was a strange haunted expression on his face – I wondered if his uncle had noticed.

It would seem not. The wee man nodded in satisfaction. Then repeated his question. "So – whit's the next step?"

The final whistle blew – a hard-fought draw. As the teams trooped off in the drizzle I noticed the giant figure of Big Neilly waiting near the changing rooms. He nodded solemnly and I waved back. Hughie had also spotted the big man.

Before I headed to Cappielow I had dropped in where the brothers were wolfing down a gargantuan breakfast dished up by their mother Jean – a diminutive woman with a sharp tongue who ruled them with a rod of iron. She had a soft spot for me since I had helped Neilly with his maths homework at school so my request was a done deal.

"Shug and Jaffa will be hanging about Cathcart Street frightening the pigeons so your family will be safe until we get this sorted."

"How do we do that?"

I took a deep breath. "The first thing is to find your medals. If Wilson is the guilty party – where would he keep the case?"

"Somewhere close. The coal bunker maybe?"

I was about to snap back a rebuke when I saw that Hughie was just holding on in no more, his cheek-bones pulled tight by pain. I wasn't doing too hot myself – my groin area had a sort of dull brooding ache that had little to do with love.

"You shouldn't be here, Hughie."

"I've never missed a match that boy's played. I'm not going to start now." He pulled out his hankie and covered his mouth for a second, coughed, and then lifted his face to the drizzle. "I'll walk Malkie down, it's no' far. I can say hello to Mary. She'll be madder than a wet hen at me."

"With every reason. You should be in your bed."

"I might stay there a few days. They have a spare room."

"Good idea."

He turned in the direction of the changing rooms and then stopped. "If you find out where he's planked it. Whit do you do then?"

I smiled as my groin suffered. "I intend to steal it back."

Barry Wilson had a large house in the posh environs of Ardgown Square; a leafy retreat where the capitalists of Greenock counted their ill-gotten gains, as my father would have put it. On the opposite side to the swanky Tontine Hotel, the place was rented and must have cost Barry a pretty packet but no doubt suited his needs and image.

I found this out from Alec Mangan who, surprisingly, had not been at all troubled when Wilson had rung the *Telegraph* threatening all kinds of reprisal. Told his editor it must have just been some joker on the sly and lit another Lucky Strike. One of Alec's few redeeming features – he just loved to cause mischief. Sadly he had been unable to find anything from his Glasgow contacts except that Barry Wilson had been involved in a money swindle as regards some building project but the case had collapsed though lack of evidence or skilfully applied bribery of the investigating polis.

Another useful fact Alec supplied was that this very Saturday night there was a big business reception at the Town Hall – all the movers and shakers. Barry would be among the honoured guests glad-handing his way to glory. But while the cat's away – the mice do play.

I slunk at a safe distance from the address in the evening gloom and watched as Barry and what looked like another Miss Glasgow, all dolled up with her cleavage safely protected from the insidious raindrops, swanned into his limo with the tell-tale number-plate *BW 303030*. It was driven by one of the flowerpot men, the other sat beside in the front. Very cosy.

Off they went. Now all I had to do was find a way in.

Luckily Rosalind was on night shift, so I'd managed to disguise my aching bones and even more luckily, I had not bruised up because she would find her path to that area by hook or by crook.

How would Sam Spade handle this?

Case the joint, no doubt.

There was a narrow wee lane at the back of the houses for the midden men to collect domestic detritus so the posh folk didn't have to actually see them and I crept along till I came to the back garden door. It was, of course, locked.

The wall was high with broken glass imbedded at the top but I noticed that there was a gap just above the door: maybe they'd run out of milk bottles.

I turned to Big Neilly – remiss of me not to mention him before but a burglar needs company – and whispered a request. "Any chance of a lift-up?"

He nodded reluctantly. "How'd ye get back though?"

Good point. "I'll stand on the bins," I replied hopefully.

Neilly shook his head, cradled his massive hands and hoicked me up so that I could scramble over like something out of *The Colditz Story*. I dropped down and sidled up through the shrubbery, rhododendron bushes, which I always associate with cemeteries – until I reached the back of the house. There was a side path that led to some French windows that looked mildewed and unused but, importantly, they had a shoogly handle that might be prised open.

Perhaps Barry was so confident that he could not envisage a surprise incursion

from the rear or perhaps the hellish Greenock weather had done me an unwitting favour and that path to the garden was rarely utilised, but by the light of my small torch, powered by Eveready batteries, I bore down on the handle and shoved inwards. If it was bolted on the other side, all would be in vain, but it wasn't – and I was in.

But it's always easier to get into something than it is to extricate yourself.

I didn't dare put on any of the lights and it was a nerve-shredding business stumbling around by faint torchlight in unknown terrain. The room I had come into was the main reception but the stairs leading upwards in the hall seemed a better bet. I was relying on Barry Wilson's ego – if indeed he had the case – where would he put it?

Somewhere he could look at it. A private place perhaps? Possibly in the company of Miss Glasgow? A comfy place. Where they could coorie doon thegither.

And there it was. On the wall. Opposite the king-size bed. The light flickered on the medals hung neatly inside the case.

In the main people are more predictable than they would like you to think but why – for God's sake – unless Hughie was right and the man had won nothing, was empty inside, just a big barrage balloon – would Wilson want to steal it? And how did he manage the theft? I had an idea about that but it was unpleasant to contemplate and could wait for the moment.

I lifted the case off its nail – could the cheapskate not have used a decent picture hook? – and trying not to gawk at certain sexual accoutrements revealed by torchlight and scattered on the bed – tucked the case under my arm and made my getaway.

And this is where I made a huge mistake that put the only person I care about into the category of Joey the Budgie. Why do it? I don't know – perhaps a suppurating desire for vengeance against all these slimy bastards that rule the roost.

It was a mistake, however, that I would regret for the rest of my life.

On the way down the stairs, my torchlight picked out a varnished wooden door that obviously led to an office or study of some kind. Curiosity killed the cat. I pushed. The door opened. In I went. There appeared to be no windows to the outside world so I chanced the light going on.

Now I had moved in category from Avenging Angel to prurient intruder. I lifted the lid of a large oak desk and keeked inside. A few paper knives but nothing much else. A small drawer to the side caught my eye. I slid it open. Nothing. I pulled too far and the whole thing came out. At the back of the drawer panel was a small key, sellotaped into position.

I could have left it there. But I was lost in a dream of Sam Spade. It cost me. The tape was easy to remove but where did the key fit? In the lower part of the desk was a small cupboard – I tried to turn the handle. It was locked. I put the key into the lock and turned. Click.

In the cupboard shelving was a single file. A binder. I flipped it open.

Maths was my strong point at school. English next. Common sense, zero. I read enough to know that this was disquieting, slammed the door shut, stuck the key back into place and found I was still holding the file as if it was unexploded dynamite.

Back out. Jammed the French windows together. Stood on the rubbish bins, passed file and case down to Neilly, scrambled back over and sweating buckets despite the cold night air – ran for my life.

I thought I was in a film but found out later – the real world plays for keeps.

Rosalind came home from night shift about seven o'clock in the morning, wolfed down the bacon and eggs I had assembled, gave me a slightly greasy kiss, muttered that I smelt like a cigarette factory and then stumbled off exhaustedly to bed. The Kidney Ward had struck again.

I was just as pleased. If I told her what I had been doing, or had in mind, she would have had a blue fit.

The night before I had thanked Neilly, sent him off to deliver the medal case to Hughie in Cathcart Street and then found Alec Mangan in his dive, The Regal Bar, close to the *Telegraph* offices, to sit beside him wreathed in Lucky Strike fumes as he leafed through the file with increasing relish.

Neither of us were qualified accountants but from what we could glean, it would seem that the books were most definitely cooked. Not only that but it appeared that, having siphoned off a fair amount of money from the gates and bank loans with Cappielow as collateral, Barry and his all year tan were preparing to make that money disappear into a fictitious firm's bank account in Glasgow – and not for the first time by the looks of it.

I left Alec salivating at the prospect of a headline bonanza but worried at the same time what the consequences of that might be, given the criminal connections Barry Wilson was rumoured to possess. My ace reporter had no wish to end up in the Clyde with a block of concrete for company.

As for me? I was on a high, the adrenaline hero, limp forgotten, Glasgow gangsters didn't scare me, the Sam Spade of the Welfare State – I should have paid more heed to Alec's reservations and I should have remembered that when Alec gets paranoid, he drinks heavy. And when he drinks heavy, he talks too much.

My plan was to take the file to a proper accountant, a friend of mine, Ross Mackie, make sure that my conclusions were correct, then let Alec break the story and the police could take it from there.

That was the plan. But they gang aft agley.

Once Rosalind had snuggled down and drifted off, I looked down at her a moment before I left. A strand of black hair had fallen over one eye and I gently prised it free. She muttered in some annoyance and then was out like a light.

I left her there. Sleeping beauty.

My first stop was Cathcart Street. Jaffa and Shug had set up a cardboard box as a table and were playing a game of three-card brag for matchsticks. They had, it would seem, become a fixture in the street for no one paid them any attention. Fresh cups of tea at their elbow indicated that Mary was on the case. "All quiet on the Western Front," said Jaffa who was the reader in the family.

"Not long now, boys," I replied and breezed up the close.

Hughie was freshly shaved and neatly turned out though the shirt was too big for him and I guessed it might be one of his brother's. He was wearing his glasses, held together with a piece of sticky tape and I assumed they had been damaged in the fracas. On the table in front of him lay the case – he had taken the medals out and was in the process of polishing them carefully. Mary was in the kitchen and I could see a large hambone sticking out of an even larger pot. Lentil soup for sure.

I suppose that I was expecting a modicum of praise but the wee man, beyond a nod of acknowledgement, went on with his cleaning – Malkie was at another table trying to assemble one of these "ship inside a bottle" gadgets that Woolworths were selling to the pure at heart. It was a fiddly business involving raising the mast inside the glass by pulling on various strings. The boy showed a surprisingly delicate touch as he manoeuvred the pieces while the pot bubbled next door in domestic bliss, yet I could sense an underlying tension.

"Ye did well," said Hughie finally. "How d'ye manage it?"

"Best you don't know," I replied. "But you can forget the retribution idea."

He said nothing and went on polishing. Malkie teased the mast erect but it seemed to give him little satisfaction. Mary was enveloped in the steam from the hambone.

I was tempted to try to garner some attention by mentioning the possibility of a greater retribution waiting for Mr Wilson but thought I'd let sleeping dogs lie. On the wall just above where the boy sat, was a photograph of a younger Hughie with a man who bore a strong liking to Malkie. A hefty specimen going slightly to fat – his arm was around Hughie and both men were grinning fit to bust. "Is that Bob?" I asked.

Hughie nodded. Malkie kept his head down. There didn't seem much else to say – I felt as if I had scored a goal but no one was celebrating.

There was another photo of two men in uniform. Army boys. From during the war it would seem, they would be the right age for that. Both stood to attention, Hughie holding a rifle and what looked like a regimental prize. Dead eye. I looked at him now with his broken specs – life changes people. The other man had sharp thin features – for some reason they rang a bell but I had enough investigations on my plate.

"Well," I remarked a touch gormlessly, "I better get back on the case."

"I thought the case was over," said Hughie sharply.

"Not yet," I replied, heading for a fall. "Not quite yet."

It took me most of the day to conclude my business. First of all to Ross Mackie, a mild-natured man who concealed a razor sharp brain behind a delicate demeanour. He agreed with my initial reaction – good to know I hadn't completely lost my mathematical marbles – and advised me to take it to the authorities because it was a complicated welter of figures and would take a wheen of time to decipher. But there was no doubt that something was and had been crooked. A clever piece of twisted bookkeeping but with the file – it could be unravelled. Hold on to it.

I took his advice and then I went looking for Alec Mangan to let him loose on a banner headline but, despite a search, the man was not to be found at the Telegraph offices or his usual dives. Though it was Sunday there were private clubs where the booze was plentiful, mind you the clientele left a lot to be desired. Alec had been drinking in some, talking big and drinking hard but then he had disappeared – that's what they told me anyway.

I even tried the Willow Bar as a last resort. Jimmy Lapsley often worked there on a Sunday to tidy up the mess – Alec might have tried to muscle in. But no.

Jimmy shook his head. "By the way," he said dolefully, "Whit were you and Rosalind up tae? I thought the ceiling was going tae thump in. You want tae control your animal instincts, John. A time and place for that sort o' thing. On a Sunday tae."

I hadn't been back all that day. An alarm bell rang like a fire drill in my head. I ran out of the pub, up the stairs, unlocked the door — Rosalind was nowhere and the place was trashed — ripped apart, all the drawers opened, papers strewn everywhere as if a wild beast had been let loose.

I stumbled into the bedroom — the sheets had been trampled to the floor and there was a thick cloying smell in the air. Chloroform of some kind.

My heart was pounding as if it would burst out of the chest cavity — in the middle of the bed lay a folded piece of paper. Once opened — the words were clear enough.

IF YOU WANT HER BACK, YOU COME AND GET HER. SOLO.

How the hell had Wilson known where to track me down?

Then I found the answer. Rosalind's black stockings lay in a heap on the floor. For want of better to do, I stooped to pick them up. My eye was caught by something near the door. I picked that up as well. A cigarette butt. *Lucky Strike.*

It was well dark by the time I got to Cappielow. A taxi straight there. Solo. Cursing my own stupidity and trying to appease the cold knot of fear that had formed in my guts. Rosalind was the only thing I had in my life. And I had put her in terrible danger through my own lunacy and selfish pride. I should have known if I took on someone as powerful and lethal as Barry Wilson

that anyone close to me would suffer the consequences.

The door that I had been unceremoniously booted from out into the street, was slightly open. A mocking invitation. I took a deep breath and walked inside.

An empty stadium is an eerie venue. Echoes of my footsteps in the silence. A few shafts of light from stray lamps in the darkness. It had finally stopped raining but the dampness seemed in the very bones of the place.

Silence.

Then a sharp click and the practice lamps came on, flooding the pitch with light. Three figures came from the side and walked out into the centre circle. Rosalind between the two heavies. No more Bill and Ben. Too deadly for that. Her hands were tied behind with a rag of some kind wrapped round her mouth. They stopped. Facing me.

I walked towards them, clutching tightly at the file. A straight swap — that was my only hope.

"So. Mr Brodie, I believe? Got the name right this time, eh?" Barry Wilson walked out from the tunnel entrance, grinning like a baboon, with a furze of hair round his head like a perverted halo. "Your friend Mr Mangan has been on the sauce all day. Shooting off his mouth about how he had the dirt on yours truly. Lucky a friend of mine heard. Tipped me off. I had a word with Mr Mangan. He sang like a lintie. All the dirt."

"Where is he now?"

"On a slow boat to China!"

Barry roared with laughter at his little joke – all the time we had been talking, I had never taken my eyes off Rosalind. Her face was white and set, gaze steady and fixed on me. Her body was rigid, temper or fear, hard to tell. The heavies were on each side, grasping her by the elbow.

"A straight swap, " I said. "I'll forget everything I know."

"Of course you will," said Barry. "The file please?"

I nodded towards Rosalind. "She comes first."

In turn, he nodded to his men who released Rosalind to walk forwards. Barry did the same so they both arrived at the one time. I handed over the file.

"Thank you," Barry remarked and then punched me full in the mouth. As I sprawled on the muddy pitch Rosalind kicked out at him but Wilson skipped nimbly aside. "Temper, temper," he chided and then turned to walk away. "You see, Mr Brodie," he called back. "I'm afraid I could not take your silence for granted, unless I arrange it for myself." As I got shakily to my feet, Bill and Ben moved unhurriedly in our direction. "I regret this action but – better safe than sorry eh? Once you disappear, that's me. King of the World!"

As he waved the file triumphantly in the air to prove a point, there was a sharp crack of sound from the darkness. A bullet hit the file and knocked it out of Barry's hands. No one moved for what seemed a lifetime then one of the heavies made a move – was it Bill or was it Ben? – for his inside pocket. Another crack. He howled in pain, clutched at his leg and fell flat on his face.

I moved to untie Rosalind and pulled away the rag.

"You stupid bastard," she said.

Into all this walked Hughie Johnstone, an old army rifle in his hands. He waved it in the direction of Wilson and the heavy. "On your faces." They did so. Hughie – master of the midfield – turned to me. "Make sure they're clean."

While he covered me, I frisked the prostrate trio. Bill and Ben had flick knives but nothing more. Barry had no weapon. Too confident by half.

Hughie looked over to Rosalind. "Are you all right, hen?"

She nodded. "They chloroformed me. Otherwise I'd have put them in the Kidney Ward."

"Chloroform? And you a nurse as well? Damned cheek."

Rosalind smiled and my heart jumped with joy – even though she was smiling at another man. "How the hell did you get here?" I asked this other man.

"Been waiting near two hours."

"But – how did you know?"

"I had a good conspirator."

Out of the darkness walked a tiny figure. Senga Baxter, horn-rims gleaming, mouth set, and now I saw the similarity to the soldier in the photo with Hughie. Explanations could wait. I took a heavy-duty air pistol out of my pocket that was in the shape of a German Luger. "You beat me to it," I remarked to Hughie.

Rosalind was black-affronted. "Where did you get that for god's sake?"

"Ming the Merciless. The owner woman. Her husband used to shoot at the pigeons. Dead now. She gave it to me as payment. A private eye needs a functioning weapon."

"I'll give ye functioning weapon," Rosalind observed grimly.

A groan from the wounded heavy brought our attention to the horizontal villains. A moment of silence then Hughie walked over and placed the muzzle of the rifle behind Wilson's head. The man whimpered in fear, but the rifle was removed and Hughie lifted his foot and accurately pressed Barry Wilson's face into the mud of Cappielow.

"Retribution," said the wee man.

Some mornings later, Hughie and I sat in the Willow Bar with two cups of Jimmy's truly terrible coffee on the table. It had a chicory essence content that would have loosened the bowels of King Kong but neither of us had the heart to complain.

The police had found Alec Mangan trussed up in the cellar of Wilson's Ardgowan residence but by that time the story had been broken by a cub reporter on the *Greenock Telegraph*, which served the miserable bugger right. Even if Alec's claim was true that he had been a chain-smoking kidnap victim, used as a front to get Rosalind to open the door – he was still a deceitful creep.

The books were still being scrutinised but it appeared that there had been embezzlement on a cosmic scale going on and eventually the whole financial edifice would have collapsed. By that time, of course, the bold Barry would have been long gone.

So now both Hughie and I were somewhat compromised public heroes but now we had our own reckoning to make.

Rosalind was still sore at me – with good reason – and though we exchanged a few terse words over the filled rolls, I had been warned that the prospects of nookie (her word, not mine) in the foreseeable future were next to nothing.

So I was feeling sore as well – plus the fact that I still had a fat lip from Wilson's punch.

"You set me up," I accused the wee man.

"How come?"

"That girl Senga Baxter – she'd tipped you off something shifty was going on at Cappielow and when the medals were stolen, you tried two birds with the one stone. You set me running like an idiot, hoping that I might just get back the medals but more than that – uncover the dirty tricks that were going on. You used me, Hughie!"

The wee man nodded soberly. "True enough – but you owe that girl Senga.

She was working extra on the Sunday in the office, heard Wilson on the extension phone telling his pals in Glasgow what was going tae happen. Her father was in the army wi' me, ye know – Willie Marshall –"

"I don't care if he was in the Boy Scouts!"

Hughie continued, unperturbed. "She phoned her father. He got me. And I got my rifle."

"I thought you were supposed to hand these things in?"

"I forgot." Hughie coughed into his hankie. "If it hadnae been for Senga – you'd be a goner."

"What about my air pistol?" I replied defensively. "I had that on hand."

"Okay for pigeons."

I now knew how players felt when they tried to pass Hughie in the midfield. You always ended up on the wrong side of the ball. But there was a deeper, darker subject to be addressed – a harder tackle. Straight in. Head up. "It was Malcolm who stole the medals, wasn't it, Hughie?"

Jimmy at this moment switched on the radio and the words of "Stranger in Paradise" filled the air while Hughie sat there like a stone. I signalled Jimmy to turn it down and Tony Bennett was reduced to a plaintive mumble as I continued. "I don't know how Wilson got to him. Money, maybe – or promised him a trial with the Juniors – but mostly Malkie did it – I would imagine – out of jealousy."

"Jealousy?"

"You and Mary. It sticks out a mile. The way she looks at you. The way you look at her." I was beginning to sound like Tony Bennett, so I switched to a tougher edge. "Bob – your brother – drowned in Largs – what was all that about?"

"He was a heavy drinker. Checked intae a hotel wi' three of his mates. They got mortal on the whisky. He got intae a fight somewhere. Lost his way. Fell in the water. Malkie thought the world of his father but he was evil bad in drink. Especially at home."

I was about to say that might have been why Bob had got plastered in a faraway place like Largs but kept my big mouth shut for a change and tried another tack. "Have you spoken with Malkie about the medals?"

Hughie coughed into his hankie – I was beginning to wonder if it was more of a smokescreen habit than the bronchial tubes of Greenock – before glancing up. Eyes blue and steady.

"I did. Last night. You are correct in your assumption. He took the spare set of keys I left at Mary's and did the deed. Not as daft as you look."

"And the assault on you?"

"Malkie told me – that he had started to feel bad at what he did. Told Wilson that he might spill the beans. The battering was tae warn him."

"They should have battered him then."

"First come, first served." A glint of humour showed in Hughie's eyes for a moment, then his face set itself in solemn lines. "He feels bad about it now, that's for sure."

It would be dealt with in the family. Even if Wilson tried to smear Malkie, who would believe him? The man was a busted flush and all his gangster pals in Glasgow would avoid him like the plague, lest they get contaminated.

Hughie took out his wallet and laid four precise fivers out on the table. "One each for Neilly and his brothers. Fourth for you. The case is closed." He stood up as Jimmy Young succeeded Tony Bennett. "Unchained Melody".

"You and Mary – what's going to happen there?"

"Time will tell," said Hughie. He nodded to me, turned and marched out, brisk of step, without another word.

I sat there with the lousy coffee, isolated, abandoned and bereft. The case was over. I would have my day in court but the case was over. Jimmy Young warbled about time only being able to do so much. I hoped that was true as regards Rosalind Connor.

"Ye want some mair of the Java?" called Jimmy the barman. I shook my head. Had enough punishment for the nonce. He turned the radio off and shuffled from one foot to the other. He of course knew, like all the town, about rumoured events at Cappielow and my possible connection to them but being a typical Greenock man he wouldn't ask unless I gave the hint. Finally, he broke the long silence.

"Ye fancy a game of dominoes?"

Coda. There has to be a coda, does there not?

About a week later, the atmosphere was still frosty at the hacienda. I sat in one corner reading *The Glass Key* and Rosalind, who at least was still in residence, sat in the other reading a nursing manual because she was sitting her exams soon to be a ward sister.

A knock at the door. Sharp. Peremptory. I opened the portal cautiously and there was the freshly spruced Hughie Johnstone, a resplendent Mary beside him, with Malkie, hair combed flat and even wearing a tie, lurking at the back.

"You are invited tae a dead posh tightener at the Tontine Hotel," announced Hughie. "I've decided tae make an honest woman of her!"

Mary gave him an affectionate shove and Malkie managed a smile. For my part, I took a deep breath to respond that celebrations were on hold *chez moi* at the moment, when a voice cut in from behind.

"Just give me a minute to get my glad rags on!" I turned to see Rosalind disappearing into the bedroom. Women are a mystery.

We took a taxi there, Hughie's treat. It was as if nothing bad had happened and all was sweetness and light. We joked, poked fun at Malkie's neckwear, which turned out to be a Glasgow Rangers tie, and arrived at the Tontine like the royal family.

While the girls sped on ahead followed closely by Malkie, my sleeve was tugged by Hughie to halt us at the door. We both turned to look back across Ardgowan Square to where Wilson's house was now no doubt in the process of being rented to another chancer.

"I saw ye once playing for the Juniors," Hughie said out of the blue. "You were better than average. A lot better."

As he turned and made for the bar, one of the waiters came out of a

side entrance and his foot slipped on the tartan carpeting. The tray he was holding, tiled, and a roll slithered off heading for the floor. It was intercepted neatly by the wee man's instep, flipped up to the knee, then the hand, finally deposited back on the tray, and without breaking stride Hughie was gone.

"He's a football man," I said as I passed the waiter. "They're a different breed."

Blizzard Books

Johnny Cook: The Impossible Job

Iain Macintosh

Attention Blizzard fans, we now do books!

Johnny Cook: The Impossible Job, by Iain Macintosh

Harton Town are in trouble. With three games left before the end of the season, they're six points adrift at the bottom of the table. They need a hero. They got a delivery driver. And not a particularly good one at that.

Johnny Cook is out of shape, out of luck and very nearly out of hair. But it wasn't always like this. Back in 1986, he was Harton's hottest young striker for almost twenty minutes before a heavy challenge ended his career on the same night it began.

Due to a ridiculous, and yet somehow plausible series of events, Cook is given the chance to save his old club from the drop. His players hate him, his chairman hates him, and his girlfriend is struggling to recall exactly what it was she ever liked about him.

It's that old-fashioned rags-to-rags, boy-has-girl, girl-doesn't-like-boy, boy-wants-to-keep-girl, girl-wants-a-boy-who-doesn't-use-farts-as -punctuation story, juxtaposed against the top level of English football and set to the music of Supertramp.

"There's no other writer quite like Iain Macintosh. I think, on balance, that's a good thing." – Jonathan Wilson

"He sent me a copy and, I have to say, it's made the most wonderful doorstop." – Mark Chapman

"Iain Macintosh, having run out of milk, once asked whether it was morally acceptable to put his wife's expressed breast milk – intended for his baby daughter – in his coffee. This book is everything you'd expect from someone like that." – Gabriele Marcotti

"It's not too long, it's got football in it and there are some rudimentary penis jokes. What's not to like?" – Patrick Barclay

168

"The enthusiast who arrives at
Hampden without a ticket will be
right out of luck."

Scotland 3 England 1

Home International, Hampden Park, Glasgow, 17 April 1937

By Paul Brown

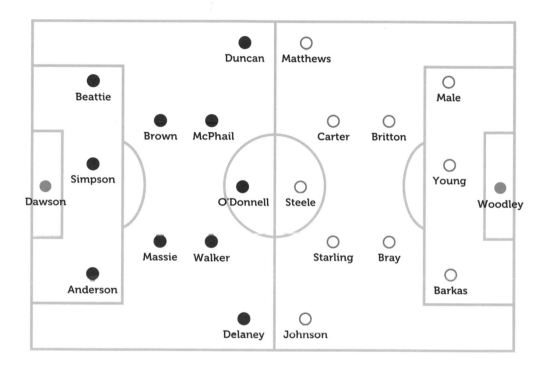

Duncan — Matthews
Beattie — Male
Brown — McPhail — Carter — Britton
Simpson — Young
Dawson — O'Donnell — Steele — Woodley
Massie — Walker — Starling — Bray
Anderson — Barkas
Delaney — Johnson

John Cairney still has his match ticket, yellowed and minus its stub, in his drawer of mementos. He doesn't remember much about the actual match. It was 78 years ago. He's 85 now, an acclaimed actor, painter and writer with a lifetime of football memories. But he does remember the vast sea of people, the ear-splitting wall of noise and the sort of collective madness that surrounded and enveloped him. "The excitement was palpable," he says. He was just seven years old, a small boy in the middle of Britain's biggest ever football crowd.

The date was Saturday 17 April 1937, and the match was Scotland versus England at Hampden Park, Glasgow. It was the first all-ticket international. The official attendance figure was given after the game as 149,407. (Some later sources give the figure as 149,547.) Once non-ticketed guests, reporters, stewards and police were taken into account, newspapers agreed that the attendance must have been close to, or in excess of, 150,000. Even judging by the lower official figure of 149,407, this was a world record attendance. It remains a British – and European – record.

It was John's first football match, and he was so excited that he'd barely been able to sleep the night before. John lived at Parkhead in Glasgow and was raised as a Celtic supporter in a football-loving family. He'd go to hundreds of subsequent matches, many with his dad, Tom, and his Uncle Phil, but few would equal the experience of that first match at Hampden in April 1937. A photo of his prized match ticket adorns the cover of his book *A Scottish Football Hall of Fame*. He's never been able to forget that immense crowd and its clamorous noise, labelled by newspapers at the time as "the Hampden Howl".

To put the size of the crowd into perspective, the 1937 attendance was three times bigger than the attendance at the most recent Scotland-England match in 2014, and more than twice as big as the attendance at the 2014 World Cup Final. In a non-football context, picture the familiar vision of the vast crowd that spreads as far as the eye can see in front of the Pyramid Stage at the Glastonbury Festival. That area has a capacity of 90,000, so imagine adding all of those folk to a 60,000 capacity crowd at the Emirates Stadium and you'll have a decent idea of what a crowd of almost 150,000 people might look like.

But what was it like to be part of such an enormous football crowd? Modern fans are unlikely to ever get the chance to find out. TV coverage and the more distanced nature of fandom,

coupled with safety concerns and other practicalities, mean there is no place for such a crowd within modern football. Existing all-seater football stadiums could not accommodate 150,000 people and it would be impractical to try to build one that could. The biggest football-specific stadium in the world at the moment is Barcelona's Camp Nou, which holds around 99,350 fans – a third fewer than Hampden in 1937 – and it is rarely close to being full. Barcelona's average attendance is currently around 73,000.

Hampden Park was the biggest football ground in the world in 1937 and it would remain so until the opening of Rio's Maracanã for the 1950 World Cup finals. Hampden already held the football attendance record, set in 1933 when 136,259 went through the turnstiles for another Scotland-England international. Reconstruction ahead of the 1937 match was supposed to increase the ground's capacity to 180,000. In fact, a safety inspection by Glasgow's Master of Works assessed the expanded capacity to be 149,969, with 14,269 seats and 135,700 standing places.

By comparison, the capacity at Wembley in 1937 was 93,000. The Empire Stadium's record attendance was 126,047, set at the 1923 FA Cup Final, known as the White Horse Final in tribute to Billy, the Metropolitan Police horse charged with keeping order after hordes of ticketless fans climbed into the ground. Certainly there were more than 126,047 people inside Wembley that day, but exactly how many is unclear, as many of them hadn't passed through the turnstiles. As a result of the 1923 chaos, Wembley's capacity was slashed.

Hampden, though, was relatively accustomed to handling crowds in excess of 100,000 for international matches and Scottish Cup Finals. The ground had been regularly expanded and improved since its opening in 1903 and the 1937 redevelopment was regarded as essential to meet the huge demand to attend internationals and finals. League matches involving the club tenants Queen's Park, meanwhile, saw only around 4,000 spectators rattling around the massive ground.

The enormous attendance for the 1937 international is particularly astonishing given the match was effectively a friendly — a dead rubber in a home international championship that had already been won by Wales. Consider also the economic climate of the 1930s, when few football fans had much disposable income. Britain was still dealing with the effects of the Great Depression and unemployment remained a major problem. (The Jarrow March had taken place just a few months earlier, in October 1936.)

There were also other distractions. Britain was consumed with preparations for the coronation of George VI, with rehearsals for parades and processions taking place in towns and cities across the nation. Yet the Scotland-England international retained utmost importance among football fans on both sides of the border. As the *Times* noted in the build-up to the game, "The Association match between England and Scotland has an appeal which is quite independent of goals and points, and not even the FA Cup Final at Wembley can surpass it in pageantry and excitement."

Internationals were traditionally an opportunity to see star players who could otherwise only be read about in newspapers or glimpsed in occasional newsreels. Tommy Walker of Hearts and Bob McPhail of Rangers were among the Scottish team's star draws. John Cairney's favourite player was the Celtic outside-right Jimmy Delaney, whom he could easily recognise from pictures on his cigarette cards. The relatively young and inexperienced England team may have been less familiar to Scottish fans. Famous favourites such as Cliff Bastin and Eddie Hapgood were missing, replaced by newer names including Stanley Matthews of Stoke and Raich Carter of Sunderland.

The scramble for tickets (or 'briefs') began in January, with fans advised to apply via their local clubs. Tickets for the ordinary terracing cost two shillings (equivalent to around £5 today). The only way to follow the game live was to be there in person, as it wasn't being broadcast on the radio due to a dispute between the BBC and the SFA. (The recently-launched BBC TV channel, meanwhile, would instead be airing "a demonstration of locomotives".)

Match-goers who intended to travel by car were required to pay an extra shilling for a colour-coded parking disc. An elaborate scheme was prepared to direct the expected 3,000 cars into the city and to suitable car parks via 14 separate routes signposted with coloured markers by the RAC. Drivers who deviated from their prescribed colour-coded routes faced a fine of £1.

In addition to more than 100,000 fans from all over Scotland, up to 50,000 were expected to travel from England in what was described as a "greater-than-ever English invasion". The railway company Great Western offered English fans "cheap trips", departing Friday evening and arriving in Glasgow on Saturday morning. The travel agent Thomas Cook advertised a deluxe excursion from London, including a pre-match sightseeing trip to Loch Lomond.

Necessary preparations were made to feed and water visiting fans. Restaurant and pub owners applied for extended licences, and civic halls were turned into mass feeding stations. Newspapers estimated that 250,000 meals would be served to match-goers. As for alcohol, according to the *Dundee Courier*, "The tonic taken if Scotland win will be sufficient to float a battleship."

A huge police operation was planned to deal with the crowd. 700 "stalwarts of the force" would be on duty in and around the ground, and detectives and plainclothes constables would mingle with the crowd to watch for pickpockets. It was publicised that the police would be "directed by radio" – an experimental method of communication at the time.

There were fears that the reconstructed Hampden Park might not be ready in time, with steel workers threatening strike action over a delayed pay rise. But by early April it was announced that work was complete. The expanded ground had 117 turnstiles, each of which, it was estimated, could cope with 40 admissions a minute, or 24,000 an hour.

As the big day approached, newspapers printed instructions for match-goers. "Remember your brief!" advised the

Dundee Courier. "The enthusiast who arrives at Hampden without a ticket will be right out of luck." Fans were instructed to arrive early ("a crowd of 150,000 cannot be accommodated in comfort if there is a last-minute rush"), and to wear a "bunnet" – a flat cap rather than a bowler hat so as not to block the view of those behind.

On the morning of the match, newspapers on both sides of the border anticipated a record-breaking occasion. "Soccer crowds invade Scotland!" reported the *Daily Mail*. The *Scotsman* heralded "football's biggest day", and predicted that the noise produced by the unprecedented crowd would hand a huge advantage to the Scottish team. "Now for the loudest-ever Hampden Howl," said the *Dundee Courier*, adding that the match promised to be "the greatest spectacle of a sporting lifetime".

England fans began to arrive in Glasgow in great numbers from the early hours, "before even the milkmen had started their rounds". They arrived in trains decorated with the colours of St George and marched into the city through heavy rain. Many wore white roses in their buttonholes. One large group was led through the streets by a man carrying a stuffed lion. Queues formed outside restaurants and tea-rooms, with many opening as early as 5am to serve the visitors with breakfasts.

Newspapers reported the story of one ticketless England fan who walked from his home in Preston to Carlisle, then hitch-hiked to Glasgow. He wandered around the city asking if anyone knew where the England team were staying, as he knew several of the players and if he could find them he could get a ticket. As one reporter remarked, "He must be Britain's super-optimist today."

By noon, tens of thousands of Scotland fans were arriving from all around the country, many of them via 150 special trains. Also arriving were 40 Scottish dockyard workers from Portsmouth, led by one Bob McDonald. "Bob is such a good organiser that the entire cost will only work out at £2 4s [equivalent to £140 today] per head," reported the *Portsmouth Evening News*. "This includes reserved train accommodation, three meals at a swagger Glasgow hotel, and tickets for the match."

After arriving at Glasgow Central, fans took a tram – or a walk – across the Clyde and south to Mount Florida, where Hampden Park is located. John Cairney was among their number, riding through the crowd on his father's shoulders, piggybacking above a stream of damp caps, the air thick with drizzle and hubbub. The route was lined with street vendors selling hats and buttonholes, yelling, "All the colours!"

At Hampden, the preparations made to ensure smooth access to the ground appeared to be successful. A correspondent from the *Motherwell Times* noted that he was able to enter the ground an hour before kick-off without standing in a queue. "Even for a man without the slightest interest in football this crowd was a wonderful sight," he wrote, also noting that women were "present in big numbers".

"Hampden Park with its throng of humanity was something to remember," the correspondent continued. "Accents heard ranged from Caithness to Devon, from Lincoln to the Western Isles. Roses, thistles, white emblems and tartan favours made a brave show. Bowler hats, thanks to the official request, were few and far between and the humble hooker-doon had a field day."

"Hooker-doon" caps provided some protection from the rain, which continued to drizzle as fans took their places on the terraces. One chap raised an umbrella, but was swiftly "told all about it", his umbrella having to withstand a barrage of orange peel and "other ammunition". Short shrift was also given to aeroplanes that circled above Hampden, trailing adverts for Cuticura medicated soap and Bile Beans laxatives. When the planes flew too low, the crowd gave them "the bird", gesturing with raised middle fingers.

John Cairney arrived through the gates at the back of the terracing, and was initially confronted by "a flat-capped, grey-coated mass", but ended up with the best view in the ground. Along with other youngsters, he was lifted into the air and passed forward over spectators' heads all the way to the front of the terrace, where he took up a position in front of the perimeter wall, just six feet from the touchline. "We had a better view than anyone in the posh stands," he says.

As kick-off approached, the crowd was treated to a programme of music involving a Scottish pipe band and community singing led by Elliot Dobie, a popular music hall and radio singer. Community singing was a familiar part of the big match experience, and spectators joined together to sing "Bonnie Banks o' Loch Lomond", "Hail Caledonia" and, with a nod to the forthcoming coronation, "God Save the King". The music and singing continued as the teams entered the field, greeted by "driving rain and ear-splitting cheers".

England came out first, led by their captain George Male, to "Heart of Oak" (the official march of the Royal Navy). Next came Scotland, led by Jimmy Simpson, to the more familiar "Scotland the Brave". Then came a voluminous wall of "shattering noise" – the Hampden Howl. "Starting on the embankment opposite the pavilion," said the *Scotsman*, "the famous cheer spread round the lofty terracing until the huge bowl echoed and re-echoed with the heartening roar that is perhaps the most notable demonstration known of enthusiasm and sporting patriotism."

Sitting at the front of the terrace, young John could not hear himself speak. He describes a wall of noise of such power that he felt he could have leant against it. It could have been a terrifying experience for a small boy, but John found himself carried along with the crowd and joined in with them, screaming and shouting "in a kind of wild hysteria". "It was never frightening," he says, "because we were safely among our own."

Male won the toss and allowed Scotland to kick off, accompanied by what the *Dundee Courier* called "the mightiest roar in international history". Within seconds, the referee blew for a foul, setting the template for a rough, stop-start game. England had the better of the first half and opened the scoring through the 20-year-old Stoke City centre-forward Freddie Steele. "A tremendous

roar seemed to shake the stadium to its foundations," Steele later recalled. "Spectators stood and clamoured all round the ground. I shall never forget that goal."

Scotland improved in the second half and scored an equaliser via a quick passing move that saw Tommy Walker beat the English defence and square the ball to Francis O'Donnell for a tap-in. The reaction was described by the *Dundee Courier* as "absolute bedlam in the most amazing crowd ring in football!" "The Hampden Howl might have been heard in the centre of the city," said the paper. "The Englishmen might well have taken fright."

The Hampden Howl did frighten the English players – a fact confirmed by Stanley Matthews. "If ever a match was won and lost by a roar, it was this one," Matthews wrote. "Those who have never heard the roar cannot appreciate the effect it has on a player. It shook me and my colleagues in the England team."

Led by Tommy Walker, and inspired by the immense crowd, the Scots began to pile pressure on the English defence. Ten minutes from time, a goalmouth scramble ended with Bob McPhail firing home from a narrow angle. And McPhail made it 3-1 in the dying minutes, scoring with a header from a free-kick. The vast majority of the crowd celebrated in a raucous frenzy. "Hampden's first all-ticket international must remain a happy memory," said the *Dundee Courier*.

As Hampden began to empty, young John began to worry about how he might find his dad – and how he could go to the toilet. A policeman told him to wait by the side of the pitch, and take a pee against the perimeter wall. Eventually, John's dad arrived and they gleefully headed back up the terracing towards the gates, the concrete steps littered with beer bottles and cigarette packets, plus the odd hat and umbrella. John recalls his dad finding half-a-crown and remarking, "Must be my lucky day!"

The exit procedure was smooth and successful. "Incredible as it sounds, the ground was practically clear 20 minutes after the game had ended," commented the *Times*. "The Hampden Park executive and the Glasgow authorities deserve every praise for their handling of 150,000 people. There were some complaints that it was not possible to see much of the game from certain sections at the top of the terracing, but those who did get a good view were conveyed to and from their places with astonishing comfort and celerity."

The *Scotsman* reflected that it had been a remarkably safe event. "Inside the ground there was relatively little crushing, although at parts the crowd were loath to move down the embankments, and this led to some discomfort on the upper tiers," the paper reported. "The number of fainting cases dealt with was 46, an unusually small total." The number of arrests was also small and reported to be no more than would be expected on a normal Saturday.

"There was no delay in getting back to the city for tea – or other refreshment," commented the *Motherwell Press*. "50,000 English football fans took possession of Glasgow after the game. It was the biggest invasion of Scottish territory since Bannockburn. It was almost as noisy as that event, but much more amicable."

Sadly, one England fan did not make it home. William Robert Bell should have returned to Bristol with his friends on the Sunday, but stayed in Glasgow as he was feeling unwell. By the Monday afternoon his condition had deteriorated, and the management of his hotel called for an ambulance. Bell was taken to Glasgow Royal Infirmary, but by the time he arrived he had died of unspecified causes.

Newspapers were quick to confirm that the official attendance of 149,407 was a world record. (They also revealed that the revenue generated from ticket sales was £12,373, equivalent to almost £800,000 today.) It was the high watermark of an unparalleled period of football fanaticism. A full English league programme was played on the same day, and there was no discernible effect on attendances. A week later, 146,433 turned up at Hampden for the Scottish Cup Final between Celtic and Aberdeen.

Hampden's huge crowds prompted calls for Wembley to be expanded. "The Ranger" in *World of Sport* wrote that Wembley's capacity of 93,000 was "totally inadequate" and claimed that demand for FA Cup Final tickets exceeded 500,000. "How long are we to tolerate this impossible position?" he asked. But Wembley's capacity would not be increased, and Hampden's would be reduced.

In the weeks that followed the international, complaints emerged from spectators who had been caught up in crushes or had been unable to see due to the size of the crowd. Newspapers reported the plight of one unnamed chap from Carnoustie who had been unable to see the game. "His lack of inches, and the height of the spectators in front, debarred him from catching a glimpse of the players in action," reported the *Arbroath Herald*. "His companions kept him informed, except when excitement held them more or less speechless."

An unnamed SFA official responded to criticism by saying there had been no crushes and that anyone who had not been able to see had "only himself to blame". However, after a complaint was raised with Glasgow Magistrates, it was recommended that subsequent attendances to be limited to 135,000. As for the chap from Carnoustie, he did not give up hope of seeing some action from the big match. "He is paying frequent visits to the cinema," reported the *Herald*, "in the hope that the newsreel will give him what he wants."

Hampden's 149,407 attendance remained a world record until the 1950 World Cup, when it was beaten twice at the Maracanã. First, 152,722 paid to see Brazil beat Spain and then 173,850 saw Brazil lose to Uruguay in the decisive final game on 16 July 1950. It's estimated that the actual attendance for that game could have been as high as 200,000. But it is the official figure of 173,850 that is recognised by Guinness as the world record, while 149,407 remains the British and European record. Neither is ever likely to be broken. Hampden's current capacity is a little over 52,000, while the Maracanã's is 78,838.

For John Cairney, the 1937 match remains a cherished memory. "The crowd was immense, and I feel privileged to have been part of it," he says. "It was an important, living experience to feel a tiny part of a sudden population of more than a hundred thousand males crammed into a football ground." He recalls being carried home on his Dad's shoulders and then telling his younger brother all about it over a bowl of soup.

John still loves football, but no longer goes to matches. He prefers the magic of his memories to the machinations of the modern game. Football, he acknowledges, has indelibly changed. "I fear we shall not see the like again of the beautiful game it once was," he says. "Or am I just an old codger who loved being a wee boy?"

THE Nightwatchman

THE WISDEN CRICKET QUARTERLY

Cricket's past is littered with great writing, and Wisden is making sure its future is too. *The Nightwatchman* is a quarterly collection of essays and long-form articles available in print and e-book formats.

Co-edited by Osman Samiuddin and Tanya Aldred, and with *Blizzard* editor Jonathan Wilson on the editorial board, *The Nightwatchman* features an array of authors from around the world, writing beautifully and at length about the game and its myriad offshoots.

Visit our web site to learn more.

www.thenightwatchman.net

178

Eight Bells

"I reckon we'll be relegated.
I'm almost certain of it."

Unexpected relegations

A selection of giants who have unexpectedly lost their place in the top tier

By Michael Yokhin

 Marseille 1979-80

Marseille fans can be excused for having had high hopes in the summer of 1979. Rumours that they were about to sign the young prodigy Michel Platini from Nancy turned out not to be true, but the squad was impressive nonetheless, with two national team stars in the classy defender Marius Trésor and the multi-talented winger Didier Six. Marc Berdoll, another member of France's squad at the 1978 World Cup, had been in superb form over the previous two seasons, scoring 32 goals. That summer, the club added Témime Lahzami, a technically gifted Tunisian who was supposed to add speed and trickery to the powerful attacking line. A first title since 1972 seemed well within reach.

The opening game in July was breathtaking. Marseille played some scintillating football in a 3-0 win over Brest, with Berdoll, Six and Témime all getting on the scoresheet. The second match was away at Paris Saint-Germain, and Six was impressive once again, scoring on the counter after 11 minutes. However, Abel Carlos equalised with a free-kick that went through the wall and Dominique Bathenay scored the winner for PSG with an outrageously free header. That was the first sign of things to come – this Marseille team were totally incapable of defending.

It was even more evident in the next fixture, when Platini went to Stade Vélodrome with St Etienne. Berdoll opened the scoring and Six found the net for his third match in a row, but *Les Verts* ran away with an easy 5-3 win. A week later, l'OM conceded five goals again in a terrible 5-0 defeat at Nancy and it became apparent that the title aspirations were unrealistic.

As defeats mounted, fans started to look for scapegoats. Témime was one of them, as the 30 year old failed to come to terms with European football. He went home in December, having played eighteen games in which he scored three goals. Six was treated even more harshly, his attitude and commitment constantly questioned. The long-haired wizard became the most hated figure in the city.

Between November and January, Marseille took just one point from eight games, conceding 23 goals. The situation became critical, but relegation with such a strong squad still seemed an impossibility. That's probably the reason why the coach Jules Zvunka, a popular former player, managed to keep his job until February, but he was eventually fired after losing on penalties to second-division Cannes in the cup. The 58-year-old Jean Robin, who hadn't worked in the first division for 16 years, was called upon to steady the ship and in his first game in charge, Marseille kept a clean sheet in a goalless draw at Nîmes, but such success was short-lived.

Trésor remained a fans' favourite despite all the trouble. When he was absent, the situation became even worse, as a modest Valenciennes showed when thrashing Marseille 6-3 at the Vélodrome, scoring three times inside the first 19 minutes.

Three home wins in succession enabled Marseille to leapfrog Lyon into 18th place, which would have meant a relegation play-off, and that offered a sense that the corner might have been turned. The next game was at Lyon, though, and l'OM lost 1-0 to slip back into the drop zone. They stayed there until the end, taking just one point from their final six fixtures. Relegation was confirmed in the penultimate week when they lost 1-0 to Nantes, who were crowned champions.

The humiliation was far from over, as a disheartened side was torn to pieces by rock-bottom Brest. Having scored just 28 goals in 37 previous fixtures, the outsiders smashed Marseille 7-2. "L'OM are dead," said the headlines. All the key players departed in the summer, and things could have got even worse for the financially stricken club. They were very nearly relegated to third division in 1981 after going into administration, but reserve-team youngsters won the final few fixtures to keep them up and save the club from extinction. Marseille were back in Ligue 1 by 1984.

 Fiorentina 1992-93

This was one of the most exciting teams Fiorentina had ever assembled, as the Cecchi Gori family who acquired the club in 1990 built a remarkable squad. Gabriel Batistuta signed in 1991, proving sceptics wrong to become a force in Serie A, even though the Viola finished 12th in his first season. He then got top partners to play with.

The temperamental German midfield dynamo Stefan Effenberg was supposed to be the leader. The Danish maestro Brian Laudrup arrived alongside him from Bayern Munich after starring for the victorious Denmark side at Euro 92. Francesco Baiano, a revelation at Zdeněk Zeman's Foggia, was the perfect striker to team up with *Batigol*. Fabrizio Di Mauro was bought from Roma to add steel to the midfield. Another interesting prospect was the Argentinian playmaker Diego Latorre, likened to Diego Maradona by some in his homeland.

Hopes were extremely high and many fans believed that the team was capable of challenging for the *Scudetto*; qualifying for Uefa Cup was a minimum target. Fiorentina's start was very promising. Latorre struggled for playing time with only three foreigners allowed, but the others found their feet almost immediately. Under the experienced coach Gigi Radice, Fiorentina played marvellous attacking football, taking the league by storm.

A 7-1 win over newly promoted Ancona, with Di Mauro and Laudrup scoring braces, served as an appetiser. Fiorentina then lost 7-3 at home to Milan in an extraordinary game, but Fabio Capello's team were obviously in the league of their own, about to run away with the title. The *Scudetto* might not have been feasible for the team from Florence, but second place most certainly was.

They thrashed the 1991 champions Sampdoria 4-0 with braces from Baiano and Batistuta, won 2-1 against Roma and then achieved their most cherished result: a 2-0 win over Juventus, who were particularly hated for having signed Roberto Baggio from them.

At the Christmas break, Fiorentina were third, just a point behind Inter, having scored 29 goals in 13 games. Relegation wasn't even a consideration. But everything changed at the beginning of 1994. On January 3, Marcello Lippi's Atalanta arrived to play on a frozen pitch at the Stadio Artemio Franchi. It was a poor game, decided by a lucky goal for the visitors, and Vittorio Cecchi Gori was enraged. Rumours of his tense relationship with Radice, who was very close to his father, Mario Cecchi Gori, had circulated in the city for a while, but nobody could imagine that the end would be so abrupt. Vittorio came to blows with the coach and fired him there and then, leaving the team in disarray.

Aldo Agroppi, named to replace Radice, was a popular figure in Florence, particularly because of his anti-Juventus views. But he had been working as a television pundit for a couple of years by this time and it was immediately clear that he was unable to manage a team of superstars. Thrashed 4-0 by Udinese in his first game in charge, Agroppi was lost and Fiorentina took just two points from the following five matches, plummeting to 14th place.

Fans were also troubled by refereeing decisions. A lot of the Fiorentina support believed the football federation wanted to see them relegated because Cecchi

Gori and Agroppi criticised it at every opportunity. To make matters worse, Viola supporters used an Italy friendly against Mexico that was staged at Artemio Franchi in March to voice their displeasure with the federation, chanting "Messico, Messico". From that point on, the situation was described as a personal war between Cecchi Gori and the federation president Antonio Matarrese. It is open to question, though, whether such an atmosphere was to blame for poor results.

Eventually, Agroppi was sacked in late April, after losing 3-0 at Juventus. He managed to win just two of his 15 games in charge, but the situation didn't improve under the club legend Giancarlo Antognoni who took the reins alongside Luciano Chiarugi for the last five fixtures. Fiorentina failed to win the first four, and slipped into the relegation zone. On the penultimate weekend, they were outraged to see Milan's defence parting like the Red Sea to enable relegation threatened Brescia to score an equaliser at San Siro — that was seen as proof that everything was corrupt.

Going in to the final round of games, Fiorentina's fate was out of their hands. They needed to beat Foggia, and did so emphatically — Batistuta and Baiano scored first-half doubles in a brilliant 6-2 triumph that offered a reminder of their form at the start of the season. However, with Brescia also winning and Udinese taking a controversial point at Roma, that wasn't enough. Fiorentina went down despite scoring 53 goals — the fifth best attacking record in the league.

Laudrup left for Milan, but Cecchi Gori managed to keep the rest of the stars in

Serie B and Fiorentina were immediately promoted. Even so, the 1992-93 season left a big scar on the collective memory of Viola fans that is still felt today.

 Kaiserslautern 1995-96

One of the most iconic pictures in Bundesliga history is that of Rudi Völler trying to console Andreas Brehme, who is weeping uncontrollably. The two close friends, World Cup winners in 1990, played against each other in an improbable relegation battle between Bayer Leverkusen and Kaiserslautern. A dramatic equaliser, scored by Markus Münch with eight minutes left, meant that Völler's team stayed up in the very last game of his career while Brehme's Lautern went down.

It was a desperate ending to the season that started with Kaiserslautern fans dreaming of the title. They had finished fourth in 1994-95, just three points behind the champions Borussia Dortmund, and were expected again to fight at the top end of the table, despite losing the Swiss star Ciriaco Sforza to Bayern. Claus-Dieter Wollitz was signed to reinforce the midfield, and the squad was already strong with the Czech pair Miroslav Kadlec and Pavel Kuka, the Germany international midfielder Martin Wagner and superb goalkeeper Andreas Reinke, not to mention Brehme.

It was a very strange season for Lautern. It's hard to say that they constantly under-performed, and some of their statistics were actually among the best in the league. They only lost 10 out of 34 matches — just three teams had fewer defeats; second-placed Bayern had 11.

They conceded 37 goals, the third-best record in the league. The champions Borussia Dortmund let in 38; Bayern conceded 48.

The problem lay in Kaiserslautern's inability to turn draws into wins. They scored just 31 goals — the lowest tally in the league — not because they played defensively but rather due to woeful finishing. With just six wins all season to go with an all-time record of 18 draws, they were doomed because Germany switched to a three-points-for-a-win system in the summer of 1995. Had two points been awarded for victories, Lautern would have survived.

It's difficult to blame the management for failing to react in time in such circumstances. Kaiserslautern won just two of their first sixteen games, but their football was more than decent and they were never outplayed. The habit of conceding late goals, as in a dramatic 3-2 loss to Bayern when they were the better side, was considered to be pure bad luck. The feeling was that things would eventually sort themselves out, because the team appeared too good to be in a relegation battle.

Every time the position of the coach Friedel Rausch seemed in danger, the team picked up a good result and he kept his job. In addition, Kaiserslautern performed brilliantly in the Cup, beating Schalke and Leverkusen on the way to lifting the trophy. By the time that happened, though, the team was relegated.

Rausch was finally sacked in late March, with the team next to bottom after 23 games. His replacement was the defensive-minded Eckhard Krautzun, a well-travelled coach, but inexperienced at the top level. "I will be considered God if we avoid relegation," he said, misunderstanding the very soul of the club. Playing for a point like ordinary outsiders was the last thing Lautern needed, but that is what they got most of the time.

In the end, a win at Völler's Leverkusen was needed to avoid the drop and Kuka put the Red Devils up after 58 minutes. Then, after Olaf Marschall was injured and Lautern put the ball out of play, Leverkusen refused to return it, scored and Münch celebrated wildly.

The town went into mourning, but the fans were jubilant just two years later. Kaiserslautern named Otto Rehhagel as coach the following season, were immediately promoted and sensationally won the title in 1998. They conceded 39 goals that season, two more than they had in 1995-96.

 4 Middlesbrough 1996-97

This was the best time to be a Boro fan. Never had the city experienced such excitement. The team was promoted to the Premiership in 1995, just in time to inaugurate the new Riverside Stadium in the top flight. The Manchester United legend Bryan Robson was the manager and the combination of his name and Steve Gibson's money enabled them to make thrilling acquisitions. The Brazilian wizard Juninho Paulista arrived from São Paulo in October 1995, and in the summer of 1996 Fabrizio Ravanelli, fresh from winning the Champions League with Juventus, was signed for £7million. Emerson, a

powerful and technically sound box-to-box dynamo, completed a £4m move from Porto.

The build-up to the season was extraordinary, with exciting friendlies against top teams such as Juventus and Internazionale. Every Middlesbrough supporter remembers the first game of the season against Liverpool, as do the players: "That was the best atmosphere I've ever experienced," said Curtis Fleming. The match was of highest quality, played with stupendous tempo, and Boro came back three times to equalise, with Ravanelli completing a hat-trick on his debut.

The next two home fixtures brought some more scintillating attacking football. West Ham were beaten 4-2 and Coventry thrashed 4-0 with Ravanelli and Juninho scoring braces. Boro were just four points off the top and Uefa Cup qualification seemed a very realistic target, especially after they won for the third time in a row at Everton.

Then everything came crashing down. The defence was not up to standard and the team proved to be extremely fragile mentally, especially after Nicky Barmby left for Everton in October having fallen out with Robson. Boro endured a 12-game run without a win and were annihilated 5-1 at Anfield before making a dreadful decision. With most of their players down with flu, the management chose not to show up for the game at Blackburn on December 21, believing they had the right to do so under the circumstances. The FA thought differently and left the Teessiders further adrift at the bottom of the Premiership by deducting three points.

Juninho continued to give his utmost on the field, but other stars started to misbehave. Emerson went awol to Brazil at Christmas. Ravanelli, disappointed with his new team, openly criticised it in the Italian press on a weekly basis and said as early as January, "I reckon we'll be relegated. I'm almost certain of it."

His compatriot Gianluca Festa was signed from Inter to strengthen the defence, which worked to an extent. Boro enjoyed a great run in March, going seven games unbeaten and giving themselves a great chance of salvation. The team's potential was evident as they reached both the FA Cup final and the League Cup final. But they only won once in their last seven fixtures, including a draw at Old Trafford after they'd taken a 3-1 lead.

Drawing 1-1 at Leeds on the final day of the season sealed their fate and Boro were relegated despite scoring 51 goals in 38 matches, Ravanelli responsible for 17 of them. The fans were angry with the FA for the points deduction which they considered unfair – but for that punishment Middlesbrough would have finished 15th instead of 19th. However, in retrospect they were much more disappointed with the team itself. All the big names left in the summer, but Boro were promoted back to the top flight immediately in 1998.

 Atlético Madrid 1999-2000

This was definitely the best squad ever to be relegated from the Primera División. With three crucial members of the 1996 double-winning team – the goalkeeper José Molina, the centre-back Santi and

the striker Kiko – still going strong, they also had the Czech midfielder Radek Bejbl, Spain defender Carlos Aguilera, the Argentinian full-back Jose Antonio Chamot, the promising schemer Ruben Baraja and the outrageously talented playmaker Juan Carlos Valerón on their books. Very promising acquisitions were made in the summer of 1999, when the prolific Dutch goalscorer Jimmy Floyd Hasselbaink arrived from Leeds, Paraguay's defensive stalwart Carlos Gamarra signed from Corinthians and the young left-back Joan Capdevila joined from Espanyol. This team was supposed to fight for the title and expectations couldn't have been higher.

The man given the responsibility to take the stars to the top was Claudio Ranieri, who arrived immediately after thrashing Atlético 3-0 with Valencia in the Copa del Rey final. That was probably the biggest reason for the fans to worry. They remembered the desperate adventure of Arrigo Sacchi during the previous season, when everything went wrong, and the double-winning Radomir Antić had to return to replace him in the middle of the season. Now another Italian came along. Could he make it where Sacchi failed?

The answer was negative from the very beginning. On the first match day, Atlético were sensationally beaten 2-0 by their neighbours Rayo Vallecano at the Vicente Calderón and the situation only got worse. Hasselbaink had a superb season, but other than that everybody underperformed. With no points from the first three games, all hopes of the title were gone by September.

There was new hope in late October, when Hasselbaink scored two brilliant goals at the Bernabéu to lead Atlético to a famous 3-1 derby win over Real, which turned out to be their last triumph against *Los Blancos* until 2013. Those celebrations were short-lived, though. Amazingly, Atlético managed to lose to nine-man Athletic and to eight-man Valencia. They scored every week but were incapable of keeping a clean sheet, which proved to be their downfall in the first half of the season.

Relegation still seemed absolutely unthinkable. Atlético were well above the drop zone in December when the real disaster struck. Just hours before the game against Oviedo, the president Jesús Gil and his board were arrested and suspended pending an investigation into misuse of club funds and tax evasion. The government appointed the administrator José Manuel Rabi to run Atlético's day-to-day operations to prevent immediate bankruptcy. Rumours circulated about illegal contracts signed by some of the stars who received tax-free money under the table. With those payments stopped, their motivation dipped and the second half of the season was desperate.

Ranieri resigned in late February, with the team in 17th place. Antić was recalled once again to save the club, but he was helpless this time. He failed to win any of his 11 league games, and the team sank like a stone. Winless since January, Atlético were relegated two weeks before the end of the season.

They managed to win their last fixture at Mallorca, after Antić had left, but that was hardly relevant. Hasselbaink scored exactly half of the team's 48 goals and he was the only one to emerge with

any credit from the fiasco. It's hardly surprising that he was the man to score in Copa del Rey final against Espanyol as well, but Atlético lost 2-1.

It took them two years to recover, both professionally and financially, and return to the Primera División.

6 Universitatea Craiova 2004-05

Spare a thought for Mihăiță Pleşan. In 2004, the 21-year-old midfielder was considered to be one of the brightest prospects in Europe. After scoring an absolutely majestic Maradona-style goal and helping Romania thrash Germany 5-1 in a friendly, he was supposed to move to a big league, and received — according the player himself at least — a very decent offer from Arsenal who had just finished their invincible season. The Universitatea Craiova president Dinel Staicu, though, refused to sell him.

Staicu wanted to win Universitatea's first title since 1991, and he looked to have the side to do so. Mircea Rednic, who had taken Rapid Bucharest to a surprise title in 2003, came to Craiova in the spring of 2004, and finished the season strongly. Before the new campaign, Universitatea brought in a raft of players from overseas whom the club's board assumed to be superior to those from the local league, but their true value was far from certain.

Rubenilson, who played alongside Rednic at Standard Liège about a decade beforehand, was the star acquisition. "I want to help the team to become champions," the Brazilian said on his arrival, but critics suggested he was a

32-year-old journeyman who had spent most of his career playing second-division football in Belgium and Spain, as well as having a spell with the Israeli minnows Maccabi Petah Tikva.

There were also the former international striker Ionel Ganea, the promising forward Mircea Ilie, not to mention Pleşan, and fans bought into Rednic's promises. Pre-season went badly, though, and journalists close to the team didn't really believe in the side. But they could never have imagined what was about to happen.

The season started with a disastrous spell of five games without a win, culminating in a 5-0 thrashing at the hands of Steaua. At that point, Staicu sold the team to his rival Adrian Mititelu, who disliked Rednic and sacked him at half-time when the team were losing 2-0 at CFR Cluj. That surprisingly helped, as Universitatea came back to win 3-2 with two goals by Pleşan, but chaos followed when Mititelu decided that he had been cheated by Staicu and refused to buy the team after all.

A bizarre week ensued in which no fewer than seven coaches took charge of the team and Rednic was eventually reinstated. By the time he came back, Staicu had sold some of the under-performing stars and the squad kept changing on weekly basis, with the president constantly bringing in cheap players from Universitatea's second-division satellite club CSM Reşiţa.

It was an absolutely extraordinary season even by Romanian standards. Universitatea used 53 different players in 30 matches, some of them taking part

in just one or two games. The situation was hopeless and the team won just once after October. There was still an element of disbelief after relegation was confirmed, bringing a 41-year stint in the top flight to an end. Fans lit candles to mourn the loss.

Rednic resigned before the fiasco was complete and the season ended with two spectacular defeats, 5-0 at Dinamo Bucureşti and 6-0 at home to Oţelul Galaţi. As for Pleşan, he has never fulfilled his potential. The only team he played for outside Romania were the Russian outsiders Volga and he now turns out for SC Universitatea Craiova, a new club built on the remains of its proud predecessor after it went out of business in 2012.

 Real Zaragoza 2007-08

July 2007 was a very unlucky month for Roberto Ayala. Three days before scoring an own goal in a 3-0 defeat to Brazil in the Copa América final that ended his international career, the Argentinian centre-back backtracked on his decision to sign for Villarreal and moved to Zaragoza instead. It turned out to be one of the worst decisions he could have made.

The Villarreal deal was agreed as early as February. Ayala knew that his seven hugely successful years at Valencia were coming to an end and chose to continue his Primera División career at their ambitious neighbours. When Zaragoza came calling, ready to pay the €6m buyout clause in his new contract, though, his head was turned. They urgently needed to replace the Barcelona-bound Gabi Milito and his experienced 34-year-old compatriot was considered the ideal solution.

It's easy to understand why Ayala thought that Zaragoza were a more attractive project than Villarreal. They were historically a much bigger club and they'd finished sixth in 2006-07, qualifying for the Uefa Cup. Victor Fernández, the coach who had masterminded the sensational Cup-Winners' Cup triumph in 1995, had done a tremendous job in his second spell at the club and the squad appeared strong enough to make the step up to qualify for the Champions League.

Diego Milito, Gabi's brother, stayed at the club, having scored 23 goals the previous season, ably assisted by Pablo Aimar, one of the best and most exciting playmakers in the league, and Andrés d'Alessandro, who was one of the many Argentinians hailed as the new Maradona. César Sánchez, the goalkeeper who had left Real Madrid in 2005 because of the emergence of Iker Casillas, was very solid. During the summer, Zaragoza added the Brazilian striker Ricardo Oliveira from AC Milan and persuaded the midfielder Matuzalém to break his contract at Shakhtar Donetsk. Francisco Pavón, of the 'Zidanes y Pavones' *galacticos* project at Real Madrid, arrived as well, and so did two central midfielders from Atlético Madrid, Peter Luccin and Gabi. This was the most expensive squad in Zaragoza history. "The club is taking firm steps forward, significant investments have been made," Ayala said. "We should at least retain our position from last season and hopefully improve on it." Everyone felt exactly the same.

The start was good. In September and October, Zaragoza won five games out of seven, only losing at Barcelona and Atlético. But a much tougher spell followed, with the defence unable to keep a clean sheet and Ayala desperately out of form. Remarkably, they took the lead in seven of nine matches but couldn't win any of them. Fernández was hastily and controversially fired after the team drew 2-2 with Mallorca to leave them just two points above the relegation zone. Reports suggested he had lost the dressing-room, but more worrying was the fact that the owner, Agapito Iglesias, tried to influence his decisions.

Javier Irureta, a much more cautious and defensive coach, who had been hugely successful at Deportivo La Coruña but failed at Betis and had been jobless since, was brought in to try to rescue the season but things just got worse. He was duly sacked after losing four games in a row. Irureta hasn't had another management job since.

In came the veteran coach Manolo Villanova. Zaragoza still had the sixth-best attacking record in the league and beating Atlético on Villanova's debut was a promising new start. They never found any consistency, though.

Ayala scored an injury-time winner against Deportivo to lift Zaragoza out of the relegation zone with three weeks of the season to go, but they only took one point from those remaining games and went down despite scoring 50 goals. Their total of 42 points would have been enough to stay up in any of the previous nine seasons, but luck wasn't on their side.

As for Villarreal, they had their best season in history, finishing runners-up to Real Madrid, 35 points ahead of Zaragoza.

8 Gamba Osaka 2012

Is it possible to get relegated with the best attack in the league and a positive goal difference? Gamba Osaka proved that it is. Their record at the end of the 34-game season read 67 goals for, 65 goals against. To put things into perspective, the champions Sanfrecce Hiroshima found the net 63 times. Niigata, who finished in 15th place, two points ahead of Gamba, and thus were safe, scored just 29 goals.

It was a bizarre adventure for Gamba, one of the top clubs in J.League history. Under Akira Nishino, they finished in the top three eight times between 2002 and 2011, winning the title in 2005, lifting the Emperor's Cup in 2008 and 2009 and claiming the Asian Champions League in 2008.

In 2011, they'd finished third, just two points behind the champions Kashiwa, and hopes were extremely high ahead of the new season after some promising purchases were made, including the Brazilian striker Paulinho, one of the most prolific scorers in Japan. The club made a significant mistake, however, in failing to offer Nishino a new contract and turning instead to the former national striker Wagner Lopes. It turned out that he didn't have a licence, so he became assistant to the well-travelled Brazilian José Carlos Serrão.

Their start was disastrous. Gamba took just one point from their first five fixtures, conceding 12 goals in the process, and that was enough for Serrão and Lopes to be shown the door. The assistant coach Masanobu Matsunami, a club legend as a player, took the reins and started well with two superb wins, but the team never found any sort of stability.

Under Nishino, Gamba had been famous for their attacking flair and gung-ho style. That continued in the 2012 season, but the goalkeeper Yōsuke Fujigaya, an important figure for years, was dreadfully out of form and his defence didn't offer much support. Results were highly unpredictable. The Brazilian striker Leandro had a good season, as did his partner Akihiro Sato, but fans never knew what would happen at the other end.

Gamba thrashed the bottom side Sapporo twice, beating them 4-0 and 7-2. They enjoyed phenomenal 5-0 away wins over high-flying Urawa and Nagoya. On the other hand, they were also beaten 6-2 at home by Kashiwa and 5-0 at Kashima.

Gamba only lost three of their last 16 fixtures and found the net in 23 consecutive games. Sensationally, that wasn't enough. They needed to beat Júbilo Iwata on the last day of the season to stay up, but conceded a goal five minutes from time to lose 2-1.

Tears were soon forgotten, though. Just like Kaiserslautern, Gamba were immediately promoted back to the top division and won the title in extremely dramatic fashion the following season. Sometimes, relegation can be a blessing in disguise. Ⓑ

The Football Supporters' Federation

By Fans, For Fans

 **INFORMING**

 **SUPPORTING**

 **CAMPAIGNING**

www.fsf.org.uk	• Legal Advice and Support	• Local Campaigns
Free Lions Magazine	• International Fans' Embassies	• National Representation
The Football Supporter Magazine	• Case Work and Consumer Advice	• Football Supporters Europe

Join the fsf today for FREE visit: www.fsf.org.uk

Contributors

The Blizzard, Issue Seventeen

Shaul Adar is the author of *Liverpool: Football, Life and Death* (in Hebrew). He writes mainly for *Haaretz* and has been based in London since 2001. Twitter: **@ShaulAdar**

David Ashton is a playwright, TV and film screenwriter; creator of the BBC Radio 4 series, *McLevy*. He has written four novels, the latest being *Nor Will He Sleep*. Also an actor, he played Dr McDuff in *Brass* and the father in The Last King of Scotland. His website is **www.david-ashton.co.uk**

Philippe Auclair is the author of *The Enchanted Kingdom of Tony Blair* (in French), *Cantona: the Rebel Who Would Be King*, which was named NSC Football Book of the Year and *Lonely at the Top*, his biography of Thierry Henry. He writes for *France Football* and *Offside* and provides analysis and commentary for ITV, RMC Sport and Radio 5 Live. Twitter: **@PhilippeAuclair**

Keith Bailie is a Belfast-based sports journalist who works for titles such as the *Belfast Telegraph*, *Belfast News Letter* and *Sunday Life*. He covers both the Northern Ireland national team and the local domestic game. He is also on the panel of podcast *The Social Club NI* and he commentates on Belgian, Portuguese and Polish football for betting websites. Twitter: **@keithjbailie**

Paul Brown is the author of *The Victorian Football Miscellany* and *All*

With Smiling Faces: How Newcastle Became United. He contributes to *FourFourTwo* and *When Saturday Comes*. Twitter: **@paulbrownUK**

Paul Brown writes for the *Daily Star*. Twitter: **@pbsportswriter**

George Caulkin has been writing about football in the north-east of England for 21 years and for the *Times* since 1998. He ghost-wrote Sir Bobby Robson's final book, *Newcastle, My Kind of Toon*, and is a Patron of the Sir Bobby Robson Foundation. Twitter: **@CaulkinTheTimes**

James Corbett is a sports correspondent and award-winning author who has reported for outlets including the BBC, the *Observer*, the *Guardian*, the *Sunday Times* and *FourFourTwo*. His books include the *Everton Encyclopedia* and his collaboration with Neville Southall, *The Binman Chronicles*. He is currently working on a book about football governance. Twitter: **@james_corbett**

Simon Curtis is a freelance football writer based in Lisbon. He contributes regularly to ESPN and *Champions* and has written for *FourFourTwo*, Reuters, WorldSoccer.com, Portugoal.net and a variety of official Uefa publications. He is currently co-writing a book on the history and influence of Portuguese football. Twitter: **@Bifana_bifana**

Miguel Delaney is an Irish-Spanish football journalist based in London, who writes for ESPN, the *Irish Examiner* and the *Independent*. He is the author of *Stuttgart to Saipan*, a history of the Ireland national team. In 2011 was nominated for Irish sports journalist of the year. Twitter: **@MiguelDelaney**

Charlie Eccleshare is a sports writer for the *Daily Telegraph*. Previously he wrote for the *Daily Mail* and the *London Evening Standard*, and has contributed to the *Guardian*. Twitter: **@cdeccleshare**

Richard Fitzpatrick is the author of *El Clásico: Barcelona v Real Madrid, Football's Greatest Rivalry*, which is published by Bloomsbury. Twitter: **@Richard_Fitz**

Conor Heffernan is an independent football writer and long-suffering Leeds United fan. He has contributed to the *Guardian*, *These Football Times* and *Sporting Traditions*. Twitter: **@PhysCstudy**

Aleksandar Holiga is an independent football writer. He writes columns for two newspapers in Croatia and has contributed to the *Guardian*, *FourFourTwo* and *When Saturday Comes* among others. Twitter: **@AlexHoliga**

Lefkos Kyriacou is a practising architect and researcher. He worked for the ESRC-funded project Conflict in Cities, focussing on Jerusalem but also working on a number of other contested cities in Europe and the Middle East. He co-authored the book *The Struggle for Jerusalem's Holy Places* and is currently

a research member of the Centre for Urban Conflicts Research in Cambridge.

Brian Oliver was sports editor of the *Observer* for 13 years and previously worked for the *Daily Telegraph*. He is now a freelance sports writer, editor and consultant.

Igor Rabiner is football and ice-hockey columnist for *Sport-Express*. He is the author of 16 books including *How Spartak Has Been Killed* (in Russian), winner in the Sports Investigation category at Knizhnoe Obozrenie's Sports Book Awards. He has been Russian Football Journalist of the Year four times.

Alexander Shea researches football ultra groups who mobilise as paramilitaries during international warfare. Based at the University of Oxford, he is currently researching the phenomenon in the former Yugoslavia, contemporary Ukraine and Armenia. Twitter: **@Alexander_Shea**

Michael Yokhin is a European football writer with a keen interest in the history of the game. He writes a regular column for ESPN and contributes to the likes of *FourFourTwo* and *Champions*. Twitter: **@Yokhin**

Blizzard Subscriptions

Subscribe to the print version of The Blizzard, *be the first to receive new issues, get exclusive Blizzard offers and access digital versions of all back-issues FREE*

Subscription Options

Set Price for Four Issues

Get a four-issue subscription to *The Blizzard* — for you or as a gift — for a flat fee including postage and packing (P&P):

UK:	£35
Europe:	£45
Non-Euorpe:	£55

Recurring Pay-What-You-Like

Set up a quarterly recurring payment for each edition of *The Blizzard*. The recommended retail price (RRP) is £12, but pay what you like, subject to a minimum fee of £6 plus P&P.

See www.theblizzard.co.uk for more

Digital Subscriptions

If the cost of postage is prohibitive, or you just want an excuse to use your new iPad or Kindle, you can set up a subscription to digital versions of The Blizzard for just £3 per issue.

See www.theblizzard.co.uk for more

Information for Existing Subscribers

The Blizzard is a quarterly publication from a cooperative of top class football journalists and authors from across the globe, enjoying the space and freedom to write about the football stories that matter to them.

Free Digital Downloads for *Blizzard* Subscribers

Whether you have taken advantage of our set price or pay-what-you-like offer, for the duration of your subscription to *The Blizzard* you are entitled to download every issue FREE.

See www.theblizzard.co.uk for more

We very much value the commitment of our print subscribers and have a policy to make available new issues, special offers and other limited access events and benefits to print subscribers first.

About *The Blizzard*

Distribution & Back Issues
Contact Information
About Issue Seventeen

Buy *The Blizzard*

We want as many readers as possible for *The Blizzard*. We therefore operate as far as we are able on a pay-what-you-like basis for digital and print versions.

Digital Version
(Current & Back Issues)

All issues of *The Blizzard* are available to download for Kindle, Android, iOS and PC/Mac at: *www.theblizzard.co.uk*.

- *RRP: £3*
- *Pay-what-you-like minimum: £0.01*

Printed Version
(Current & Back Issues)

Purchase a physical copy of *The Blizzard* in all its luxurious, tactile, sensual glory at: *www.theblizzard.co.uk*. If you haven't felt our rough textured cover-varnish and smelled the inner genius, you haven't properly experienced its awesome true form. Read it, or leave it on your coffee table to wow visitors.

- *RRP: £12* (+P&P)
- *Pay-what-you-like min: £6* (+P&P)

Contact *The Blizzard*

All advertising, sales, press and business communication should be addressed to the Central Publishing Office:

> *The Blizzard*
> Ashmore Villa,
> 1, Ashmore Terrace,
> Stockton Road,
> Sunderland,
> SR2 7DE

Email: info@theblizzard.co.uk
Telephone: +44 (0) 191 543 8785
Website: www.theblizzard.co.uk
Facebook: www.facebook.com/blzzrd
Twitter: @blzzrd

About Issue Seventeen

Editor Jonathan Wilson
Publisher The Blizzard Media Ltd
www.theblizzard.co.uk
Design Daykin & Storey
www.daykinandstorey.co.uk

Copyright

Stroke is the third biggest killer and the leading cause of severe adult disability in the UK.

Please remember us with a gift in your will

Behind much of the Stroke Association's unique work are people just like you – people who want to do something powerful and lasting through their Will.

To find out more about leaving a gift in your Will please call us on **020 7566 1505** or email **legacy@stroke.org.uk**

stroke.org.uk

Registered as a Charity in England and Wales (No 211015) and in Scotland (SC037789). Also registered in Isle of Man (No 945) Jersey (NPO 369) and serving Northern Ireland.